D1062873

Nietzsche in Anglosaxony

Nietzsche in Anglosaxony

A study of Nietzsche's impact on English and American literature

Patrick Bridgwater

Leicester University Press 1972

First published in 1972 by Leicester University Press
Distributed in North America by Humanities Press Inc., New York

'Nietzsche' from W. H. Auden's *New Year Letter* reprinted
by permission of Faber and Faber Ltd and Random House Inc., New York

Designed by Arthur Lockwood
Set in Linotype Baskerville
Printed in Great Britain by Western Printing Services Ltd, Bristol
Bound by James Burn (Bookbinders) Ltd., Esher
ISBN 0 7185 1104 2

Contents

7 *Preface*

9 *Chapter One*
Nietzsche in England

21 *Chapter Two*
Apollo and Dionysos: Walter Pater and Arthur Symons

37 *Chapter Three*
Stellar friendship: George Moore and Nietzsche

48 *Chapter Four*
"That insane belov'd philosopher" (John Davidson)

56 *Chapter Five*
Man and Superman (H. G. Wells and Bernard Shaw)

67 *Chapter Six*
"That strong enchanter" (W. B. Yeats)

91 *Chapter Seven*
Subjective fantasies: Herbert Read and Edwin Muir

104 *Chapter Eight*
The pagan Infinite: D. H. Lawrence and J. C. Powys

114 *Chapter Nine*
"A very dangerous experiment"
(Nietzsche in Georgian England)

132 *Chapter Ten*
The "men of 1914" and Nietzsche

149 *Chapter Eleven*
Nietzsche and American literature

163 *Chapter Twelve*
Fictional Supermen: Jack London and Theodore Dreiser

173 *Chapter Thirteen*
Zarathustran images: John Gould Fletcher

184 *Chapter Fourteen*
"In his sphere, the master" (Eugene O'Neill)

191 *Chapter Fifteen*
"Formidable poetry" (Wallace Stevens)

202 Postscript

208 Notes

223 Bibliography

235 Index

Preface

Few writers have been more influential than the 'last metaphysician', Friedrich Nietzsche. His impact on German literature has been the subject of many studies, usefully summarized by Peter Pütz in his *Friedrich Nietzsche* (Stuttgart, 1967). However, his influence extended far beyond the borders of German-speaking Europe, and for a time was strongly felt in the Anglo-Saxon world. Although there are several excellent studies of Nietzsche's impact on particular British and American writers, there has been no study of the subject as a whole. The object of the present survey is to fill this gap and to show just how strong and widely felt Nietzsche's impact was. The dimensions of the subject and some of its aspects will probably come as a surprise to many readers.

My debt to scholars who have already ploughed portions of the field is obvious and considerable, as is the debt to the staff of the Inter-Library Loan department of Leicester University Library, who so patiently and efficiently ordered a great deal of literary bric-à-brac.

An earlier version of the chapter on W. B. Yeats and Nietzsche appeared in *Affinities: Essays in German and English Literature*, ed. R. W. Last, London: Oswald Wolff, 1971.

Nietzsche's works are quoted in contemporary English from *The Complete Works of Friedrich Nietzsche*, ed. Oscar Levy (18 vols, 1909–13), which is the most complete, and most widely available, English edition, and which is also the edition read by the majority of writers under discussion. References are, however, given in such a form that passages can be located in any German or English edition.

P. B.

Chapter One

Nietzsche in England

Wyndham Lewis was stating a simple fact when he wrote in 1926 that "A few years after his dramatic exit from the stage [in 1900], he [Nietzsche] became the greatest popular success of any philosopher of modern times."[1] Equally justified was John Willett's comment in his recent wide-ranging study of Expressionism that "the force of Nietzsche's ideas was immense throughout Europe ... One after another of the figures [of the expressionist generation] was swept off his feet by Nietzsche's aggressive affirmations of life".[2] That the key to twentieth-century German literature, and especially poetry, is to be found in Nietzsche's ideas, will hardly be disputed. His view of art as the last metaphysical activity within European nihilism – to use Gottfried Benn's useful paraphrase – is, after all, as important as Wilhelm Worringer's later statement that mimesis has nothing whatsoever to do with art. But what of the impact of Nietzsche's ideas on British and American literature? Does not Wallace Stevens, for instance, in effect echo Nietzsche in his statement that "After one has abandoned a belief in God, poetry is that essence which takes its place as life's redemption"?[3]

Robert Graves,* whose essay on 'Nietzsche' in *The Crowning Privilege* (1955) amounted to an anti-German diatribe on the subject of Nietzsche's supposed Germanism, stated quite categorically that "The Nietzschean cult in England has been confined to a very small group consisting mostly of Scots; the one prominent person to champion him has been Bernard Shaw".[4] Now it is true that Nietzsche's impact was most strongly felt by Scottish – *and Irish* – writers. And it is true that he marginally influenced Bernard Shaw, though Shaw hated being labelled, let alone Nietzschefied, and in fact owed more to Schopenhauer and Wagner than to Nietzsche. There are detailed parallels between *Thus Spake Zarathustra* and *Man and Superman* (in the Epistle Dedicatory to which Shaw acknowledges the *kinship* of Nietzsche), but the fact still remains that Shaw, concerned as he was with "the struggle between human vitality and the artificial system of morality", was a fellow-iconoclast rather than a disciple of Nietzsche; this is attested by his own writings on Nietzsche in the late 1890s. Yet in consequence of this obvious intellectual kinship Nietzsche has become known to all too many English readers as the 'mad' grandfather of Shaw's Superman and himself (as Robert Graves rightly observes) a kind of "Shavian paradox"; after all, Nietzsche entered the canon of English criticism as "the greatest, if the maddest, man of letters of modern Germany".[5] In more general terms, however, Robert Graves' statement is simply not true, although it does represent a common misconception. What of W. B. Yeats, for instance? Yeats is presumably not mentioned as one of the "prominent persons" to champion Nietzsche because Robert Graves happens to share Raymond Mortimer's view of Yeats as "a bower bird collecting bright coloured rags and pebbles"; but even seeing Yeats in these terms, it should be obvious that one of the main sources of such "bright coloured rags and pebbles" was Nietzsche's work. And Yeats is only one of a number of important modern poets to have fallen heavily for Nietzsche's ideas.

A far more reliable starting-point is Michael Hamburger's statement that:

* Robert Graves, incidentally, went off to war in 1914 with a copy of Nietzsche's *Poems* in his kit-bag.

> Even if his [Nietzsche's] impact here was never as strong or immediate as his impact on the Continent, a tremor in the atmosphere rather than an earthquake, that tremor can be felt in the works of W. B. Yeats, James Joyce, T. E. Hulme and Wyndham Lewis, in the circle around A. R. Orage and other groups representative of 'advanced' opinion up to the thirties.[6]

Though basically true, this too needs modifying in several respects. Nietzsche's *real* influence on the Continent was scarcely 'immediate'; in Germany, as in England and France, the Nietzscheanism of the 'nineties was mostly a matter of surface imitation – it was not until almost a generation after his mental collapse in 1889 that Nietzsche's ideas really began to bite. In England his influence is seen much more clearly, and is far more significant, in the cases of John Davidson, W. B. Yeats, Edwin Muir and Herbert Read (only one of whom is specifically mentioned by Hamburger), than in the cases of Joyce, Hulme (who was influenced more strongly by Wilhelm Worringer) and Wyndham Lewis. And so far as the first four are concerned, the impact of Nietzsche's ideas caused, at least temporarily, rather more than a 'tremor': Davidson soon had three whole volumes of Nietzsche by heart, Yeats was "enchanted" and Muir "intoxicated" by Nietzsche, whose effect on Herbert Read was "cataclysmic".

From the "disruptive 'nineties" onwards, when he was first felt to be a "rousing revolutionary influence" (Ernest Rhys), Nietzsche was very much in the air, both in London, and in Dublin and Glasgow. At the beginning of the 1890s, of course, he was known only to the few who read German. The first reviews of his work to attract attention in literary circles, by the Scottish poet John Davidson, appeared in *The Speaker* (28 November 1891) and *Glasgow Herald* (18 March 1893); the earliest references to Nietzsche in the literature of the period are to be found in George Egerton's *Keynotes* (1893), where we read: "we agreed that Friedrich Nietzche [sic] appealed to us immensely",[7] and in Davidson's *Sentences and Paragraphs* (1893). The year 1895 saw the publication of the first extended treatment of the subject in English in Max Nordau's essay 'Friedrich Nietzsche' which appeared as Chapter V of Book III ('Ego-Mania') of his controversial and bestselling *Degeneration* (1895). Nordau's attitude is clear: Nietzsche is a "pronounced maniac", the philosopher of "ego-mania". Fortunately, perhaps (at least from the point of view of the present study), Nordau's virulent attack on Nietzsche, which anticipates the sort of thing being written 20 years later in a fury of chauvinistic self-righteousness, does not seem to have had much effect. The main reason for this will have been that none of Nietzsche's works was yet available in English, so that very few English readers would have been in a position to dispute Nordau's verdict.

It was in the following year, 1896, that general interest in Nietzsche's ideas began in this country; 1896 saw the publication of the first two volumes of the first English translation, *The Collected Works of Friedrich Nietzsche* (ed. A. Tille). In welcoming the appearance of this edition, which was to remain incomplete, W. Wallace referred to Nordau's "fairly clever piece of journalistic work":

> Report of Nietzsche on this side of the Channel has been heard now and again; but of knowledge, as distinct from notoriety, there is no great amount. Perhaps the majority of such English readers as take interest in these matters have gained their acquaintance with him, and their estimate of his ideas, from the chapter devoted to him in Max Nordau's *Degeneration*.[8]

Equally, and indeed perhaps more importantly, 1896 also saw the publication of Havelock Ellis's series of three articles on Nietzsche in *The Savoy*[9] – the first extended sympathetic essay in English. Prefacing his brilliant essay with the words "I do not come forward as the champion either of Nietzschianism or Anti-Nietzschianism", Havelock Ellis wrote of Nietzsche as "the greatest spiritual force which has appeared since Goethe", "a great critic of life"; he concluded by declaring that "the nineteenth century has produced no more revolutionary and aboriginal force." His enthusiasm went with knowledge, and to this day his essay is as good as anything of its kind.

In addition to his articles in *The Savoy*, reprinted in his *Affirmations* (1898) and *Selected Essays* (1936), Havelock Ellis also wrote on Nietzsche in the Paris *Weekly Critical Review*;[10] the latter article, reprinted under the title 'The Genius of Nietzsche' in Ellis's *Views and Reviews, First Series: 1884–1919* (1932), contained the comment:

> During recent years several of Nietzsche's books have been translated into English, but with an enthusiasm which was, to say the

> least, injudicious. The English publishers exclusively brought forward the latest, the most extravagant, the most insane portions of his work, and it is not surprising that, except among those extravagant persons to whom extravagance naturally appeals, Nietzsche has until lately found few English readers. Now at length one of the sanest and most truly characteristic of his works [*The Dawn of Day*] has appeared in ... translation ... and at last, even in England, Nietzsche is beginning to find appreciators and admirers ... he has at last gained serious recognition in England.[11]

While there is too much generalization here, Ellis's comment – in April 1903 – does confirm that Nietzsche began to receive serious recognition in England in about 1902. Indeed, it is clear in retrospect that 1902 marked the opening of the 'Nietzschean decade' in English literature.

It is not generally known that Mrs (Edith) Havelock Ellis also wrote on Nietzsche in her *Three Modern Seers* (1910). She argues there that Nietzsche, "a modern Lucifer of the intellect", is "a tonic like quinine", and goes on: "As a tonic, a necessary tonic, Nietzsche's philosophy is very valuable. As a gospel it is, for some of us, quite inadequate." This is a protest against the 'Nietzscheism' (in the full sense of that once so pregnant word) of the first decade of our century, a phenomenon which is well illustrated by the fact that Henri Lichtenberger's *La philosophie de Nietzsche* (1898) became, when translated by J. M. Kennedy, *The Gospel of Superman* (1910). Edith Ellis took exactly the same view of Nietzsche in her article 'Nietzsche and Morals' in *Forum*.[12]

Less of a landmark in Nietzsche-criticism than Havelock Ellis's articles in *The Savoy*, but also important in the present context, is a long since forgotten review-article, 'The Ideals of Anarchy – Friedrich Nietzsche', in *The Quarterly Review* (October 1896),[13] which takes the form of an almost equally sympathetic summary of Nietzsche's life and ideas; published anonymously, the article was in fact by W. F. Barry, who also wrote on Nietzsche in his *Heralds of Revolt* (1904). Nietzsche, the "madman and genius" whose Zarathustra is "the Mohammed of Darwinism", is seen – as early as 1896 – as "the hero as well as the prophet of free-thinkers"; he is praised for having, in his "headlong, iridescent style ... stated the question of science", praised for having written "the Bible of

Positivism"; the reviewer echoes Tille's comment on Nietzsche's "immense rhetorical power and rhapsodic gift".

Taken together, Ellis's and Barry's articles were such as would be likely to arouse interest in the translations which were just appearing, and – since the readerships of *The Savoy* and *The Quarterly Review* were presumably very different – to arouse interest in both literary and literary-minded circles. In fact, once his work began to appear in English, Nietzsche very soon began to make an impact on English literature (John Davidson, H. G. Wells, G. B. Shaw). The English translations were *very* widely reviewed when they began to appear in 1896; in the years 1896–9 in particular there were countless – mostly anonymous – reviews of his work in the British press, and between 1896 and 1914 virtually every literary periodical of any importance carried review-articles on Nietzsche. The main reason for this is, I think, that Nietzsche's arrival in England was timely; he may have been "the expiring voice of the old nineteenth-century romanticism in philosophy" (James G. Huneker), but at the turn of the century he seemed to stand for liberation from the nineteenth century, and more especially from Victorianism; his initial appeal was to the anti-Victorian intellectual.

On 27 May 1898 Hubert Bland lectured to the Fabian Society on 'Frederick Nietzsche: a Child in a China-shop'. "Nietzsche," Bland said, "is veritably a child in a china-shop, a clever, audacious, naughty child":

> One after another he picks out our most cherished articles of virtù ... and flings them upon the floor in an ecstacy of impish glee ... we must not take our child in the china-shop with too great a seriousness, for he is a sturdy urchin whose very naughtiness comes from a superfluity of red corpuscles in the blood. If he does shatter our delicate Dresden shepherdesses ... there will be so much less left for the housemaid to dust. And when we have swept away the pieces ... we may perhaps bring ourselves to realize that our treasures were but worthless rubbish after all.[14]

This reaction is both very English, and also highly characteristic of the time. The child-in-a-china-shop image points forward to Nietzsche's reception in Georgian England, where he was met with something of the same bland complacency. The refusal to take this "sturdy urchin" too seriously marks the most important difference between English and German reactions to Nietzsche; and yet much of the present study will be concerned with writers who, in the next two decades, took him, at least temporarily, very seriously indeed. One reason why Nietzsche attracted such widespread attention at the turn of the century is that given by Hubert Bland: that he was a fine antidote to current sentimentality and to the tendency to carry morality into every sphere of life; Nietzsche's "campaign against morality" was welcome because "We are all in danger of being done to death by Ethical Societies".[15] Nietzsche became the spokesman of the anti-Victorian movement; with him the New Paganism of the 1880s returned with a vengeance.

But of course if Nietzsche stood for modernism in his "campaign against morality" and in his metaphysics and theology, he stood no less resolutely against modernism in the political context, which makes his impact on Fabians such as Bernard Shaw, Rupert Brooke, and Eric Gill ostensibly surprising. Even more bitter than his attacks on Christianity are his repeated attacks on democracy as such. For some of his English readers this was his real importance. A case in point is that of Edward Garnett. In 1899 Garnett published in *The Outlook*[16] a review-article on 'Nietzsche' which was later reprinted in his *Friday Nights* (1929). In his very sympathetic review Garnett argues that: "It is *because* Nietzsche challenges Modernity, *because* he stands and faces the modern democratic rush ... because he opposes a creative aristocratic ideal to negate the popular will ... that he is of such special significance".[17] More particularly, he is full of praise for Nietzsche's anti-conformism: "Nietzsche is undoubtedly the deepest, though most biassed, psychologist of human institutions that our century has seen. His analysis of the Christian ... ideal ... is ... the most telling and brilliant psychological analysis ever made".[18]

Whether Nietzsche is defined as the champion or the opponent of Modernity, however, does not matter; what matters, and what accounts for his impact in England, is the fact that it was precisely the "transvaluation of values" that was, in one way and another, the central problem facing the generation of 1890–1914. Nietzsche might not be approved, but he could not easily be ignored; as Gertrud Burdett wrote in the *New Century Review*, "In judging ... Nietzsche, it is well to bear in mind that we are living in a time of intellectual unrest, and of social discontents; that ... *we are ripe for new teachings, and longing for new ideas*"[19] (my italics).

The first English novel with a Nietzschean hero, W. H. Mallock's

The Veil of the Temple, appeared in 1904, having been serialized in *The Monthly Review* the previous year. Mallock's knowledge of Nietzsche may be uncertain – his name is misspelt several times – but there is no doubting his enthusiasm:

> you should read Nietzsche ... he had no fear of the cliff. He stood on the very edge, and heard the sea roar beneath ... Nietzsche, whatever his merits otherwise, is of all modern thinkers the one who has been foremost in seizing the new moral ideas which the world's new knowledge suggests to us ... and in pushing them to their most startling conclusions. He alone has dared to attack Christianity not only as a system of dogmas, but as a system of democratic philanthropy – to denounce its tenderness for the weak – to deride it as the morality of slaves – to declare that the victories of the future will not be with the weak, but with the strong; and to tell us that this is the true message of science ... Nietzsche is the only explorer who sets his prow towards the ocean and steers his course by the light of the stars only.[20]

Previously Mallock had mentioned Nietzsche in his *Aristocracy and Evolution* (1898).[21]

Another early admirer of Nietzsche was John Addington Symonds' friend Vernon Lee (pseudonym of Violet Paget), who published an article on 'Nietzsche and the Will to Power' in 1904,[22] and included a chapter on Nietzsche in her *Gospels of Anarchy* (1908). So far as John Addington Symonds himself is concerned, it is interesting to note the parallel between Nietzsche and Symonds drawn by W. F. Barry in his article 'The Ideals of Anarchy':

> In many ways ... we are reminded of an unhappy English genius and New Pagan, John Addington Symonds, whom Nietzsche not a little resembled. Both were outwardly diffident, at heart self-sustained and intractable; in either the capacity for mental suffering, heightened by illness and introspection, gave a keen sense of what pleasure there might be in life, were health its normal condition; each luxuriated in music yet was an imbecile in mathematics; and both combined an intense love of the Greek and Roman literature with the modern feeling for landscape, especially for the pictured shores of the Riviera, and high Alpine regions like the Engadine in which they found a home. Both, finally, turning from metaphysics as delusion, and convinced that

> religion, above all in its Christian dogmatic form, was the ruin of art and the chief hindrance to man's advancement, devised in its stead an Epicurean stoicism, or rule of pleasure founded upon the mystery of pain, with the mortality of the soul to put a sting into it, and death as the great deliverance.[23]

There are other parallels too, for instance the predilection of both men for Venice and Davos, and for the Italian Renaissance; both were influenced by Jacob Burckhardt's view of the Renaissance. Nietzsche's debt to Burckhardt is well known; what is not so well known is that in the Preface to his *Renaissance in Italy: The Age of the Despots* (1875), Symonds wrote: "It would be difficult indeed for me to exaggerate the profit I have derived from the comparison of my opinions with those of a writer so thorough in learning and so delicate in his perceptions as Jacob Burckhardt." There is, of course, no question of Symonds being influenced by Nietzsche; a number of his friends (Havelock Ellis, Arthur Symons, Vernon Lee) were to write about Nietzsche, but Symonds himself died in 1893, several years before Nietzsche's work became at all well known in the literary circles in which he moved.

Although Oscar Levy's edition of *The Complete Works of Friedrich Nietzsche* only appeared in 1909–13, Nietzsche's impact on English literature was arguably greatest in the years 1902–12. This is not as strange as it may seem, for by the turn of the century Nietzsche's potentially most influential individual works were available in English in A. Tille's incomplete and financially unsuccessful editions (*The Collected Works of Friedrich Nietzsche*, 3 vols, London: Henry & Co., 1896–7; *The Works of Friedrich Nietzsche*, 4 vols, London: T. Fisher Unwin, 1899–1903). Thomas Common may have written in 1906 of "the cold reception which Nietzsche has met with in England and America",[24] but by 1906 this "cold reception" had given way to widespread enthusiasm in advanced intellectual circles, although it did, admittedly, take the First World War to make his work sell in this country. As was emphasized in an editorial in *The Nation*,[25] those who were most drawn to Nietzsche were the "Socialistically inclined":

> Nietzsche has become quasi-popular for two reasons: first, as a mere writer, as a poet of startling phrases and occasional insight, but with no systematic doctrine; and, secondly, as one of the innumerable forces of change and of rebellion against the existing

> order of things. It is a fact, we believe, that nowhere will you find more men who regard Nietzsche favorably or tolerantly than among those Socialistically inclined: they feel and welcome the destructive energy of the man, while caring little that his programme of construction is entirely opposed to their own.

In other words, it was his views on ethical and religious questions that drew the "Socialistically inclined" to Nietzsche; evidently his views on socialism and democracy were not yet widely known.

Within a little more than a year, however, this "quasi-popularity" had given way to violent anti-Nietzscheanism. This anti-Nietzscheanism, which, as we shall see, played a significant part in the intellectual warfare of 1914–15, marked the virtual end of his influence except on those who had already fallen under his spell (though there are exceptions), while in the post-1918 world Nietzsche's very name was taboo, and "the free individual, the Nietzschean superman, disappeared like a chimera in the darkness".[26] It was probably this reaction against Nietzsche, combined with the obscurity of so much of the evidence, that led Gertrud von Petzold to write in 1929: "There is no denying that in general Nietzsche found little recognition in English literature ... The only writer openly to declare his allegiance to Nietzsche was John Davidson".[27] This is simply not true, for by 1929 not only John Davidson, but also W. B. Yeats, Edwin Muir, and Herbert Read, to say nothing of the Americans Jack London and Eugene O'Neill, had declared their indebtedness to Nietzsche, while a number of other important writers were clearly indebted to him in varying degrees.

However considerable the cult of Nietzsche among British intellectuals and writers in the first decade of the twentieth century, there were of course at the same time those (*pace* Nordau) to whom his name was anathema. Foremost among the latter was G. K. Chesterton, who missed few opportunities to decry "poor Nietzsche" and the "effronteries of Zarathustra". In *Heretics* (1905), Chesterton described Nietzsche as representing the "pretentious claim of the fastidious" to superiority, and added: "Nietzsche's aristocracy has about it all the sacredness that belongs to the weak ... It is an aristocracy of weak nerves";[28] arguing from this not entirely unreasonable point of view (cf. the hysterical quality of Nietzsche's language), he even went on, less reasonably, to state that "Nietzsche and the *Bow Bells Novelettes* have ... the same fundamental character; they both worship the tall man with curling moustaches and Herculean bodily power, and they both worship him in a manner which is somewhat feminine and hysterical".[29] If this seems to go beyond the proper bounds of criticism, it is in *Orthodoxy* (1909) that Chesterton is most outspoken:

> Nietzsche ... preached ... egoism. That, indeed, was simple-minded enough; for Nietzsche denied egoism simply by preaching it ... Nietzsche had some natural talent for sarcasm: he could sneer, though he could not laugh; but there is always something bodiless and without weight in his satire, simply because it has not any mass of common morality behind it. He is himself more preposterous than anything he denounces. ... the whole weakness of Nietzsche, whom some are representing as a bold and strong thinker. No one will deny that he was a poetical and suggestive thinker; but he was quite the reverse of strong. He never put his own meaning before himself in bald abstract words ... Nietzsche always escaped a question by a physical metaphor, like a cheery minor poet ... Nietzsche is truly a very timid thinker. He does not really know in the least what sort of man he wants evolution to produce.[30]

Chesterton's criticism is partly shrewd enough; Nietzsche's aggressive physical metaphors do cover any number of intellectual sins of omission. But it is also for the most part brilliantly predictable; it has every appearance of being prompted (under the influence of Max Nordau, surely) by a distaste for contemporary Nietzscheanism rather than by any profound knowledge of Nietzsche's own writings: *it* is *all* bald abstractions. It is also vintage Chesterton. Until August 1914, however, Chesterton's views were those of the minority; most contemporary *literati* fell for Nietzsche hook, line and sinker, and to those who opposed his influence one might apply Romain Rolland's comment on German Nietzscheanism, made in a letter to Malwida von Meysenbug in 1899: "Nietzsche dominates even those who fight him."

Finally, before proceeding to examine individual writers' reactions to Nietzsche, it should be stressed that it was Nietzsche's *ideas* that were to be so influential, and more especially his *poetic* ideas or myths (e.g. of Eternal Recurrence). So far as style or the "art of getting meaning into words" is concerned, Ezra Pound was not being entirely unjust when he wrote in his 'How to Read' that "Nietzsche made a temporary commotion", and left it at that. Nietzsche's imagery did, however, impress some poets (e.g. John Gould Fletcher, and maybe Isaac Rosenberg); and obviously his ideas would have attracted far less attention if they had not been so forcefully and strikingly expressed. At this stage it is worth pointing out too that Nietzsche owed his very considerable impact to the "totally inadequate" early translations of his work; hardly any of the British and American writers in question read his work in the original. The Levy edition, which collected the early translations, may have left much to be desired, but rarely can a translation of a modern œuvre have exercised such powerful influence on so many important writers. Much the same is true as regards critical works, for it was the early hagiographical expositions, rather than the early essays by academic philosophers, that helped to generate enthusiasm for Nietzsche in literary circles. The whole story is in fact one of subjective reactions and, frequently, of creative misconceptions.

Chapter Two
Apollo and Dionysos: Walter Pater and Arthur Symons

Walter Pater's first essay, 'Diaphaneitè', was written in July 1864, at which time Nietzsche had just left school; Pater's first published 'Greek' essay, on 'Winckelmann', appeared in 1867, some four years before *The Birth of Tragedy*. Yet because of the close parallels between 'A Study of Dionysus' (1876) and Nietzsche's famous first book, Pater has repeatedly been seen as a kind of proto-Nietzschean. It is therefore with Walter Pater and his disciple Arthur Symons that our study must begin.

In his essay on 'Nietzsche and the Nietzscheans'[1] Michael Hamburger wrote that: "At least one English writer, Walter Pater, was among that élite whose recognition established Nietzsche as an international figure when he was scarcely read in Germany." In fact there is no evidence to support this statement: Pater never mentioned Nietzsche in his writings or letters, let alone 'recognized' him in the way implied. It is true, however, that Pater's name has frequently been linked with Nietzsche's. The first critic to describe at length some of the striking affinities between the two writers was Arthur Ransome, who wrote in 1913:

> He [Pater] has never been compared to Nietzsche. Yet no student of Pater's *ideas* could avoid such a comparison, fantastic as it may seem ... Before *The Birth of Tragedy* was written, Pater had distinguished Apollo and Dionysus ... as the particular deities of opposed artistic tendencies. At one with Nietzsche in his conception of the relative nature of truth, though he shrank from carrying it to battle *à l'outrance*, he says almost what Nietzsche says of the evil influence of 'the ideal,' 'the absolute,' on European thought ... Mildly, as if it did not matter, he murmurs what Nietzsche shouted: The European mind will never be quite sane again ... And he traces its insanity, as Nietzsche might have traced it, through the Neo-Platonists, *The Imitation*, Spinoza, Descartes, Malebranche, Leibniz, Berkeley. ... And in his criticism of the Sophists, he shows that he is aware ... of the theory of two moralities, one of the ruler and another of the ruled. ... He shared Nietzsche's dislike of dialectic, because in approaching the condition of mathematical speculation [,] philosophy denudes itself of personality ... [The] portraits [of Heraclitus, Parmenides, and Pythagoras], inset in [*Plato and Platonism*] ... are curiously suggestive of paragraphs of Nietzsche's *Early Greek Philosophy*. They are ruled by just such a conception of truth ... so characteristic of the man who preached rather than denounced his version of the Eternal Recurrence.[2]

Arthur Ransome's points are good ones, and are particularly interesting in that they mostly concern *Plato and Platonism*, a work which has not normally been linked with Nietzsche's name; but it must be stressed that he is only drawing a – pretty convincing – parallel, not describing an 'influence'. And of course the parallels can be extended: both Nietzsche and Pater advocated living a life of sustained ecstasy: Zarathustra's commandments "Be hard!" and "Ready must thou be to burn thyself in thine own flame" are paralleled in Pater's definition (in the famous Conclusion to his *Renaissance*) of "success in life" as being "To burn always with this hard, gemlike flame, to maintain this ecstasy", and in his crystal-imagery. Marius is obliged, in truly Nietzschean fashion, to construct "the world for himself in great measure from within". And so on.

More recently some Pater scholars have assumed that the essay 'A Study of Dionysus' (1876) shows an unacknowledged debt to Nietzsche's early writings. In this essay Pater does after all make a distinction between two opposite tendencies in ancient Greek art which roughly correspond to Nietzsche's 'Apollo' and 'Dionysos':

> Hence, all through the history of Greek art, there is a struggle, a *Streben*, as the Germans say, between the palpable and limited human form, and the floating essence it is to contain. On the one hand, was the teeming, still fluid world, of old beliefs ... a world [of] Titanic vastness ... On the other hand, there was that limiting, controlling tendency, identified with the Dorian influence in the history of the Greek mind, the spirit of a severe and wholly self-conscious intelligence ... ending in the entirely humanised religion of Apollo.[3]

Pater later elaborated this distinction between 'European' (or 'centripetal') and 'Asiatic' (or 'centrifugal') art-forms which are, indeed, associated with Apollo and Dionysos respectively; the terms 'centripetal' and 'centrifugal' were presumably borrowed from Schopenhauer's *Die Welt als Wille und Vorstellung*. It must be stressed, however, that there is no evidence that Pater was influenced by Nietzsche's analysis of the 'Apollonian-Dionysiac duality', or indeed that he ever read *The Birth of Tragedy*, which first appeared in German in January 1872. There is, in fact, every reason to suppose that we are faced here with a *parallel* only, albeit a close one. Having said this, the parallel is worth examining briefly. Nietzsche, after all, writes of "that measured limitation, that freedom from the wilder emotion, that philosophical calmness of the sculptor-god [Apollo]" as opposed to the "titanic-barbaric nature of the Dionysian", "those Dionysian emotions ... in the augmentation of which the subjective vanishes to complete self-forgetfulness";[4] he contrasts the "inbursting flood of the Dionysian" with the "austere majesty of Doric art".[5] On the basis of such distinctions he speaks of "The Apollonian appearances in which Dionysos objectifies himself"[6] and defines Greek tragedy as the "objectivation [= objectification] of a Dionysian state ... the Apollonian embodiment of Dionysian perceptions".[7] Indeed, not only do Pater and Nietzsche describe ancient Greek art as the product of opposing objective (Apolline) and subjective (Dionysian) tendencies; they are agreed that it reached its zenith when these opposing tendencies were united:

> Thus ... the intricate relation of the Apollonian and the Dionysian in tragedy must ... be symbolized by a fraternal union of the two deities: Dionysos speaks the language of Apollo; Apollo, however, finally speaks the language of Dionysos; and so the highest goal of tragedy and of art in general is reached. [Nietzsche][8]

> These two tendencies, then, met and struggled and were harmonized in the supreme imagination, of Pheidias, in sculpture – of Aeschylus, in the drama. [Pater][9]

Pater's famous statement that "All art aspires to the condition of music" reflects his ideal of a totally balanced or harmonized art, an ideal which, as we have just seen, he shared with Nietzsche, who wrote of "the only possible relation between poetry and music ... : the word, the picture, the concept ... seeks an expression analogous to music."[10] For both men Goethe stood as the supreme embodiment of the balanced artistic personality. Similarly, Pater's view of Italian Renaissance art as combining the centrifugal and the centripetal parallels Nietzsche's view of Greek tragedy as combining Apollonian and Dionysian elements.

Coming back to the distinction between 'Apollo' and 'Dionysos', it is true, as G. C. Monsman has said,[11] that Nietzsche conceives of Dionysos as subjective and 'centrifugal', and of Apollo as objective and 'centripetal'. Contrasting Homer, "the aged dreamer sunk in himself, the type of the Apollonian naïve artist", with Archilochus, "the subjectively willing and desiring man", Nietzsche remarks that "here the 'objective' artist is confronted by the first 'subjective' artist."[12] Pater, for his part, also identifies the subjective tendency with the "teeming, still fluid world" of Dionysos (cf. Nietzsche's reference to the 'Dionysiac flood-tide'), while stating that the 'Dorian' ("objective") tendency is embodied in the religion of Apollo. Both writers in fact contrast the Dionysian art of the flood with what Nietzsche, using Pater's favourite metaphor, calls "the Apollonian light-picture".[13] For both men Apollo stands for order, Dionysos for disorder. G. C. Monsman has commented on this general parallel: "One would be tempted to see a borrowing from Nietzsche on Pater's part were it not for two considerations: first,

Pater seems to have thought in these terms from ... 1864 ... , and second, there is an important difference between Nietzsche and Pater in the rendering of the personality of Dionysus".[14] The first point here is a valid one: since Pater analyses the Apollonian personality in 'Diaphaneitè' (1864), and then applies this analysis to Greek art in 'Winckelmann' (1867), there can be no question of borrowing from Nietzsche. It is hardly true, however, to argue that 'for Pater the personality of Dionysus is somewhat more complex than it was for Nietzsche".[15] After all, in 'Diaphaneitè' and 'Winckelmann' it is Apollo, and not Dionysos, who holds Pater's attention; and when he then comes to write 'A Study of Dionysus' (1876), his statement that Dionysos is "twofold", "a Doppelgänger", is itself completely in line with Nietzsche's view. In *The Birth of Tragedy* Nietzsche writes of "the mysterious twilight of the Dionysian",[16] adding that "In his existence as a dismembered god, Dionysos has the dual nature of a cruel barbarized demon, and a mild pacific ruler",[17] and that "The one ... Dionysos appears in a multiplicity of forms".[18] Monsman surely oversimplifies when he implies that Nietzsche's Dionysos is a single abstract cipher, whereas Pater's is a truly mythical *Doppelgänger*: "For Nietzsche, Dionysus was merely a personification of a component in an abstract philosophical scheme. Pater's handling of the god, on the other hand, is poetically far superior, for he introduces him as a protagonist not merely in an ideological pattern but in a truly mythic pattern."[19] This is arguably both to overrate Pater and to do Nietzsche less than justice. Pater's treatment of Dionysos may or may not be poetically superior; the real point is that it is quite different from Nietzsche's. On this particular point a more reliable guide is W. F. Barry, who in his article 'The Ideals of Anarchy' was one of the first critics to note the parallels between Pater and Nietzsche:

> For an English reader, probably the speediest way into [*The Birth of Tragedy*], would be through Walter Pater's meditations on 'Dionysus, the spiritual form of fire and dew,' on the Bacchanals of Euripides, the myth of Demeter and Persephone, and the romantic elements – so he terms them – in Hellenic religion. But Nietzsche takes a grander sweep ... Profoundly observant of the recurring cycles in [Greek] civilization, he goes beyond Pater and the folk-lore which is content to deduce the Eleusinian

> mysteries from corn and wine. He sees in them a philosophy encompassing all the mythologies.[20]

Pater's conception of Dionysos is in fact hardly more complex than Nietzsche's. When all is said and done, Pater's Dionysos is a vegetation-god with unmistakable *fin-de-siècle* characteristics; there is a parallel between Pater's "chthonian god", who, "like all the children of the earth, has an element of sadness", and Yeats' "sad and desirous" 'nineties Dionysos. Nietzsche's Dionysos may be essentially an abstract component in an ideological pattern, but this pattern is also a "truly mythic" one, and Nietzsche's Dionysos is a grandiose abstraction whose shattering sorrows make the "sadness" of Pater's god look rather anaemic. Besides, the patron-god of Pater's imaginative world is Apollo rather than Dionysos; for Pater it is Apollo who is the symbol of cultural rebirth, whereas with Nietzsche this rôle is assigned to Dionysos. While it is therefore true that the terms 'Dionysian' and 'Apollonian' belong fully as much to Pater's thought as to Nietzsche's,[21] the crux of the matter is that these terms, which both writers arrived at independently within very few years of one another (Nietzsche first set forth the antithesis 'Apollonian: Dionysian' in a lecture on 'The Dionysian Principle' written in 1870[22]), have in part quite different connotations in their respective works.

One reason for the, in part, very close parallels between Pater's and Nietzsche's views of Greece may be that both men apparently drew on Karl Ottfried Müller's *Die Dorier* (1824).[23] In *Plato and Platonism* Pater several times referred to Müller, his debt to whom is obvious. But what of Nietzsche? The passage in *The Birth of Tragedy*[24] where he writes "Apollo could not live without Dionysos" appears to echo Müller's statement that "[Apollo's] character could only be shown in opposition with a system of hostile attributes and powers";[25] Nietzsche's view in the same context that "I can only explain to myself the *Doric* state and Doric art as a permanent war-camp of the Apollonian" is again Müller's view precisely. Pater's distinction between the Apollonian and the Dionysian may also reflect the thinking of one of his pupils at Oxford: Gerard Manley Hopkins.

In his unfinished Platonic dialogue *On the Origin of Beauty* (12 May 1865), Hopkins formulated two theories of beauty which are important for his own later poetry. After stating that beauty consists in the judicious blending of regularity with variety, he proceeds to distinguish between two different kinds of beauty, symmetrical ('diatonic') and asymmetrical ('chromatic') beauty. Diatonic beauty is characterized by formal balance and emotional restraint; chromatic beauty, by contrast, is irregular, unrestrained, intense. *Here* already is the basic distinction between what Nietzsche, seven years *later*, was to term 'Apollo' and 'Dionysos'. When Pater makes similar distinctions in his own later work, it therefore seems clear that he is elaborating ideas which he had held for some time, ideas which both gave Hopkins his starting-point and which were no doubt further clarified by Hopkins' treatment of them. Quoting Humphrey House's remark that "I have seen a suggestion somewhere that [Hopkins'] dialogue was written for Walter Pater",[26] Professor W. H. Gardner states that "*On the Origin of Beauty* almost certainly owes something to Hopkins' intercourse with Pater".[27] In fact one can be more specific and say that Hopkins' distinction between 'diatonic' and 'chromatic' beauty is almost certainly indebted to Pater's own first essay, the 'Diaphaneitè' of July 1864. In this grossly neglected essay, which contains the seeds of so much of his later work, Pater is feeling his way towards a definition of the Apollonian type of man or artist, and, in what was to be his characteristic Hegelian manner, he makes a series of distinctions between 'diaphaneitè' and its opposites, viz.:

clear crystal nature fine edge of light pure white light	breadth of colour
restraint	violence
simplicity and repose	struggle
innocence	wisdom
harmonious	confused, unmusical
transparency	intransparency
wholeness of nature	(lack of restraint)

Once these distinctions have been noted, it seems highly likely that Hopkins' *On the Origin of Beauty* was prompted by his tutor's 'Diaphaneitè'. Hopkins will have sought to elaborate Pater's concept of 'diaphaneitè' into a theory of 'diatonic' beauty, and to show that the opposite quality also forms the basis of a different kind of ('chromatic') beauty. The parallel between 'diatonic' beauty and 'diaphaneitè', and between 'chromatic' beauty and the 'breadth of colour' which Pater opposed to 'transparency', speaks for itself. Hopkins' statement that 'the diatonic scale, you know, leaves out, the chromatic puts in the half notes" appears to echo Pater's reference to "those evanescent shades, which fill up the blanks between contrasted types of character." Now if this identification of his source is right, it means that Hopkins is partly elaborating Pater's concept and is partly carrying it further (again in the Hegelian manner of the 1860s) by positing its antithesis. It also seems likely that Pater's thought will have been helped forward by his pupil's essay; after 1865 Pater's criticism becomes much more obviously dialectic (European: Asiatic, Classic: Romantic, objective: subjective, Doric: Ionian, centrifugal: centripetal, masculine: feminine, mind: soul, etc.) in that it proceeds by way of the Hegelian dialectic which he absorbed at Oxford, a dialectic in which he may well have followed the lead of his brilliant pupil.

There is a further point which is worth making about Pater's little-known essay. This is that 'Diaphaneitè' is the source of some of the most memorable passages in the 'Winckelmann' essay of 1867, cf.:

the tumultuary richness of Goethe's nature	the tumultuous richness of Goethe's culture
This colourless, unclassified purity of life ... blending and interpenetration of intellectual, moral and spiritual elements	This colourless, unclassified purity of life, with its blending and interpenetration of intellectual, spiritual, and physical elements
The beauty of the Greek statues was a sexless beauty; the statues of the gods had the least traces of sex. Here there is a moral sexlessness, a kind of impotence, an intellectual wholeness of nature, yet with a divine beauty and significance of its own	[identical]

The way in which Pater incorporated passages from 'Diaphaneitè' into 'Winckelmann' not only proves that 'diaphaneitè' is an *Apollonian* quality; it also suggests that he would not have wished his essay of 1864 to be published since he had already used some of the best things in it in 1867.

It therefore seems incontrovertible that precisely those elements in Pater's work which have been seen as 'Nietzschean' are in fact already present in his thought from 1864 onwards, eight years before Nietzsche published his first work. Arthur Symons' comment in his *Plays, Acting, and Music* (1903) that "There are many pages, scattered throughout his work, in which Pater has dealt with some of the Greek problems very much in the spirit of Nietzsche"[28] remains basically true, although it would be more accurate to say that Pater deals with such problems in the *manner* of Nietzsche, for when all is said and done Pater's 'spirit' is not Nietzsche's; there is *nothing* in his later work that *need* have come from Nietzsche, even if he knew Nietzsche's work, which is very doubtful. It therefore seems both unnecessary and unjustified for critics to continue to speak of Pater's indebtedness to Nietzsche. This being so, it is time that we turned our attention to Pater's 'disciple', Arthur Symons, who enthused over Nietzsche more than any other writer of the 'nineties generation.

Although he came across Nietzsche's name by 1896 at the latest, Arthur Symons' interest in Nietzsche dated from about 1902. It is misleading to imply, as Roger Lhombreaud has done,[29] that Symons knew of Nietzsche by 1891. Quoting from Symons' essay on 'Beethoven' in the *Studies in Seven Arts* (1906):

> Germany has had both poets and philosophers, who have done great things; but it has done nothing supreme except in music. Dürer created a very German kind of beauty; philosophers from Kant to Nietzsche have created system after system of philosophy, each building on a foundation made out of the ruins of the last ... Goethe, excellent in all things, was supreme in none.[30]

Lhombreaud implies that this passage is "reprinted" from notes which Symons made on the occasion of his visit to Germany in July 1891; no evidence is adduced in support of this claim. In view of Symons' lack of knowledge of and sympathy with things German at that time, it seems highly unlikely that he should have been the first English man of letters to hear of Nietzsche; it is far more likely that this reference to Nietzsche dates from 1904, the year in which the essay on Beethoven was written; by 1904 Symons had known Nietzsche's work for several years.

As editor of *The Savoy* (1896), Symons will have read the series of articles on Nietzsche by Havelock Ellis, with whom he enjoyed a "memorable friendship". But it was not until about 1902 that Symons got to know Nietzsche's work at first-hand. In his *Plays, Acting, and Music* (1903), he included a chapter entitled 'Nietzsche on Tragedy' which takes the form of a review of *L'Origine de la Tragédie, ou Hellénisme et Pessimisme*;[31] in this review, first published in *The Academy and Literature*,[32] he writes:

> I have been reading Nietzsche on the Origin of Tragedy ... with the delight of one who discovers a new world, which he has seen already in a dream. I never take up Nietzsche without the surprise of finding something familiar. Sometimes it is the answer to a question which I have only asked; sometimes it seems to me that I have guessed at the answer. And, in his restless energy, his hallucinatory vision, the agility of this climbing mind of the mountains, I find that invigoration which only a 'tragic philosopher' can give. ... The whole book is awakening; in Nietzsche's own words, 'a prodigious hope speaks in it.'

Most of the rest of the essay is a summary of Nietzsche's argument in *The Birth of Tragedy*; but this summary too shows that Symons found Nietzsche's ideas and style sympathetic; he writes of Nietzsche's "argument which has itself the ecstatic quality of which it speaks", of his "astonishing figures of speech", and compares his treatment of the Greek theme with Pater's, praising Nietzsche's "more rigorous logic". In view of his friendship with Havelock Ellis and John Davidson, and the fact that by then much of Nietzsche's work was already available in English, it seems strange that Symons should have discovered Nietzsche as late as 1902 and that he should have read him first in French – though one feels that this is also characteristic. Besides, he also read *The Saturday Review*, in which Shaw had written on Nietzsche. However, it was no doubt because of the delight with which he found himself reading *The Birth of Tragedy* in 1902, that Symons went on to read *Thus Spake Zarathustra* and *Dawn of Day* several years later; by 1907, as we shall see, his aesthetic fascination had given way to a more vigorous acceptance of Nietzsche.

Symons also mentions Nietzsche elsewhere in *Plays, Acting, and Music*. In 'The New Bayreuth', for instance, he alludes to *The Birth of Tragedy* in these terms: "The music, as in Nietzsche's interpretation, was the 'Dionysiac' element, the vital principle; the rest was the picture, the human illusion, which the music held back into its place, on the other side of the gulf".[33] The allusion here is to Nietzsche's analysis of Wagner's *Tristan und Isolde* in *The Birth of Tragedy*,[34] where he writes of "the Dionysian primordial element of music", "the Apollonian illusion ... the assiduous veiling during the performance of tragedy of the intrinsically Dionysian effect", "the innermost abyss of things". Symons repeatedly refers to Nietzsche in connexion with Wagner; thus in 'Parsifal and the Pathetic Symphony'[35] there is a reference to Nietzsche, whose name is, however, misspelt; and there is another reference in 'The Ideas of Wagner'.[36]

In *Studies in Seven Arts* (1906) Nietzsche is – inevitably – mentioned a number of times in the essay 'The Problem of Richard Strauss'; one comment – "Nothing so unlike Nietzsche was ever written as the 'Also sprach Zarathustra' of Strauss"[37] – implies that Symons knew Nietzsche's *Thus Spake Zarathustra* by this time; in fact he probably read it in 1906, for he quotes from it in his book on Blake (see below). In the essay on 'Beethoven' Symons also quoted Schopenhauer's view of music ("Music, as Schopenhauer has made clear to us, is not a representation of the world, but an immediate voice of the world"[38]), which he will have gleaned either from *The Birth of Tragedy*,[39] or from Wagner; at this time of his life Symons was, like George Moore, under Wagner's spell.

At this time (1906/7) he was also, if not 'influenced', at least most impressed by Nietzsche's work. This is shown by the most significant piece of evidence in this context, Symons' book *William Blake* (1907), the Introduction to which contains not only a detailed examination of the many parallels between Blake and Nietzsche (which also caught Yeats' eye), but also Symons' longest, most significant, and most eulogistic comment on Nietzsche, beginning:

> Thought to-day, wherever it is most individual, owes either force or direction to Nietzsche, and thus we see, on our topmost towers, the Philistine armed and winged, and without the love or fear of God or man in his heart, doing battle in Nietzsche's name against the ideas of Nietzsche. No one can think, and escape Nietzsche.[40]

This is one of the most acclamatory statements on Nietzsche by a writer of the 'Nineties generation. And Symons goes on to give a sympathetic and well-informed summary of what Nietzsche's philosophy means to him:

> The philosophy of Nietzsche was made out of his nerves and was suffering … Nietzsche's mind is the most sleepless of minds; with him every sensation turns instantly into the stuff of thought; he is terribly alert, the more so because he never stops to systematize; he must be for ever apprehending. He darts out feelers in every direction, relentlessly touching the whole substance of the world. His apprehension is minute rather than broad; he is content to seize one thing at a time, and he is content if each separate thing remains separate; no theory ties together or limits his individual intuitions. What we call his philosophy is really no more than the aggregate of these intuitions coming to us through the medium of a remarkable personality. His personality stands to him in the place of a system. Speaking of Kant and Schopenhauer, he says: 'Their thoughts do not constitute a passionate history of the soul.' His thoughts are the passionate history of his soul. It is for this reason that he is an artist among philosophers rather than a pure philosopher. And remember that he is also not, in the absolute sense, the poet, but the artist. He saw and dreaded the weaknesses of the artist, his side-issues in the pursuit of truth. But in so doing he dreaded one of his own weaknesses.[41]

Given that it was written at a time when 'Nietzscheism' was far more widespread than knowledge of the philosopher's work, this is surely excellent criticism. Enthusiasm is tempered with first-hand knowledge. The numerous quotations from Nietzsche, that occur when Symons is discussing parallels between Blake and Nietzsche, show that by 1907 he had read not only *Thus Spake Zarathustra*, but also *Dawn of Day* (from which most of his quotations are taken).

The parallels which he proceeds to draw between Blake and Nietzsche are particularly interesting because writers like Yeats and Read were to come to Nietzsche via Blake. He writes:

> The Marriage of Heaven and Hell anticipates Nietzsche in his most significant paradoxes, and before his time, exalts energy above reason, and Evil, 'the active springing from energy,' above Good, 'the passive that obeys reason.' … When Nietzsche says [in *Dawn of Day*]: 'Let us rid the world of the notion of sin, and banish with it the idea of punishment,' he expresses one of Blake's central doctrines … [Blake], like Nietzsche, hated asceticism … 'Put off holiness,' he said, 'and put on intellect.' And 'the fool

> shall not enter into heaven, let him be ever so holy.' Is not this a heaven after the heart of Nietzsche? ... Yet, to Nietzsche, with his strange, scientific distrust of the imagination, ... there comes distrust, hesitation, a kind of despair, precisely at the point where Blake enters into his liberty. 'The habits of our senses,' says Nietzsche [in *Dawn of Day*], 'have plunged us into the lies and deceptions of feeling.' ... Blake said, 'The tigers of wrath are wiser than the horses of instruction,' and it is partly in what they helped to destroy that Blake and Nietzsche are at one; but destruction, with Blake, was the gesture of a hand which brushes aside needless hindrances, while to Nietzsche it was 'an intellectual thing,' the outer militant part of 'the silent, self-sufficient man in the midst of a general enslavement, who practises self-defence against the outside world, and is constantly living in a state of supreme fortitude.'[42]

Although these and other comments shed not a little light on Symons' view of Nietzsche, it must be remembered that he is elucidating not Nietzsche, but Blake; Nietzsche is used to explain and even to justify Blake to the reader of 1907, which throws an interesting incidental light on the relative popularity of the two writers at the time:

> And so, like Nietzsche, but with a deeper innocence, he [Blake] finds himself 'beyond good and evil', in a region where the soul is naked and its own master. Most of his art is the unclothing of the soul ... After *Zarathustra*, *Jerusalem* no longer seems a wild heresy. People were frightened because they were told that Blake was mad, or a blasphemer. Nietzsche, who has cleared away so many obstructions from thought, has shamed us from hiding behind these treacherous and unavailing defences.[43]

In justifying Blake, Symons may have written "Nietzsche has come after Blake, and will pass before Blake passes",[44] but the fact remains that in his *William Blake* he comes forward as the advocate not only of Blake, but of his successor, Nietzsche, to whom he sees all contemporary thought as variously indebted. His own enthusiasm speaks for itself.

Two years later, in *The Romantic Movement in English Poetry* (1909), Symons repeated his parallel between Blake and Nietzsche, quoting verbatim from his *William Blake*: "And so, like Nietzsche, but with a deeper innocence, he finds himself 'beyond good and evil', in a region where the soul is naked and its own master".[45] It seems quite possible that the comparison of Blake and Nietzsche may have been prompted by Symons' memory or re-reading of the essays by Yeats (on Blake) and Havelock Ellis (on Nietzsche) in *The Savoy*. When he began work on his *William Blake*, it would have been natural to re-read Yeats' essay; if he did so, he would have been likely to re-read Ellis's essay too. Symons' view of Blake certainly parallels Yeats' view, which they must have discussed together; and a few of the passages from *Dawn of Day* which Symons quotes were also quoted by Havelock Ellis.

Despite Arthur Symons' reading of *The Birth of Tragedy*, *Thus Spake Zarathustra*, and *Dawn of Day*, and his evident enthusiasm for Nietzsche in the first decade of the present century, there is no reason to suppose that he was himself 'influenced' by Nietzsche in any meaningful sense. True, there are passages in his essays of the period which *might* reflect on his reading of Nietzsche, cf. these lines from 'A Censor of Critics' (in *Studies in Prose and Verse*, 1904): "The world is becoming more and more democratic, and with democracy art has nothing to do … [The crowd] is powerful now, it must have … the slave's revenge on its masters." But, although they were written in 1902, when Nietzsche may well have been in the front of his mind, there is no reason to suppose that these lines do in fact echo Nietzsche's views directly (Arthur Symons was an 'aristocrat of letters' long before he read Nietzsche); and even if they do, this is no more than an isolated instance. In general, it is much more likely that Nietzsche simply helped Symons to clarify and express more forcefully ideas which he already held – which is exactly what he did for Symons' friend Yeats. Thus the lines written in 1900 – "the first duty … of every man … is to escape from material reality into whatever form of ecstasy is our own form of spiritual existence"[46] – sound 'Nietzschean' enough, but since Symons was hardly aware of Nietzsche by 1900, it is merely a question of a parallel, a parallel which helps to explain the fascination which Nietzsche's writings clearly held for Symons. Nietzsche's ideas tend in fact to parallel Symons' ideas. A case in point is Symons' view of the dance.

Although Symons, like Yeats, appears to have first read Nietzsche in 1902, there is a very close resemblance between his view of the dance as expressed in 1897 in the poem 'The Dance':

cast adrift in unchainable ecstasy,
Once, and once only, heart to heart, and soul to soul,
For an immortal moment we endured the whole
Rapture of intolerable immortality[47]

and Nietzsche's description of Dionysian ecstasy in *The Birth of Tragedy*:

> Dionysian emotions awake, in the augmentation of which the subjective vanishes to complete self-forgetfulness ... Under the charm of the Dionysian not only is the covenant between man and man again established, but also estranged, hostile or subjugated nature again celebrates her reconciliation with her lost son, man. ... In song and in dance man exhibits himself as a member of a higher community: he has forgotten how to walk and speak, and is on the point of taking a dancing flight into the air. His gestures bespeak enchantment ... he feels himself a god ... Man is no longer an artist, he has become a work of art ... In the Dionysian dithyramb man is incited to the highest exaltation of all his symbolic faculties; something never before experienced struggles for utterance – the annihilation of the veil of Mâyâ.[48]

Under this condition of ecstatic self-transcendence, "each one feels himself not only united, reconciled, blended with his neighbour, but as one with him, as if the veil of Mâyâ had been torn and were now merely fluttering in tatters before the mysterious Primordial Unity".[49] Then, indeed, to quote from Yeats' notes for the first *Vision*, "unity of being [is] perfectly attained".[50] Symons' image of the two dancers whose "two souls rushed together and were one" is, of course, analogous to Yeats' gyres which whirl until "unity of being" is attained; but both images have a common analogue in the above passage from *The Birth of Tragedy*. The passage in Symons' 'The World as Ballet' (1898), in which he says that the dancers "dissolve the will into slumber", again parallels Nietzsche's passage about Dionysian emotions, "in the augmentation of which the subjective vanishes to complete self-forgetfulness."

The dance is an important symbol in the thought not only of Yeats and Symons, but also of Nietzsche; for all three writers it is the symbol of self-transcendence, of what they variously call "Primordial Unity" (Nietzsche), "unity of being" (the state of equilibrium of the Thirteenth Cycle: Yeats), "possession and abandonment, the very pattern and symbol of earthly love" (Arthur Symons).[51] But while Yeats and Symons presumably exchanged views on this subject when they were living together at Fountain Court, it seems unlikely that either of them received any initial stimulus from Nietzsche (unlike John Gould Fletcher who a decade later used Nietzschean terminology to describe his reaction to Nijinsky). Both writers appear not to have read Nietzsche until 1902. We therefore seem to be faced by another of those parallels which enable us to speak of a characteristically ''Nineties' view of things common to England and Germany. This in turn stresses both how much of a quintessentially ''Nineties' figure Nietzsche was, and how basic to the 1890s was his concept of 'Dionysian art'.

Arthur Symons was, as I have said, an 'aristocrat of letters' (who made something of a cult of solitude) long before he read Nietzsche. What we see in his work is not so much the influence of Nietzsche, as the vitalism which is so typical of the 1890s. It is, surely, significant that when he read *The Birth of Tragedy* he delighted in some of Nietzsche's ideas because they were somehow 'familiar'; in other words, because they corresponded with his own inarticulate inner thoughts. To call Arthur Symons a 'Nietzschean', as Oscar Levy did, is to go too far, although there *was* at least one genuine Nietzschean among his fellow-members of The Rhymers Club: John Davidson. Before considering Davidson, however, we must take account of an admirer of Pater and friend of Symons – George Moore.

Chapter Three
Stellar friendship: George Moore and Nietzsche

Although George Moore may not be the most obvious figure to find in the present context, he had many friends and acquaintances who were interested in Nietzsche (including Édouard Dujardin, Daniel Halévy, Theodore de Wyzewa, W. B. Yeats, Arthur Symons, John Eglinton, and Havelock Ellis), and his name crops up at several important points in our story: Moore knew Theodore de Wyzewa, author of the article which sparked off John Davidson's enthusiasm for Nietzsche; he was in touch with Havelock Ellis in 1896 and knew *The Savoy*, in which Ellis's historic articles appeared; and he was 're-introduced' to Yeats in 1902 by John Quinn, who was just then recommending Yeats to read Nietzsche.

Chameleon-like as ever, George Moore plays an ambiguous part in the present story. In *Salve*, the second volume of *Hail and Farewell*,[1] he wrote of himself: "There is very little Nietzsche in me, but this much of him I remember, that we must pursue our courses valiantly, come what may." Though not the only reference to Nietzsche in his work, this is the only passage in which Moore links Nietzsche with himself. Now since Moore, a self-proclaimed 'Objectivist', is not at his most objective when writing about himself, it will be as well to consider his statement in some detail.

In his *The Life of George Moore* (1936), Joseph Hone quoted Moore as saying in 1904: "I find not only my Protestant sympathies in the *Confessions* [*of a Young Man*] but a proud agnosticism and an exalted individualism which in certain passages lead the reader to the sundered rock about the cave of Zarathustra".[2] This comment is, to say the least, ambiguous: it is simply not clear whether Moore is alluding to *Thus Spake Zarathustra* as the source of or a parallel to "certain passages" in his *Confessions of a Young Man* (1888, 3rd edn: 1904). Hone comments:

> The reference to Nietzsche is interesting, because Moore, as John Eglinton recalls for me, caught a good deal from the German ... philosopher of whom he had heard much earlier from Dujardin. I myself remember his admiration for his friend, Daniel Halévy's *Vie de Nietzsche*; it was in this way that biography should be written, he said.[3]

Incidentally, Joseph Hone, biographer of George Moore and W. B. Yeats, should be reliable on this subject since he himself took an interest in Nietzsche; in addition to translating Halévy's *The Life of Friedrich Nietzsche* (1911), he published an article on 'Nietzsche and Culture' in the *Contemporary Review*.[4] Now George Moore corresponded with Édouard Dujardin, editor of *La Revue Wagnérienne* and *La Revue Indépendante*, from November 1886,[5] and Dujardin was by all accounts one of the earliest of the French Nietzscheans. Moore himself refers to his friend's enthusiasm for Nietzsche in *Conversations in Ebury Street*: "It will never be clear to me whether it was Kant or Nietzsche or Palestinian folk-lore that interrupted the successful administration of *Fin de Siècle*".[6] And in *Hail and Farewell*[7] he refers to Dujardin's habit of invoking "Schopenhauer and Nietzsche" in the context of discussions about Wagner. Moore therefore may very well have heard about Nietzsche from Dujardin in 1886–7, while he was working on *The Confessions of a Young Man*, which was serialized in Dujardin's *Revue Indépendante* in 1888; Dujardin was a man of many enthusiasms, but his enthusiasm for Wagner and Nietzsche dates from this time.

Besides, if the *Confessions* do echo *Thus Spake Zarathustra* at certain points, as Moore implied they do, it would certainly follow that his knowledge of Nietzsche could only have come from Dujardin; there were, after all, no English or French translations of Nietzsche's work available in the 1880s, and George Moore could not read German.[8] Indeed, although many writers in the period 1880–1914 knew French – compare the immense influence of French Naturalists and Symbolists on other writers besides Moore in the 1890s – few could read German, which still tended to be regarded as a "gross tongue, partially redeemed by Heine" (Lionel Johnson). Besides, Moore claimed, in 1906, to "know nothing of German literature";[9] he accordingly resolved to consult Kuno Meyer, who assured him that Nietzsche was among the great German writers.[10] In this case Moore's modesty seems to have got the better of him, for he greatly admired Schopenhauer and Wagner, and was also fond of referring to Goethe and Heine.

The *Confessions of a Young Man* has been called an attempt to introduce 'diabolism' to the English mind, 'diabolism' being both a Victorianism for what Moore himself called the "proud agnosticism" of the work, and a word with positively Nietzschean connotations (compare Bernard Shaw's recognition of Nietzsche as a fellow-'Diabolonian'); indeed, one suspects that John Eglinton's maiden aunt was not alone in regarding George Moore as "a child of Hell".

Now let us turn our attention to the *Confessions* in order to see if there are, in fact, any echoes of ideas from *Thus Spake Zarathustra* there; since Moore at this time could only have heard of certain Nietzschean ideas at second hand, the actual phrasing is unimportant. There are, firstly, a number of passages in which Moore expresses his love of "the great pagan world of marble and pomp and lust and cruelty, that my soul goes out to and hails as the grandest",[11] the "antique world, its plain passion".[12] Such views parallel Nietzsche, of course; but they appear to derive from Pater and Gautier, for Moore writes: "I too am of their [Pater's and Gautier's] company – in this at least I too love the great pagan world, its bloodshed, its slaves, its loathing of all that is feeble".[13] This brings us to the next point, Moore's preference for "the strong": "the terrible austere laws of nature which ordain that the weak shall be trampled upon, shall be ground into death and dust, that the strong shall be really strong – that the strong shall be glorious, sublime".[14] Here there is an even closer parallel with

Nietzsche's views as expressed, particularly, in works after *Thus Spake Zarathustra*; but here too there is nothing specifically Nietzschean – Moore may well simply be expressing the love of vitality that is part and parcel of *fin-de-siècle* aestheticism; there is, for instance, a clear parallel with Yeats' aristocratic ethic here. Allied to this glorification of brute strength is the disdain for 'weak' virtues such as pity:

> Pity, that most vile of all vile virtues, has never been known to me. The great pagan world I love knew it not ... The light which I, a pagan, standing on the last verge of the old world, declare to be darkness, the coming night of pity and justice which is imminent, which is the twentieth century.[15]

Here we are indeed close to Nietzsche, the Nietzsche of *Thus Spake Zarathustra*, who wrote: "So much justice and pity [do I see], so much weakness. ... Pity maketh stifling air for all free souls".[16] In this case the parallel is so close that Moore's idea could have come from Nietzsche, the more so since he goes on "Man would not be man but for injustice",[17] which accords with Nietzsche's statement that "injustice is necessary";[18] but it could equally well simply be a logical development of his previously quoted ideas. Personally, I suspect Dujardin's influence here.

Scattered throughout the *Confessions* are a number of other ostensibly 'Nietzschean' remarks, for instance: "Terrible is the day when each sees his soul naked, stripped of all veil ... Art is ... individuality ... Education destroys individuality ... Democratic art! Art is the direct antithesis to democracy ... the pale socialist of Galilee ... I hate Him and deny His divinity."[19] These and other similar remarks are closely paralleled at a number of points in Nietzsche's work; but here too one can only say that there is no evidence that any of them derive from Nietzsche even at second hand. They may simply show George Moore at his shocking best. True, the emphasis on individuality in art *may* have been reenforced by Dujardin's accounts of Nietzsche's attitude, the more so since it is allied with something rather like the transvaluation of values ("In his search for new formulas, new moulds, all the old values must be swept aside. The artist must arrive at a new estimate of things"[20]); but from such 'evidence' it is really impossible to tell whether 'Pagan Moore', as he was called for some time after the appearance of the *Pagan Poems* in 1881, did catch much of

Nietzsche from Dujardin in 1886–7 or later. On balance Schopenhauer seems a far more likely source than Nietzsche for many of the 'Nietzschean' passages in *Confessions.* The book contains a number of references to Schopenhauer – "Schopenhauer, oh, my Schopenhauer!"[21] – which show that Moore was under his spell in the late 1880s, and remained under it for some time; an aphorism like "Terrible and imperative is the voice of the will to live"[22] is glossed by the remark "If you had read Schopenhauer you would know that the flesh is ... the eternal objectification of the will to live".[23] Moreover, Joseph Hone reports that "when adding sixty pages to the third edition of the *Confessions* he [Moore] emphasized the importance of these new pages, since they enabled him to accentuate the philosophy of the book, that of Schopenhauer, who 'alone helps us to live' and 'alone shows us the real good and leads us from the real evil.' "[24] What Pater called the "personal and uncontrollable" element in *Confessions* is therefore more likely to be connected with Moore's knowledge of Schopenhauer than with what he may or may not have heard of Nietzsche from Dujardin.

There is in fact no real evidence in *Confessions* to support Moore's own statement, made in 1904, that certain passages in the book "lead the reader to ... Zarathustra." There is not a little that could pass as Nietzschean were the book first published in 1904; but in 1888 Moore's "proud agnosticism" clearly derives from Shelley, his "exalted individualism" from Gautier, and his love of the "great pagan world" from Pater. It seems possible, in fact, that in 1904 George Moore was claiming the then-fashionable Nietzsche as an ally, or was simply getting his dates muddled (as he often did). Be this as it may, he could not have *read* any Nietzsche by 1888; by *1898*, on the other hand, he clearly *had* read at least a few pages of Nietzsche.

In 1887 Moore got to know Theodore de Wyzewa, who reviewed 'A Mere Accident' in the *Revue Indépendante.* In 1891 Wyzewa published in *La Revue Politique et Littéraire* the article on Nietzsche which was to attract the attention of John Davidson. While there is no evidence that George Moore read the article, Wyzewa is likely to have sent him a copy; if he did, the article, coming on top of Dujardin's enthusiasm, might have prompted Moore to take an interest in Nietzsche. Moore certainly took considerable interest in the intellectual life of Paris, and from 1891 onwards (as opposed to 1896 onwards in England) Nietzsche's philosophy was discussed in most of the important reviews there. Both Schopenhauer and then Nietzsche came in on the wave of French Wagnerism, and to this extent Moore's attitude is typical of intellectual Paris in the 1880s and 1890s: he is interested in Wagner, Schopenhauer, and Nietzsche, *in that order*. To a lesser extent English Nietzscheanism also came in on the Wagnerian wave. We have seen that Arthur Symons came to Nietzsche via Wagner, and what was probably the first review of a work by Nietzsche in the English press, a review of *Richard Wagner in Bayreuth*, appeared in *The Athenaeum*[25] and amounted to a few lines at the end of a long review of Wagner's *Ring*, viz.: "The disciples and supporters of the Wagnerian system will find a most able exponent and champion thereof in ... Nietzsche ... whose essay is worthy of study." Leaving aside George Moore's literary Wagnerism,[26] it is rather later that we find him, according to Hone, enthusing over Daniel Halévy's *Vie de Nietzsche* (1909); Moore knew Halévy well, and was a neighbour of his in the Rue de la Tour des Dames in the late 1880s.

Now after recalling Moore's admiration of Halévy's Nietzsche-biography, Hone continues:

> Two of the most successful of his paraphrases resulted from this acquaintance, the one at the close of 'Resurgam' (*Memoirs of My Dead Life*) from Nietzsche's poem of the Eternal Return, the other in *Evelyn Innes*, where Ulick Dean bids farewell to the opera singer (the symbol of the two ships which have crossed paths), from Nietzsche's page on 'Stellar Friendship'.[27]

Unfortunately it is not clear from the context whether "this acquaintance" refers to Moore's acquaintance with Nietzsche's work or with Daniel Halévy. This is unfortunate because while Moore certainly does paraphrase Nietzsche's *The Joyful Wisdom* in *Evelyn Innes* (1898), there is no conclusive evidence as to how he came to know the passage in question. The English translation did not appear until 1910, and even the French translation only appeared in 1901, as part of the complete edition begun by the *Mercure de France* in 1898.* It is most likely that Moore first heard

* There was, however, an early French equivalent to Common's anthology: *A travers l'œuvre de Frédéric Nietzsche*, ed. P. Lauterbach and A. Wagnon (Paris: A. Schulz, 1893). Though there is no evidence that George Moore knew the book, it is another possible source for his knowledge of Nietzsche's passage on "Stellar Friendship".

of Nietzsche's passage on "Stellar Friendship" from Daniel Halévy on one of his visits to Paris; Halévy started writing on Nietzsche in 1892, and in his *The Life of Friedrich Nietzsche* he was to quote the passage in question. Otherwise, Moore could have heard of the passage from Dujardin; Nietzsche's passage summarizes his relationship with Wagner, and it was Wagner who loomed so large both in Dujardin's interests and in *Evelyn Innes.*

If there is some doubt about the source of Moore's knowledge, there is no doubt at all that Ulick Dean's farewell letter does paraphrase Nietzsche. In view of its importance, his letter must be quoted at length:

> Alas, from our first meeting, and before it, we were aware of the fate which has overtaken us. ... We are ships, and the destiny of ships is the ocean, the ocean draws us both: we have rested as long as may be, we have delayed our departure, but the tide has lifted us from our moorings. With an agonized heart I watched the sails of your ship go up, and now I see that mine, too, are going aloft, lifted by invisible hands. I look back upon the bright days and quiet nights we have rested in this tranquil harbour. Like ships that have rested a while in a casual harbour, blown hither by storms, we part, drawn apart by the eternal magnetism of the sea ... In the depths of our consciousness ... there lies a certain sense that our ways are different ways, and that we must fare forth alone, whither we know not, over the ocean's rim; and in this sense of destiny we must find comfort ... Ours is the same adventure, though a different breeze fills the sails, though the prows are set to a different horizon ... But, Evelyn, my heart is aching so ... the wide ocean which lies outside the harbour is so lonely ... 'May we not meet again?' my heart cries from time to time; 'may not some propitious storm blow us to the same anchorage again, into the same port?' Ah, the suns and the seas we shall have sailed through would render us unrecognisable, we should not know each other. Last night I wandered by the quays, and, watching the constellations, I asked if we were divided for ever, if, when the earth has become part and parcel of the stars, our love will not re-appear in some starry affinity, in some stellar friendship.[28]

This is a paraphrase of the following passage from *The Joyful Wisdom*:

> *Stellar Friendship.* – We were friends, and have become strangers to each other. ... We are two ships, each of which has its goal and its course; we may ... cross one another in our paths, and celebrate a feast together as we did before, – and then the gallant ships lay quietly in one harbour and in one sunshine, so that it might have been thought they were already at their goal, and that they had one goal. But then the almighty strength of our tasks forced us apart once more into different seas and into different zones, and perhaps we shall never see one another again, – or perhaps we may see one another, but not know one another again; the different seas and suns have altered us! That we had to become strangers to one another is the law to which we are subject: just by that shall we become more sacred to one another! ... There is probably some immense, invisible curve and stellar orbit in which our courses and goals, so widely different, may be comprehended as small stages of the way, – let us raise ourselves to this thought! ... And so we will believe in our stellar friendship.[29]

Even Evelyn's reflections on Ulick Dean's letter derive from Nietzsche: "The symbol of the ships seemed ... to express the union and the division and the destiny that had overtaken them ... in her vision ships hailed each other as they crossed in mid-ocean. Ships drew together as they entered a harbour. Ships separated as they fared forth, their prows set towards different horizons."[30]

The facts of this 'borrowing' speak for themselves. Moore has simply taken Nietzsche's passage and reproduced it bit by bit, expanding it as he does so. The final phrase in Ulick Dean's letter – "stellar friendship" – points directly to his unacknowledged source. Although he has improved upon Nietzsche's passage and turned it into the most memorable thing in his own novel, it could be argued that he has not sufficiently improved upon his model to justify borrowing it in this way. The fact that Nietzsche's work was unknown in England at the time may have had something to do with it.

Now Moore again refers to this passage and again uses Nietzsche's metaphor in some revealing lines in *Salve*, where he writes about Father Tom Finlay's *New Ireland Review*, to which he contributed in 1902:

> We shall not meet again, and if we do, of what use? We are like ships; all and sundry have destinies and destinations. There is

> very little Nietzsche in me, but this much of him I remember, that we must pursue our courses valiantly, come what may. Father Tom and I had lain side by side in harbour for a while, but the magnetism of the ocean drew me, and I continued to write, feeling all the while that my stories were drawing me away from Catholic Ireland.[31]

Since he uses it again in this way, Moore must have been pleased with his Nietzschean borrowing in *Evelyn Innes*. This autobiographical passage is not only the only passage in his work in which Moore writes of his own attitude to Nietzsche; it is also revealing that he here casts himself in the role of Nietzsche to Father Tom's Wagner, wheras in *Evelyn Innes* he was using the metaphor from the point of view of his Wagnerian heroine. In this passage from *Salve* Moore also provides the reference to Nietzsche that had been lacking in the novel, thus proving that the two ships metaphor there does in fact derive from Nietzsche. The self-dramatization in *Salve* is typical both of Moore, and of Nietzsche, whose work Moore claimed to have largely forgotten by 1912.

The other borrowing from Nietzsche, dating from 1906, is less blatant. I refer to this passage from 'Resurgam' at the end of *Memoirs of My Dead Life* (1906):

> What a ceaseless recurrence of the same things! ... At the end of ... some billion years, the ultimate moment towards which everything from the beginning has been moving, will be reached; and from that moment the tide will begin to flow out again, the eternal dispersal of things will begin again ... I believe that billions of years hence ... I shall be sitting in the same room where I sit now, writing the same lines that I am now writing.[32]

The idea here, though not the wording, echoes the idea which Nietzsche formulated in *The Joyful Wisdom*:

> This life, as thou livest it at present, and hast lived it, thou must live it once more, and also innumerable times; and there will be nothing new in it, but every pain and every joy and every thought and every sigh, and all the unspeakably small and great in thy life must come to thee again, and all in the same series and sequence – and similarly this spider and this moonlight among the trees, and similarly this moment, and I myself. The eternal

> sandglass of existence will ever be turned once more, and thou with it, thou speck of dust![33]

Nietzsche elaborated this idea in *Thus Spake Zarathustra*:

> Everything goeth, everything returneth; eternally rolleth the wheel of existence. Everything dieth, everything blossometh forth again; eternally runneth on the year of existence.
> Behold, we know what thou teachest: that all things eternally return, and ourselves with them, and that we have already existed times without number, and all things with us.
> Thou teachest that there is a great year of Becoming, a prodigy of a great year; it must, like a sand-glass, ever turn up anew, that it may anew run down and run out: – I come again … *not* to a new life …
> – I come again eternally to this identical and selfsame life, in its greatest and its smallest, to teach again the eternal recurrence of all things.[34]

It may well be that it is not the *Confessions*, but the passage from 'Resurgam', which leads the reader back to the sundered rocks about Zarathustra's cave. By 1906 Moore could have read *Thus Spake Zarathustra* in English.

George Moore remains enigmatic to the end. John Eglinton's reported statement that Moore "caught a good deal" from Nietzsche, is not confirmed by an examination of the facts. John Eglinton, the critic of the Irish literary revival, who wrote under the pseudonym William Magee, was himself interested in Nietzsche; in his *Anglo-Irish Essays* (1917) he devoted a chapter to 'A Way of Understanding Nietzsche'; while approving of Nietzsche's moral relativism, he criticized the superman-idea as "a little crazy". Since Moore apparently put himself out to impress Eglinton, he may have feigned a somewhat exaggerated interest in Nietzsche for the younger writer's benefit. Eglinton did not meet Moore until 1898; in the period 1898–1906 Moore must have found himself talking about Nietzsche, at least occasionally; after all, Nietzsche was very much in the air at this time, and Moore could hardly have avoided him, even if he had wanted to. Indeed, it is likely, especially in view of the occasional presence of W. B. Yeats and John Eglinton, that some of the ideas which were thrown about at George Moore's Saturday evening at-homes in Dublin in the first decade of the century were

Nietzschean ones. Moore delighted in 'naughty' ideas, of which Nietzsche was considered the epitome. In addition we know that Moore heard of Nietzsche from Dujardin, probably as early as 1886–7, although it must be stressed that the *Letters from George Moore to Éd. Dujardin* contain neither reference nor allusion to Nietzsche; and Hone reports that Moore admired Halévy's Nietzsche-biography – which did not appear (in French) until 1909.

So far as Nietzsche's impact on George Moore is concerned, then, our findings are mainly negative. Moore's own comment that "certain passages" in the *Confessions of a Young Man* "lead the reader to ... Zarathustra" must, surely, be taken with a pinch of salt; the fact is that there are some passages which could be, but none which need be Nietzschean; there is no evidence to substantiate the idea that *Confessions* was the first English literary work to echo Nietzsche. It is much more likely that the 'Zarathustran' passages in the book echo Shelley, Pater, Gautier and Schopenhauer, and the ideas of the late 1880s in general. There is, after all, much that sounds 'Nietzschean' in these ideas; André Gide for one found Nietzsche less exciting because he had already read Oscar Wilde, and Thomas Mann too noted how many of Nietzsche's aphorisms might have been written by Wilde (and vice versa). Even the cult of Dionysos was by no means restricted to Nietzsche; Swinburne, for instance, was a student of the cult.

The first book by George Moore that is demonstrably indebted to Nietzsche is *Evelyn Innes* (1898). There and in *Memoirs of My Dead Life* (1906) Moore paraphrases Nietzsche – but only once in each book. The paraphrase used in *Evelyn Innes* is used again in *Hail and Farewell* (*Salve*), although in both cases it is an allusion to Wagner – the major German enthusiasm of Moore's life and the major influence on *Evelyn Innes* – as much as to Nietzsche. It is a curious fact that Moore used Nietzsche as a kind of emotional crutch when writing about parting and death. To speak of any significant 'indebtedness' to Nietzsche would be ridiculous; and besides, Moore was not enough of an ideas-man to be at all plausible as proto-Nietzscheite. Moore borrowed ideas and metaphors wherever he could find them. A few happened to come from Nietzsche. *Voilà tout*. In retrospect Moore's own statement that "there is very little Nietzsche in me" must be accepted. It is time that we passed on to a writer who has not only been said to be, but actually was indebted to Nietzsche: John Davidson.

Chapter Four
"That insane belov'd philosopher" (John Davidson)

The first British writer to take real notice of Nietzsche was the Scottish poet John Davidson (1857–1909), who discovered his work in 1891; in the United States the critic James Huneker had begun to enthuse about Nietzsche three years previously, in 1888. True, Davidson was already a 'Nietzschean' before he discovered Nietzsche, in the sense that "formal Nietzschean thought merely intensified tendencies that already possessed him".[1] But Nietzsche's impact on the Scottish poet in November 1891 was nonetheless considerable, so considerable that when the body of John Davidson was found in Mounts' Bay in March 1909, R. A. Scott-James claimed in a London daily newspaper that he had been murdered by Nietzsche.

Davidson first came across Nietzsche's ideas in 1891 in an article by Theodore de Wyzewa.[2] Wyzewa, who had seen Nietzsche, though he appears not to have met him, described him as "l'étonnant Frédéric Nietsche [sic] ... l'homme le plus remarquable de la littérature allemande contemporaine";[3] his continued misspelling of the philosopher's name argues against a sound first-hand knowledge of his work, and the article is in fact based mainly on biographical information culled from *Die Gesellschaft*[4] and an enthusiastic reading of *Human, All Too Human*.

Davidson was so impressed by Wyzewa's fervent article that he published an abridged adaptation of it under the title 'The New Sophist' in *The Speaker* (28 November 1891); a second, longer version appeared in the *Glasgow Herald* on 18 March 1893. The first book by Davidson to refer to Nietzsche was the aphoristic miscellany *Sentences and Paragraphs* (1893), which contained a small selection of aphorisms (from *Human, All Too Human*), taken from his own *Speaker* article and from Wyzewa, together with the following commentary based on his two previous articles:

> No writer is less German than Nietzsche. His style is that of a Frenchman: he has a profound horror of dissertation. All his writings are collections of aphorisms; and all ideas disgust him when he has considered them for a short time. His writing is a succession of imagery of the most concrete order, but always with a symbolic value. There is no trace of sentiment – everywhere a morbid sense of reality, incapable of satisfying itself with any thought of man's heart. His irony is altogether different from the ordinary German humour – dry, bitter, cruel, and as perfectly under control as that of Swift. He would be satisfied could he find one certainty. He has compared himself to Diogenes, who went in broad day with a lantern seeking a man. '*My* misfortune,' said he, 'is that I cannot even find a lantern.' He is the Nihilist of philosophy.
>
> 'In the beginning was nonsense, and the nonsense came from God, and the nonsense was God.' That is Nietzsche's theory of the universe. All is illusion – metaphysic, science, religion, art.
>
> Nietzsche's is the most unphilosophic mind that ever attempted philosophy. He is a great poet seeking a system, instead of taking things on trust. He starts from nothing, and ends in nothing. He proves and disproves, believes and disbelieves everything; and he is as uncertain of the Nihilism to which he always harks back as he is of witchcraft.
>
> Nietzsche always regarded his Nihilism as a preface to a

> positive doctrine. But he failed to unlearn the habit of doubt, until he went mad, and discovered that 'indubitably it was he who had created the world.'
>
> Goethe felt and suffered as much as Nietzsche, but being stronger, saw through the Brocken spectre of self, which interrupted Nietzsche's view wherever he turned.[5]

For all his enthusiasm, the Scottish poet was not really 'influenced' by Nietzsche at this stage, although the germ was implanted; as yet he knew Nietzsche's work only at secondhand, hence the rather vague nature of the above commentary, which is again a re-hash of his *Speaker* article; he has not learnt any more about Nietzsche since 1891. All Davidson's writings on Nietzsche in the period 1891–3 are based on Wyzewa; there is no development in his attitude because, not reading German, he was not in a position to add to his as yet scanty knowledge of Nietzsche's work. And if he knew little enough of the work, he was pretty critical towards it: "After all, Niet[z]sche's Nihilism is little more than a recrudescence of Sturm und Drang"[6] – "Any man who has work to do in the world, any man who has children, any man who enjoys ordinary health is furnished with an answer to Nietzsche".[7] There is an obvious contrast between these early judgments, which are at least his own, and that contained in his 'Tête-à-tête' (*The Speaker*, 17 June 1899). Here Davidson described Nietzsche as "A great man; a man of unexampled divulsive power" and recommended Englishmen to read him, saying: "Such a tonic the world of letters has not had for a thousand years. Nietzsche set himself, smiling, to dislodge the old earth from its orbit; and – it is something against such odds – the dint of his shoulder will remain for ever." In thus commending Nietzsche he used one of the latter's favourite metaphors and applied to him his own definition of 'active nihilism'.

This changed, now truly Nietzschean attitude is explained by the fact that in 1897/8 Davidson, finding himself "at cross purposes with life," turned to philosophy, and more especially to Nietzsche's works, the first English translations of which had just begun to appear. From 1898 onwards allusions to Nietzsche began to appear in his work in such numbers that a contemporary reviewer dubbed him "a poetic disciple of Nietzsche", and in 1902 Davidson himself, while rebutting the idea of discipleship, wrote that "a year or two ago I knew by heart the three published volumes of the English translation of Nietzsche".[8] These three volumes were: *The Case of Wagner* ... (a selection), tr. Th. Common, 1896; *Thus Spake Zarathustra*, tr. A. Tille, 1896; and *A Genealogy of Morals*, tr. W. A. Haussmann, 1897. That Davidson "steeped himself thoroughly in the translations of Nietzsche's work as they appeared in the last years of the century"[9] is clear. It is also evident that it was the despair to which he was reduced in the late 1890s, his agonized search for "the relation of the Soul of Man to the Universe" that made Davidson turn to Nietzsche's work with such desperate urgency. In Nietzsche he found a man who, like himself, had heard "the cat-call of the Sphinx". John Davidson's fundamental belief that "There is no such thing as naked reality" is, after all, the foundation on which Nietzsche's whole mythical artifact is built.

Looking back in 1913, Holbrook Jackson argued that the influence of Nietzsche had been beneficial:

> Early association with the ideas of Nietzsche had directed Davidson's innate pessimism into channels of creative inquisitiveness and speculation. He learnt more from Nietzsche than did any other poet of his time, but he never became a disciple. He learnt of that philosophical courage which Nietzsche called 'hardness', and used it Nietzsche-wise in his continual questioning and revaluing of accepted ideas. He was imbued also with the German philosopher's reverence for power. But he did not accept the Superman doctrine.[10]

Apart from the last sentence, which we shall see to be mistaken, this is an excellent summary. But not all contemporary critics shared Holbrook Jackson's view that Nietzsche's influence was beneficial. In his *Orthodoxy* (1909), G. K. Chesterton wrote that John Davidson, who was capable of writing excellent poetry, had taken to writing "laborious metaphysics" in defence of Nietzsche's doctrine of will; for good measure he added that "All the will-worshippers, from Nietzsche to Mr Davidson, are really quite empty of volition".[11] But then whereas Holbrook Jackson was himself a Nietzsche-enthusiast, Chesterton was quite the opposite.

Davidson's position in 1897 is stated in his *New Ballads:* "Night – it was always night/And never a star above." The parallel with Nietzsche is brought out particularly clearly by W. B. Yeats' later condemnation of Nietzsche in the words "But why does Nietzsche think that the night has no stars, nothing but bats and owls and the insane moon" (see Chapter Six below), which appear to echo Davidson's lines. For the man reduced to such despair the appeal of Zarathustra's "Only from the grave can there be resurrection" is obvious. Davidson shared Nietzsche's view of Christianity, of democracy, and of the rationalism and determinism of the nineteenth century; he too believed in the individual's right to self-determination, and rejected all external authority and moral sanctions. That he would find many of Nietzsche's ideas sympathetic was therefore inevitable. Nietzsche's *Freigeist*-ideal, his insistence on the relativity of all moral values, his announcement of the death of God and consequent rejection of the Christian morality of the past, all these are reflected in Davidson's work, particularly in the period 1902–8, as are the myths of the Superman and of Eternal Recurrence.[12] The Man-of-Power or Man-God of Davidson's egoistic creed –

> Henceforth I shall be God; for consciousness
> Is God: I suffer; I am God: this Self,
> That all the universe combines to quell,
> Is greater than the universe; and *I*
> Am that I am. To think and not be God? –
> It cannot be.[13]

is closely related to the Superman. What is both original and grotesque is the Scottish poet's admixture – a decade later – of Nietzscheanism and jingoism: "The Englishman is the Overman; and the history of England is the history of his evolution".[14] This is absurd, of course; and yet the popularity of W. E. Henley's 'Unconquerable':

> Out of the night that covers me,
>   Black as the pit from pole to pole,
> I thank whatever gods may be
>   For my unconquerable soul.
>
> In the fell clutch of circumstance
>   I have not winced nor cried aloud;
> Under the bludgeonings of chance
>   My head is bloody, but unbow'd.

suggests that Imperial Man was bound to be particularly susceptible to the Superman-idea.

Similarly Davidson's theory of endless evolution and devolution will have been confirmed by the idea of Eternal Recurrence, that "eternal cirque of heinous agony". Nietzsche also helped Davidson to arrive at his own view of poetry as the product of suffering. In general terms it is true to say that "He assimilates from Nietzsche ... only those aesthetic ideas which complement or complete his own";[15] the admixture of eclecticism and independent-mindedness is highly characteristic. But at times Davidson's borrowings go almost too far. The 'Parable' in his *The Treatment of an Empire-Builder* (1902), for instance, is closely modelled on Nietzsche's parable of the madman seeking God in *The Joyful Wisdom*, cf. passages like these:

> A Protagonist came into the market-place, and began to sing songs that had not been sung before.
>
> When they had killed the Protagonist they were struck with astonishment, and exclaimed to each other, 'Why, the Protagonist is dead! Who can have done this?'

Although this particular borrowing does not seem to have been noticed before, contemporary reviewers did see this third *Testament* as Nietzschean; the review in *The Academy*[16] was headed 'A Prophet of Nietzsche', and declared:

> This 'empire-builder' is very frankly Mr. Davidson, and only at the close, when he has done hot-gospelling, remembers ... his supposed character. The gospel ... is largely one of the fundamental function and necessity of pain in the world. But it goes further than this. It proclaims that the strong egoist alone is happy ... and that his happiness is purchased by the suffering of the weak and altruistic ... It is a terrible gospel, but scarce new – though it may be new in song. For this, surely, is the gospel of Nietzsche; and it might be written, 'Nietzsche is great, and Davidson is his prophet.'

This is precisely the sort of generalization and Nietzschefication that annoyed Davidson and prompted his letter to the Editor of the *Daily Chronicle* dated 22 May 1902:

> SIR, – I should be glad if you would allow me to point out that I am not a disciple of Nietzsche. The gist of Nietzsche, so far as I know him, will be found in my play, 'Smith: a Tragic Farce,' written in 1886, long before I had even heard the name of

> Nietzsche. It is true that in the conversation of the beasts in the 'Testament of an Empire-Builder', the Hackney quotes directly from 'that insane belov'd philosopher' ('The Genealogy of Morals,' if I remember rightly); but it will be observed that it is the Hackney who does so. I cannot understand why an intelligent being should be, or should be supposed, the disciple of anyone.
>
> I should like to say also that it is not necessary to identify me with the speakers in my 'Testaments.' In the dramatic presentation of any character, if it is to be vital at all, there must be an alloy of the personality of the writer; to that extent I will be found in my 'Testaments.'
>
> If you can give me the space, let me add a word for Nietzsche. There are signs of a Nietzsche panic in certain quarters; and the word 'overman' is supposed to be an index of evolution in humanity. This seems to me very foolish. Nietzsche has nothing to tell the Englishman of the 'overman'; the Englishman is the 'overman'; in Europe, in Asia, Africa, America, he holds the world in the hollow of his hand. Moreover, he has been stated in our literature again and again, the outstanding instances being these:– Marlowe's 'Tamburlaine,' Shakespeare's 'Richard III,' Milton's Satan, Carlyle's Cromwell. A year or two ago I knew by heart the three published volumes of the English translation of Nietzsche, and found them as literature very admirable and exciting; but so far as his philosophy goes in these volumes, Nietzsche seems to me to have laid a wind-egg in a mare's nest. – I am, &c.,
> JOHN DAVIDSON.

This letter was reprinted in *The Academy*[17] at Davidson's request. It is clear that he strongly objected to being described as a 'disciple' of Nietzsche (what writer would not?); when *Holiday and Other Poems* appeared in 1906, he expressed the hope that this time there would be "no tiresome tattle about ... Nietzsche."

Whatever his reservations about Nietzsche's philosophy, Davidson absorbed a great deal of it; he could not have three whole volumes of Nietzsche by heart without doing so. In general, his debt to Nietzsche is sufficient to justify J. B. Townsend's comment that the following lines from *The Triumph of Mammon* (1907) amount to "shameless ingratitude, if not gross misrepresentation":[18]

> He posed as Zoroaster, and led us back
> To Dionysos: not our mark at all;

The past is past. And, for his prophecy? –
Why, Florimond, this Nietzsche was a Christian …
His Antichrist is Christ, whose body and blood
And doctrine of miraculous rebirth,
Became the Overman: Back-of-beyond,
Or – what's the phrase? – Outside good-and-evil:
That's his millennium, and we'll have none of it.

There may be more than a grain of truth in Davidson's comment that "this Nietzsche was a Christian" but for him now to reject the whole of Nietzsche because the German philosopher did not share his own "Lucretian materialism" (G. B. Shaw), is in the circumstances grotesque.

With John Davidson it is not so much particular ideas that matter as the whole tenor of Nietzsche's work and the strength of his personality and personal example. Davidson's whole attitude to Nietzsche is itself wholly Nietzschean (cf. Nietzsche's attitude to Schopenhauer), and nowhere more so than when he is denying Nietzsche (cf. Nietzsche's attitude to Socrates and Christ). Despite *The Triumph of Mammon*, the respect which the Scottish poet felt for the German philosopher is well documented: he calls Nietzsche "a great man; a man of unexampled divulsive power", "the most divulsive force in the history of letters", "the most potent influence in European thought of our time", and "the most powerful mind of recent times".

Although John Davidson was a kindred-spirit rather than a disciple of Nietzsche, enough has been said to disprove Bernard Shaw's remark that "Davidson had nothing whatever to do with Nietzsche or his philosophy".[19] Indeed, Hugh MacDiarmid, himself influenced by Davidson, is surely right to stress the vital significance of "The relation of John Davidson's thought to Nietzsche's".[20] The crux of the matter is that Davidson's ideas are most characteristic and most significant when they are closest to Nietzsche.

It was because Davidson dared to criticize the writer with whom he had so much in common that Oscar Levy wrote of him as "a true Nietzschean … though one more intoxicated than inspired by Nietzsche."[21] But this verdict is not unjust; it is certainly juster than it was meant to be!

Chapter Five
Man and Superman (H. G. Wells and Bernard Shaw)

An ambiguous marginal figure in the present context is H. G. Wells, of whom Bernard Bergonzi wrote in 1961: "Whether or not he read the English translations of Nietzsche and Tille's introduction, when they appeared in 1896, is uncertain".[1] In fact it seems fairly certain that Wells did read Tille's edition of *The Collected Works of Friedrich Nietzsche*, two volumes of which appeared in 1896, since in June 1897 we find Thomas Common defending Nietzsche against Wells' accusation of "blackguardism",[2] a charge which Wells made in *Natural Science* (April 1897): "The tendency of a belief in natural selection as the main factor of human progress, is, in the moral field, towards the glorification of a sort of rampant egotism – of blackguardism in fact, – as the New Gospel. You get that in the Gospel of Nietzsche."[3] It was no doubt this comment by Wells that Thomas Common had in mind when he wrote in his Introduction to *Beyond Good and Evil*[4] that "H. G. Wells's semi-serious writings seem like a coarse and crooked refraction of the ideas of Nietzsche, whom he was accustomed to malign." In fact the passage quoted appears to be the only one in which Wells 'maligns' Nietzsche; but Common was apt to exaggerate when defending his master. Now Wells evidently charged Nietzsche with the "glorification of a sort of rampant egotism – of blackguardism" because he took him to believe in the need for inferior individuals to be coerced by their superiors; it appears, in other words, that Wells disapproved of the Superman idea and the glorification of 'master-morality' at the expense of (democratic) 'slave-morality'. Had he known his Nietzsche better, he would perhaps have realized that the "gospel of discipline and education" which he advocated instead of the "Gospel of Nietzsche" was very close indeed to Nietzsche's concept of *Züchtung* (it is precisely 'discipline and education' that the German word implies).

If H. G. Wells knew Nietzsche's work to the extent of cheerfully accusing him of the "glorification of ... blackguardism", we should hardly expect to find what looks very much like the influence of Nietzsche in *The Island of Dr. Moreau* (1896) and later works. Only a few years after Wells had denounced Nietzsche, G. K. Chesterton commented that Wells' *The Food of the Gods* (1904) was "in essence a study of the Superman idea";[5] adding that "Nietzsche summed up all that is interesting in the Superman idea when he said, 'Man is a thing which has to be surpassed,' " Chesterton made it clear that he did not consider Wells to have added anything interesting to Nietzsche's idea. More recently Bernard Bergonzi has pointed out that the chapter 'Dr. Moreau Explains' in *The Island of Dr. Moreau* contains "something very like Tille's attempt to assimilate Nietzsche and Darwin".[6] We have seen that Wells is likely to have read Tille's introduction to *The Collected Works of Friedrich Nietzsche* (in vol. XI, containing *The Case of Wagner*, *The Twilight of the Idols*, and *The Antichrist*); he is less likely to have known Tille's book *Von Darwin bis Nietzsche* (1895). In his introduction Tille had written of the "task of transvaluing the intellectual currency of our time," and, as Bergonzi says, "Moreau can stand as a symbol of the Nietzschean transvaluation of values".[7]

Now it was, of course, the Superman who was to accomplish the 'transvaluation of values', and it was to the development of the Superman that Nietzsche saw human evolution as being directed. It was this view which Wells described as blackguardly; and yet in

The Sleeper Wakes (1898) we find what appears to be a straight echo of Nietzsche's doctrine of the Superman as formulated in *Thus Spake Zarathustra*, Tille's translation of which came out in 1896:

> The hope of mankind – what is it? That some day the Over-man may come, that some day the inferior, the weak and the bestial may be subdued or eliminated. Subdued if not eliminated. The world is no place for the bad, the stupid, the enervated. Their duty ... is to die! The death of the failure! That is the path by which the beast rose to manhood, by which man goes on to higher things ... The coming of the aristocrat is fatal and assured. The end will be the Over-man – for all the mad protests of humanity.[8]

These words, spoken by Ostrog, amount to a paraphrase of Nietzsche – Tille had used the word Overman to translate *Übermensch* – and more especially of his definition of man as "a connecting-rope between the animal and the overman" in the Prologue to *Thus Spake Zarathustra.* Are we to assume that Ostrog is a blackguard, or that H. G. Wells was trying to have his cake and eat it?

Incidentally, in connexion with Nietzsche and Darwinism – and it will be evident from this brief discussion of H. G. Wells that Nietzsche also came in partly on the Darwinian wave – it is interesting to note that Thomas Common apparently wrote urging T. H. Huxley to read Nietzsche as early as 1894. In a letter to Thomas Common dated 23 March 1894, Huxley replied that he intended to read Nietzsche;[9] there is no evidence that he did so.

Be this as it may, with Wells' *The Sleeper Wakes* the Superman arrived on the English literary scene. It is therefore time to move on to Bernard Shaw. Although the story was never confirmed by Shaw, Thomas Common wrote in 1906 that the value of Nietzsche's works "is attested by the fact that the greatest English author and dramatist, Mr. Bernard Shaw, read the MS. of the book of Nietzsche extracts [*Nietzsche as Critic*, *Philosopher*, *Poet and Prophet*, ed. Th. Common, 1901] with approval, and afterwards carried it himself to the publisher's [Grant Richards'] office, where he recommended that it should be issued".[10]

In the 'Epistle Dedicatory' to *Man and Superman* (1903), Shaw remarked that Nietzsche was "among the writers whose peculiar sense of the world I recognize as more or less akin to my own" – a remark which means a good deal less than it might otherwise seem to mean since Nietzsche is listed alongside Bunyan, Blake, Hogarth, Turner, Goethe, Shelley, Schopenhauer, Wagner, Ibsen, Morris, and Tolstoy! Shaw does not acknowledge any specific indebtedness to the doctrine of the Superman, although in 'The Revolutionist's Handbook' he does say that "The cry for the Superman did not begin with Nietzsche, nor will it end with his vogue." However, since Shaw also writes there that "We must replace the man by the superman", it is hardly surprising that critics have ever since linked Shaw's Superman with Nietzsche's; indeed, Shaw is the only British writer who wrongly enjoys – if that is the word – the popular reputation of having been influenced by Nietzsche. One of the first critics to link Shaw's Superman with Nietzsche's was G. K. Chesterton, whose comment is particularly interesting since it not only further illustrates his own attitude towards Nietzsche, but was written at the height of British Nietzscheanism when Chesterton tended to see Nietzsche under every woodpile. In *Heretics* he commented that "Mr. Shaw ... has even been infected to some extent with the primary intellectual weakness of his new master, Nietzsche, the strange notion that the greater and stronger a man was the more he would despise other things".[11] To speak of Nietzsche as Shaw's "new master" was, of course, ridiculous. But Chesterton proceeded to amplify this comment considerably in his book on Shaw:

> ... Shaw's discovery of Nietzsche. This eloquent sophist has an influence on Shaw and his school which it would require a separate book adequately to study ... Nietzsche ... was a frail, fastidious, and entirely useless anarchist. He had a wonderful poetic wit; and is one of the best rhetoricians of the modern world. He had a remarkable power of saying things that master the reason for a moment by their gigantic unreasonableness ... All that was true in his teaching was this: ... the mere achievement of dignity, beauty, or triumph is strictly to be called a good thing ... Nietzsche imagined he was rebelling against ancient morality; as a matter of fact, he was only rebelling against recent morality ...
>
> Nietzsche might really have done some good if he had taught Bernard Shaw to draw the sword, to drink wine, or even to dance. But he only succeeded in putting into his head a new superstition ... I mean the superstition of ... the Superman.

In one of his least convincing phrases, Nietzsche had said that

> just as the ape ultimately produced the man, so should we ultimately produce something higher than the man. The immediate answer, of course, is sufficiently obvious: the ape did not worry about the man, so why should we worry about the Superman? If the Superman will come by natural selection, may we leave it to natural selection? If the Superman will come by human selection, what sort of Superman are we to select? If he is simply to be more just, more brave, or more merciful, then Zarathustra sinks into a Sunday-school teacher; the only way we can work for it is to be more just, more brave, and more merciful; sensible advice, but hardly startling. If he is to be anything else than this, why should we desire him, or what else are we to desire? These questions have been many times asked of the Nietzscheites, and none of the Nietzscheites have even attempted to answer them.[12]

Chesterton's comments on Shaw make almost as good reading as Shaw's comments on Nietzsche (see below); they are interesting more as illustrating his own reaction to the doctrine of the Superman than for their relevance to Shaw's play. The way in which Chesterton labelled him a "Nietzscheite" and said "Nietzsche might ... have done some good if he had taught Bernard Shaw ... to dance" must have made Shaw dance – with rage. Despite detailed parallels between *Thus Spake Zarathustra* and *Man and Superman*, Shaw, with his concern with "the struggle between human vitality and the artificial system of morality", was a fellow-iconoclast rather than a disciple of Nietzsche. While he was clearly impressed by Nietzsche's Superman, and by Nietzsche's *style*, the context in which his own Superman appears has little to do with "the lyrical Bismarck". Chesterton was simply the first of many critics to make a mountain out of a single word. Another to do so was Oswald Spengler. In *The Decline of the West*[13] Spengler asked: "In how far is Shaw the pupil and fulfiller of Nietzsche?" Skating over the first part of his question, he argued that Shaw was "the one thinker of eminence" to have consistently advanced in the same direction as Nietzsche, namely towards "productive criticism of Western morale"; he wrote of *Man and Superman* as the "final synthesis of Darwin and Nietzsche", and claimed that "The Will-to-Power, translated to the realistic, political and economic domain, finds its expression in Shaw's *Major Barbara*."[14] In fact Spengler took it for granted that Shaw is the 'pupil' of Nietzsche, and only showed, more convincingly than most, the parallels between the Irish playwright and the German philosopher.

In the early years of the century Bernard Shaw suffered almost as much as John Davidson at the hands of critics who sought to tar him with the Nietzschean brush. Thus on 13 March 1910 the dramatic critic of *The Sunday Times*, reviewing the Frohman Repertory production of Shaw's *Misalliance* and Granville Barker's *The Madras House*, wrote that "Shaw is Nietzsche strengthened with the cream of Irish wit, and ... Barker is Nietzsche diluted with sterilised milk of Bernard Shaw." An anonymous correspondent ("E.F.B.") took exception to this clever but absurd statement in a letter which is well worth rescuing from the limbo in which it has lain for 60 years:

> Nietzsche and Shaw have one point in common, and one only – dislike for the present state of things. But ... Mr. Shaw wages war against society, because it is not socialistic enough for his taste. Nietzsche wages war against society because it is socialistic ... Mr. Shaw's gospel is the gospel of levelling, Nietzsche's gospel is the gospel of inequality. Mr. Shaw would destroy the present social system because it possesses forms, conventions, and class distinctions which his anarchical soul abhors ... Nietzsche, on the contrary, is the apostle of aristocracy and privilege ... as philosopher ... Nietzsche has nothing in common with Shaw.[15]

At this point the correspondent, evidently a Nietzschean, goes on to attack Shaw. But there is much truth in the lines quoted, as there also is in his statement that "Nietzsche's philosophy covers so wide a field that isolated texts may be picked out to support any cause, and unfortunately the Socialists are as unscrupulous in quoting Nietzsche as the devil in quoting Scripture."

In the 'Preface to Major Barbara' (1905), Bernard Shaw provided some timely "First Aid to Critics" on the subject of his supposed indebtedness to Nietzsche:

> I first heard the name of Nietzsche from a German mathematician, Miss Borchardt, who had read my Quintessence of Ibsenism, and told me that she saw what I had been reading: namely, Nietzsche's Jenseits von Gut und Böse. Which I protest I had never seen, and could not have read with any comfort, for want of the necessary German, if I had seen it.

> Nietzsche, like Schopenhauer, is the victim in England of a single much quoted sentence containing the phrase 'big blond beast.' On the strength of this alliteration it is assumed that Nietzsche gained his European reputation by a senseless glorification of selfish bullying as the rule of life, just as it is assumed, on the strength of the single word Superman (Übermensch) borrowed by me from Nietzsche, that I look for the salvation of society to the despotism of a single Napoleonic Superman, in spite of my careful demonstration of the folly of that outworn infatuation. But even the less recklessly superficial critics seem to believe that the modern objection to Christianity as a pernicious slave-morality was first put forward by Nietzsche. It was familiar to me before I ever heard of Nietzsche.

With regard to *The Quintessence of Ibsenism* (1891), what Shaw says seems conclusive, particularly since Helen Zimmern's translation of *Beyond Good and Evil* did not appear until 1905. Similarly there seems to be no reason to doubt him when he says that the view of Christianity as a slave-morality was familiar to him long before he had ever heard of Nietzsche. There remains: the word 'Superman'. The crux of the matter is that Shaw was, like Davidson, "a Nietzschean before he ever heard of Nietzsche";[16] at the same time he was, in many ways, the absolute opposite of a Nietzschean.

Shaw's other comments on Nietzsche, in review articles and letters, modify this impression without changing it substantially. He first wrote about Nietzsche in 'Nietzsche in English' (*The Saturday Review*, 11 April 1896), a review of the first volume (*Nietzsche contra Wagner, &c.*, tr. Thomas Common) of *The Collected Works of Friedrich Nietzsche* (London: Henry & Co., 1896). Though he is at his most Shavian, by no stretch of the critical imagination could Shaw be said to be over-enthusiastic:

> Whilst I am still at large I may as well explain that Nietzsche is a philosopher – that is to say, something unintelligible to an Englishman. To make my readers realize what a philosopher is, I can only say that *I* am a philosopher ... Nietzsche is worse than shocking, he is simply awful: his epigrams are written with phosphorus on brimstone. The only excuse for reading them is that before long you must be prepared to talk about Nietzsche or else retire from society, especially from aristocratically minded society ... since Nietzsche is the champion of privilege, of

> power and of inequality. Famous as Nietzsche has become – he has had a great *succès de scandale* to advertise his penetrating wit – I never heard of him until a few years ago, when, on the occasion of my … 'The Quintessence of Ibsenism,' I was asked whether I had not been inspired by a book called 'Out at the other side of Good and Evil' by Nietzsche. The title seemed to me promising; and in fact Nietzsche's criticism of morality and idealism is essentially that demonstrated in my book as at the bottom of Ibsen's plays. His pungency; his power of putting the merest platitudes of his position in rousing, startling paradoxes; his way of getting underneath moral precepts which are so unquestionable to us that common decency seems to compel unhesitating assent to them, and upsetting them with a scornful laugh: all this is easy to a witty man who has once well learnt Schopenhauer's lesson, that the intellect by itself is a mere dead piece of brain machinery, and our ethical and moral systems merely the pierced cards you stick into it when you want it to play a certain tune. So far I am on common ground with Nietzsche. But not for a moment will I suffer any one to compare me to him as a critic. Never was there a deafer, blinder, socially and politically inepter academician … To him modern Democracy, Pauline Christianity, Socialism, and so on are deliberate plots hatched by malignant philosophers to frustrate the evolution of the human race and mass the stupidity and brute force of the many weak against the beneficial tyranny of the few strong. This is not even a point of view: it is an absolutely fictitious hypothesis: it would not be worth reading were it not that there is almost as much evidence for it as if it were true, and that it leads Nietzsche to produce some new and very striking and suggestive combinations of ideas. In short, his sallies, petulant and impossible as some of them are, are the work of a rare spirit and are pregnant with its vitality.

The whole tone here makes it quite clear that Shaw is writing of a fellow-iconoclast who threatens to steal some of his own thunder, not of one whom he recognizes in any sense as a master. He approves of Nietzsche's criticism of morality and idealism as being close to Ibsen's and his own, and he admires Nietzsche's aphoristic brilliance. But that is all. In social and political terms he regards Nietzsche as "inept".

If some of Shaw's criticism suggests that he did not take Nietzsche very seriously, the opposite is suggested by his long-forgotten letter in *The Eagle and the Serpent* (15 April 1898), which is worth quoting in full:

> Dear Sir, – Mr. Common's suggestion of Nietzsche Society may possibly prove fruitful. Since the foundation of the Fabian Society in 1884, no organ of a new popular development of social philosophy has been formed among us. It is noteworthy that the Fabian Society was formed by the division of a pre-existing group into two sections; one, the Fabian Society, taking up the political and economic side of the social question; and the other, then called the Fellowship of the New Life, and still in existence as the New Fellowship, taking up the ethical and philosophical side. The result is noteworthy. The Fabian Society has exercised a great influence, and has attained perhaps, the maximum of success possible to such organizations. The New Fellowship, though composed largely of the same men, has exercised practically no influence at all, because it had no really new ideas. There was nothing to be learned from it that had not already been learned from the best of the Unitarians. Like them, it sought to free social and personal ideals and duties from superstition; but it laid even greater stress on the sacredness of the ideals and duties than the comparatively easy-going superstitious people did. It was not until after 1889, when Ibsen and Nietzsche began to make themselves felt, that the really new idea of challenging the validity of idealism and duty, and bringing Individualism round again on a higher plane, shewed signs of being able to rally to it men beneath the rank of geniuses who had been feeling their way towards it for two centuries. Had the New Fellowship started with any glimmering of this conception, their history might have been different. As it is, it seems to me quite possible that a Nietzsche Society might hit the target that the Fellows of the New Life missed, and might repeat on the ethical plane the success of the Fabian Society on the political one. Yours faithfully, G. Bernard Shaw.

Latter-day Unitarian, revitalized New Lifer, and ethical bedfellow of the Fabian Society: this is one of the more mind-boggling of Nietzsche's literary re-incarnations! But Shaw's letter does show that he took Nietzsche seriously as a moral philosopher and champion of

Individualism (the "champion of inequality" seems to be forgotten); besides, we have already noted a contemporary critic's comment that Nietzsche was taken most seriously by the "Socialistically inclined", among whom Shaw certainly belongs. In view of Shaw's letter, it is interesting to note that a reviewer in the *Fabian News* wrote of A. R. Orage's *Nietzsche, The Dionysian Spirit of the Age*, that it was "badly wanted in England".

In 'Giving the Devil his Due' (*The Saturday Review*, Supplement, 13 May 1899), a review of the first two volumes (*A Genealogy of Morals, and Poems*, tr. W. Haussmann; *Thus Spake Zarathustra*, tr. A. Tille) of *The Works of Friedrich Nietzsche* (London: Fisher Unwin, 1899), Shaw described Nietzsche as "a Devil's Advocate of the modern type". After tracing the history of 'Diabolonianism' from Blake to Ibsen, he went on:

> After the dramatist came the philosopher. In England, G.B.S.: in Germany, Nietzsche. Nietzsche had sat at the feet of Wagner, whose hero, Siegfried, was also a good Diabolonian. Unfortunately, after working himself up to the wildest enthusiasm about Wagner's music, Nietzsche rashly went to Bayreuth and heard it – a frightful disillusion for a man barely capable of 'Carmen'. He threw down his idol, and having thus tasted the joys of iconoclasm (perhaps the one pursuit that is as useful as it is amusing), became an epigrammatic Diabolonian, took his stand 'on the other side of good and evil'; 'transvalued' our moral valuations; and generally strove to rescue mankind from rulers who are utterly without conscience in their pursuit of righteousness.

The rest of Shaw's review, amusing as it is, has little to do with Nietzsche. What he says about Nietzsche here strongly suggests that he had belatedly been reading the volume he reviewed on 11 April 1896, which included *Nietzsche contra Wagner*! The affinity between Shaw and the "epigrammatic Diabolonian" of whom he writes, is evident in his characteristic definition of iconoclasm as "perhaps the one pursuit that is as useful as it is amusing".

Bernard Shaw's various writings about Nietzsche show that he took an interest in the philosopher's work right from the publication of the first translations (Thomas Common's version of *Nietzsche contra Wagner, &c.*, and Alexander Tille's version of *Thus Spake Zarathustra*) in 1896, recognized Nietzsche as a kindred-spirit, a fellow-iconoclast whose "sense of the world" was "more or less akin" to his own, and took over the word 'Superman' from Nietzsche (only to use it in a different context); eventually, of course, the Shavian word displaced the word 'Overman' used by the early translators. Otherwise Shaw seems to have had his doubts about Nietzsche and to have been surprisingly *little* influenced by him, considering that he once called *Thus Spake Zarathustra* the "first modern book that can be set above the Psalms of David at every point on their own ground."

It is ironical that while H. G. Wells' debt to Nietzsche has largely gone unnoticed, G. B. Shaw has frequently been credited with an indebtedness to Nietzsche which he was himself – rightly – at pains to deny. Shaw, popularly supposed to be the most 'Nietzschean' of British writers, was in fact much less indebted to Nietzsche than most of the other writers under discussion, though his comments on Nietzsche admittedly make good reading.

Chapter Six
"That strong enchanter" (W. B. Yeats)

It was in 1902 that Nietzsche was discovered by the major English-language poet whom he was to influence most strongly: W. B. Yeats. Yeats, like Herbert Read ten years later, came to Nietzsche after an enthusiastic reading of William Blake, and in the context of his work the juxtaposition of Blake and Nietzsche is particularly significant. It may be assumed that Yeats first became acquainted with Nietzsche's work through Havelock Ellis's brilliant series of articles in *The Savoy*, to which he was himself a leading contributor.*

* No. 1 of *The Savoy* (January 1896) contained two love-poems and a story by Yeats; No. 2 (April 1896) contained the first part of Havelock Ellis's 'Friedrich Nietzsche', together with Yeats' 'Rosa Alchemica' and 'Two Poems Concerning Peasant Visionaries'; No. 3 (July 1896) included the second part of Havelock Ellis's 'Friedrich Nietzsche' and the first part of Yeats' essay 'William Blake and His Illustrations to the Divine Comedy', as well as the poem 'O'Sullivan Rua to Mary Lavell'; No. 4 (August 1896) contained the third and last part of Havelock Ellis's essay on Nietzsche and the second part of Yeats' essay on Blake.

Havelock Ellis's conclusion was striking enough: that "the nineteenth century has produced no more revolutionary and aboriginal force"; but there is no evidence that Yeats was prompted to pursue the subject in 1896. Yeats could also have heard of Nietzsche from John Davidson in their Rhymers' Club days. But in fact his real interest in Nietzsche's work dates from summer 1902, when John Quinn lent him Thomas Common's 'choice selections', *Nietzsche as Critic, Philosopher, Poet and Prophet* (1901). This is the book, publication of which Bernard Shaw is said to have recommended; in his introduction Thomas Common wrote: "I have specially to thank Mr. George Bernard Shaw for the interest he has taken in the work and for valuable suggestions he has furnished with reference to arrangement and other matters." The copy of the book which Yeats read, now in the possession of Northwestern University Library, contains extensive underlinings and several significant manuscript annotations in Yeats' hand.* Yeats was so enthralled by Nietzsche that in September 1902 he wrote to Lady Gregory:

> I have written to you little and badly of late, I am afraid, for the truth is you have a rival in Nietzsche, that strong enchanter. I have read him so much that I have made my eyes bad again ... Nietzsche completes Blake and has the same roots – I have not read anything with so much excitement since I got to love Morris's stories which have the same curious astringent joy.[1]

He added that Nietzsche's thought "flows in the same bed as Blake's, but still more violently";[2] the parallel seems to have struck him forcefully, for in the revised edition (1903) of his *Ideas of Good and Evil* he repeated the simile, writing of "Nietzsche, whose thought flows always, though with an even more violent current, in the same bed Blake's thought has worn".[3] He will have seen at once that Blake (with his 'Marriage of Heaven and Hell') and Nietzsche (with his 'Beyond Good and Evil') are at one in rejecting conventional moralities, and that the same antinomies which Blake celebrated are celebrated in Nietzsche's own 'prophetic book': *The Birth of Tragedy* (Yeats' favourite work by Nietzsche, to which he refers in several letters written in 1903). Later, in *A Vision*, he sig-

* For information in this connexion I am indebted to Dr Richard D. Olson, formerly Curator of Rare Books and Special Collections in the University Library, Northwestern University, and to his successor, Mr R. Russell Maylone.

nificantly referred to the "antithetical wisdom" of men like Blake and Nietzsche who are "full of morbid excitement". The wisdom he admired was, of course, humanitarian wisdom, for, as Louis MacNeice noted,[4] Yeats agreed with Blake, and with the early Nietzsche, that Science is the tree of Death; he later called it the religion of the Suburbs. We have seen that one of the first critics to elaborate the many parallels between Blake and Nietzsche was Yeats' friend Arthur Symons.

In a letter to John Quinn dated 15 May 1903 Yeats referred to Nietzsche's two art-sponsoring deities, Apollo and Dionysos:

> I have always felt that the soul has two movements primarily: one to transcend forms, and the other to create forms. Nietzsche, to whom you have been the first to introduce me, calls these the Dionysiac and the Apollonic, respectively. I think I have to some extent got weary of that wild God Dionysus, and I am hoping that the Far-Darter will come in his place.[5]

It is clear from this that Yeats accepted Nietzsche's distinction between the principles of Dionysos and Apollo, passion and form. Indeed, he was already in the habit of referring to these "two movements" of the soul in occult terminology as "the Transfiguration on the Mountain" and "the Incarnation". No doubt it was partly the many parallels between Nietzsche's work and the occult literature with which he was already familiar, that made Yeats so receptive to Nietzsche. In a letter to ('A. E.') Russell dated 14 May 1903, he made use of Nietzsche's distinction to describe his own changed aesthetic:

> I am no longer in much sympathy with an essay like 'The Autumn of the Body', not that I think that essay untrue. But I think I mistook for a permanent phase of the world what was only a preparation. The close of the last century was full of a strange desire to get out of form, to get to some kind of disembodied beauty, and now it seems to me the contrary impulse has come. I feel about me and in me an impulse to create form, to carry the realization of beauty as far as possible. The Greeks said that the Dionysiac enthusiasm preceded the Apollonic and that the Dionysiac was sad and desirous, but that the Apollonic was joyful and self sufficient. Long ago I used to define to myself these two influences as the Transfiguration on the Mountain and

> the Incarnation, only the Transfiguration comes before the Incarnation in the natural order.[6]

Clearly Yeats is in part ascribing to Nietzsche's terms meanings of his own; his "sad and desirous" 'nineties muse is an absolute travesty of Nietzsche's Dionysos, for, as Jane Harrison said, summarizing Nietzsche: 'Dionysos breaks all bonds; his motto is limitless Excess, Ecstasy".[7] But Yeats has also understood Nietzsche well, for it is precisely the "impulse to create form, to carry the realization of beauty as far as possible" that Nietzsche's Apollo represents, while Dionysos stands for "the contrary impulse", the impulse to "transcend forms".

In *The Birth of Tragedy* Apollo and Dionysos represent opposed human and artistic impulses. Nietzsche himself does not stress the idea of alternating Apolline and Dionysian cycles, though this follows from his cyclic view of history and the fact that he sees these two interacting artistic impulses as imparting character to the epochs which they dominate. It is therefore reasonable to conclude with M. I. Seiden that on reading Thomas Common's 'choice selections' in 1902, Yeats will have accepted three cardinal principles: "the great man is a protagonist in that drama which is the historical process; history alternates, in cycles of endless recurrence, between Dionysian (or anarchic) and Apollonian (or severely disciplined) epochs or civilizations; and each new age, the opposite to whatever it succeeds, brings with it a 'transvaluation of values' ".[8] Although Seiden did not know which of Nietzsche's works Yeats read in 1902, his comment is confirmed by Yeats' own later statement in *On the Boiler* (1939): "When a civilization ends, task having led to task until everybody was bored, the whole turns bottom upwards, Nietzsche's 'transvaluation of values' ".[9] The hour-glass metaphor here suggests that Yeats was thinking of Zarathustra's pronouncement of the doctrine of Eternal Recurrence (see below). Nietzsche's distinction between Apollo and Dionysos as historical opposites is subsumed in Yeats' later terms 'primary' and 'antithetical'.

Although Nietzsche's basic thesis in *The Birth of Tragedy* is that "art owes its continuous evolution to the Apollonian-Dionysiac duality", his 'Apollo' and 'Dionysos' represent not only artistic impulses, but basic forms of human consciousness – what Yeats, in his first reference to Nietzsche, called "two movements" of the "soul". They are the two faces of "the original Oneness, the ground of Being, [which,] ever-suffering and contradictory, time and again has need of rapt vision and delightful illusion to redeem itself." Nietzsche himself saw art as the only remaining hope or means of restoring the broken unity of man with nature. But art takes these two basic forms: the Apollonian art of masks, and the Dionysian art of tragic ecstasy. He regarded the ancient Greek's Apollonian consciousness as "a thin veil hiding from him the whole Dionysiac realm": Apollonian control and symmetry superimposed on Dionysian tragic awareness. In view of Yeats' statement that he felt an "impulse to create form", it is Apollonian art which is immediately relevant here; we shall return to Dionysos presently in connexion with Yeats' definition of tragedy. Now Apollonian art is the art of masks: unable to face tragic reality, the Apollonian artist masks it with illusion, the "veil of Mâyâ"; he is the "objective" as opposed to the "subjective" artist; he is the "Apollonian poet" as opposed to the "Muse poet", to use Robert Graves' terms which echo Nietzsche's. But, as I have said, the "separate art realms of *dream* [Apollo] and *intoxication* [Dionysos]" ultimately stand for different types of human consciousness and therefore of personality. This is where we come back to Yeats, for it is clear that Yeats will have found his doctrine of psychological dualism – self and antiself – confirmed by Nietzsche; after all, Nietzsche's all-important doctrine of self-overcoming (*Selbstüberwindung*) really means the overcoming of antiself by self. Nietzsche, like Yeats, is very much concerned with the relationship between the self and its mask; as Richard Ellmann has rightly said, "According to Nietzsche, the superman wears a mask he has designed for himself, while 'the objective man', whom he (and Yeats after him) describes as a 'mirror', creeps into 'a God's mask'. In the one case personality is asserted, in the other rejected".[10] It is after his reading of Nietzsche that 'mask' becomes a favourite term of Yeats. There is an obvious parallel between (i) the dialogue between self (*Hic*) and antiself (*Ille*) in the poem 'Ego dominus tuus' (cf. also the poem 'A Dialogue of Self and Soul'), and (ii) Zarathustra's communing with his own soul (= antiself) in 'Of the Great Longing'[11] or his distinction between 'I' and 'Self', for, as Nietzsche says, "Man is hard to discover, and hardest of all to himself; often the spirit belieth the soul." More generally, both Nietzsche's view of Apollo as the "divine image" of the individual self, and his view of the Superman (see below) as totally subjective man, will have confirmed Yeats in his view of the Self. Nietzsche will certainly have "taught Yeats ... to have confidence in his thought and in his subjective synthesis",[12] though it seems unlikely that he – of all people – taught Yeats to "think calmly";[13] Nietzsche is, after all, an *hysterical* thinker. Yeats even – at times – shared Nietzsche's premiss: that the individual creates his own world, what is known as reality being only a "mythology" (Nietzsche) or "phantasmagoria" (Yeats). In both cases this view goes back to Schopenhauer, whose philosophy lies behind the whole of *The Birth of Tragedy*, and whom Yeats greatly admired ("Schopenhauer can do no wrong in my eyes – I no more quarrel with him than I do with a mountain cataract", he wrote to Sturge Moore).

This brings us to the religious aspect of the question. Yeats was evidently disturbed by Nietzsche's rejection (in *The Birth of Tragedy*) of Platonic thought and his condemnation (in *Thus Spake Zarathustra* and elsewhere) of Christian spirituality. Beside the contrast of "master morality" and "slave morality", i.e. of subjective and objective morality, in *Nietzsche as Critic* ... ,[14] Yeats wrote:

Night	{Socrates Christ}	one god	night ... denial of self in the soul turned towards spirit, seeking knowledge.
Day	Homer	many gods	day ... affirmation of self, the soul turned from the spirit to be its mask and instrument when it seeks life.

This annotation shows both that Nietzsche helped Yeats to establish the pattern of opposition between self and soul which is implicit in much of his later work, and that Yeats has substituted Christ for Nietzsche's Dionysos. Yet when he came to write *The Resurrection* in 1927, Yeats did so "out of his confident belief that Dionysos worship, in its pure form as a mystery religion [= Orphism], was a more primitive faith of the same order as Christianity".[15] Though he later studied the whole Dionysos myth in more detail, Yeats' early interest in the myth – which came from Nietzsche – is shown by the poem 'The Magi' (1914), in which Dionysos-worship and Christianity are already juxtaposed:

> Now as at all times I can see in the mind's eye,
> In their stiff, painted clothes, the pale unsatisfied ones
> Appear and disappear in the blue depth of the sky

With all their ancient faces like rain-beaten stones,
And all their helms of silver hovering side by side,
And all their eyes still fixed, hoping to find once more,
Being by Calvary's turbulence unsatisfied,
The uncontrollable mystery on the bestial floor.[16]

The description of the Dionysian Mysteries here could well have come from *The Birth of Tragedy;* it shows the aesthetic fascination which Dionysos held for Yeats, for all his ultimate moral misgivings. Nietzsche, for his part, knew very well that the myth of "the god who is destroyed, who disappears, who relinquishes life and then is born again" (Plutarch) is common to Orphism and Christianity; the Orphic adepts conferred on Dionysos' passion and resurrection a mystic sense that makes his identification with Christ understandable. It may well be that Nietzsche came to insist so desperately on Dionysos and Christ being opposites because he knew, or feared, that they were not opposites at all, and that his own Dionysian doctrine was a super-Christian doctrine.

More than anything else in Nietzsche, it will have been the vision of Eternal Recurrence, as annunciated in *Thus Spake Zarathustra*, that caught and held Yeats' attention. In the third part of the book ('Of the Vision and the Riddle', cf. Yeats' *A Vision*), Zarathustra first tells of his shattering vision of eternity as a gateway with two paths leading from it in opposite directions, and later finds the courage to spell out the idea of Eternal Recurrence: at the end of a Great Year of Becoming the hour-glass of the universe is reversed so that all things run their course again. Now while it is true that Yeats' own cyclic theory is more elaborate than and in some respects quite different from Nietzsche's doctrine of identical recurrence, there can be little doubt that here as elsewhere he received a considerable stimulus from Nietzsche, whose ideas were largely derived from the same sources as his own. It should be stressed, however, that the idea of eternal recurrence was familiar to Yeats long before he read Nietzsche; to that extent Yeats – like John Davidson and Bernard Shaw – was a 'Nietzschean' long before he read Nietzsche. In 1885 Mohini Chatterjee told him that "Everything that has been shall be again", and Yeats duly incorporated this wisdom into the poem 'Kanva on Himself' which ends "For as things were so shall things ever be".[17]

Nietzsche's myth of Eternal Recurrence is clearly indebted to

Pythagoras' doctrine of the "Great Year", and to Heraclitus, the "dark" philosopher who "seems to hint at a 'cycle of life'".[18] In his lectures on *The Pre-Platonic Philosophers* Nietzsche referred to the recurrence in his exposition of Pythagoras, and in the second of his *Thoughts Out of Season* he repudiated the Pythagorean doctrine of eternal recurrence – but only because in his view events do not recur within the span of *known* history. With this proviso he accepted Pythagoras' doctrine. Later, in the section on *The Birth of Tragedy* in *Ecce Homo*, he referred to Heraclitus, the prophet of "eternal Becoming" whom he admired so deeply: "The doctrine of the 'Eternal Recurrence', i.e. of the unconditional and infinitely repeated circulation of all things – this doctrine of Zarathustra *might* have been taught by Heraclitus. At least the Stoics, who inherited almost all their principal ideas from Heraclitus, show traces of it." The last remark is particularly suggestive since Nietzsche was in the habit of referring to himself as the "last of the Stoics". Though the evidence is inconclusive, it seems fairly clear that Heraclitus believed in a cycle of life, though not necessarily in the idea of *identical* recurrence. There are also parallels between Nietzsche and various Indian religions (which he knew, though probably not as well as Yeats) on this point; quite apart from the symbolism of the Buddha, there is a passage in the Theravada Scriptures from the Pali Canon which connects with Nietzsche's doctrine and provides an analogue for some of Yeats' ideas in *A Vision*: "Verily, this world has fallen upon trouble! One is born, and grows old, and dies, and falls from one state, and springs up in another. And from this suffering, no one knows any way of escape, even from decay and from death." In *A Vision* Yeats noted that in both the Vedas and the Upanishads there are analogues to his own cyclic theories. And of course this passage from the Pali Canon is remarkably close to Heraclitus: "One and the same thing are the living and the dead, the waking and the sleeping, the young and the old; the former change and are the latter, the latter change in turn and are the former".[19]

Another likely source for Nietzsche's idea of Eternal Recurrence is the Orphic doctrine of the 'circle of birth' or 'cycle of births' or 'wheel of fate and birth',[20] the idea which is found as part of Plato's arguments for immortality in the *Phaido*: to Plato it was already an *ancient* doctrine that "the souls of men that come Here are from There and that they go There again and come to birth from the dead." The Wheel as such had its place in Orphic ritual. What is important in the present context is that in the case both of Orphism and of Nietzsche, this cyclic doctrine is the ultimate expression of our moral responsibility as human beings. For Orpheus the Wheel was a "cycle of ceaseless purgation" (Jane Harrison). And of course Nietzsche's doctrine of Eternal Recurrence – a 'sorrowful weary Wheel' indeed – was essentially a private myth, a surrogate for the Christian concept of personal immortality in which he no longer believed; it also, incidentally, provided a moral sanction to replace the Christian one. Pythagoras, Heraclitus, Orphism in general, Plato, Indian philosophy – these are also among Yeats' main sources for his esoteric cyclic philosophy, which of course differed sharply from Nietzsche's in that Yeats believed that it was possible – exceptionally – to escape from the Great Wheel of Incarnations; this belief was as essential to Yeats as the opposite belief was to Nietzsche.

One of the basic ingredients of Yeats' personal myth is the eternal conflict between Being and Becoming, the supernatural and the natural. Here too he will have found his ideas part confirmed, part contradicted by Nietzsche who is also very much concerned with just this conflict, though Nietzsche tends to reject the idea of Being in favour of "the eternal and exclusive Becoming, the total instability of all reality, which continually works and becomes and never is".[21] For Nietzsche the replacement of stable Being by a totally instable and ever haphazardly changing Becoming is an inevitable consequence of the "death of God".

After this outline of the main basic ideas which Yeats obtained from, or found confirmed by Nietzsche, we are in a position to consider Yeats' (mostly unpublished) annotations in the copy of Thomas Common's *Nietzsche as Critic* ... which he read in 1902.* His underlinings and annotations show that his interest was caught above all by Nietzsche's views on *morality*, and more especially by the sections on "Master-Morality and Slave-Morality" from *Beyond Good and Evil*[22] and the *Genealogy of Morals*.[23] Almost all his annotations relate to this aspect of Nietzsche's work; most imply his agreement, a few imply his disagreement with Nietzsche. Thus Yeats clearly agreed with Nietzsche's statement that "designations

* I am most grateful to Mr R. Russell Maylone, Curator of Rare Books and Special Collections, Northwestern University Library, for copies of Yeats' annotations and for permission to make use of them.

of moral worth everywhere were at first applied to *men*, and were only derivatively and at a later period applied to actions",[24] which he underlined. Like Nietzsche, he is interested in the actor rather than the action; in particular, he is concerned with the 'noble man' and his 'aristocratic' morality – his annotations show that this is where the fascination of Nietzsche's writings lies for him in 1902. Nietzsche's statement that "He who has not had a hard heart when young, will never have a hard heart"[25] is qualified by Yeats with the words "but 'hard' surely in the sense of scorning *self* pity." This is a typical reaction: Yeats seems to have approved the more conservative passages in "Master-Morality and Slave-Morality"; his underlinings mostly concern such passages and express tacit agreement, whereas his actual annotations as such tend to express disagreement with Nietzsche's more outspoken statements. Thus he underlines the phrase "[profound reverence for] *age and tradition* [– all law rests on this double reverence]",[26] but shortly afterwards adds this note:

> Yes, but the necessity of giving remains. When the old heroes praise one another they say, 'he never refused any man.' Nietzsche means that the lower cannot create anything, cannot make obligations to the higher.

This shows again that Yeats' sympathies are with the "noble" or "higher" man; but he evidently has moral reservations about Nietzsche's remark that "one has only obligations to one's equals",[27] which is altogether too arrogant for him. Nietzsche's illustration of "dual-morality" – "According to slave-morality, the 'evil' man also excites fear; according to master-morality, it is precisely the 'good' man who excites fear"[28] – is underlined by Yeats; but again he adds a note in the margin:

> In the last analysis the 'noble' man will serve or fear [?] the weak as much as the 'good' man, but in the first case the 'noble' man creates the *form* of the gift [,] in the second the weak.

Though unfortunately not clear, this must be reckoned a further modification of Nietzsche.

An interesting group of annotations connects with the doctrine of the Self, and here Yeats is basically in agreement with Nietzsche. As a starting-point we may take Yeats' note referring to Nietzsche's comments on the "*ressentiment* movement":[29]

> Nietzsche . . . opposes organization from restraint – denial . . . to organization from power – affirmation. Yet his system seems to lack some reason why the self must give to the selfless or weak or itself perish or suffer diminution – the self being the end.

For Yeats the Self is indeed "the end"; beside Nietzsche's remarks on the law-book of the Manu under the heading 'The Natural System of Ranks and Castes',[30] he writes:

> A sacred book is a book written by a man whose self has been so exalted (not by denial but by an intensity like that of the vibrating vanishing string) that it becomes one with the self of the race.

In effect this shows Yeats' acceptance of Nietzsche's fundamental doctrine of self-overcoming (*Selbstüberwindung*). But he also sympathizes with Nietzsche's caste-system. In the same context we find Yeats evidently impressed by Nietzsche's comment on the "highest caste" – "It is only the most intelligent men who have licence to beauty, to the beautiful; it is only in them that goodness is not weakness" – which he marks emphatically in the margin.[31] On the same page he defines Nietzsche's "rulers" by writing: "Rulers, that is to say the living, or wholly free, wholly self moving." Nietzsche goes on to write of "the second caste", which includes "noble warriors"; in the margin Yeats writes: "soldiers they obey life". Beside Nietzsche's comments on "the mediocre" (those in the field of "business activity"), Yeats notes: "business, the unfree, they serve things, not life." These particularly interesting annotations show that Yeats had no hesitation in accepting Nietzsche's "Natural System of Ranks and Castes" and himself distinguished between (i) the wholly free or self moving, (ii) those who serve life, and (iii) those who serve things, not life. The essential aristocratism, the "morality of 'style' "[32] of both writers is once again revealed, as is their overriding concern with *quality* of life. Yeats clearly agrees with Nietzsche that "complete automatism of instinct" is "the prerequisite for every kind of superiority, for every kind of perfection in the art of living".[33] Perfection in the art of living – that is the ultimate concern of Yeats and Nietzsche alike.

The last (for the present) important annotation by Yeats is found in the margin of 'Zarathustra's Teaching'; Nietzsche writes:

> Lo, I teach you the overman!

> The overman is the meaning of the earth. May your will say: the overman *shall be* the meaning of the earth.
>
> I conjure you my brethren, *remain true to the earth*, and do not believe those who speak to you of supernatural hopes![34]

Beside this famous passage Yeats wrote:

> Yet the 'supernatural life' may be but the soul of the earth [,] out of which man leaps again when the circle is complete.

That Yeats thus links the 'superman' with his own cyclic doctrine is particularly interesting since Zarathustra's vision of the 'Eternal Recurrence' is only to be revealed later in Common's anthology.[35] It is tempting to apply to Yeats his own basic comment on Nietzsche: "How full he is of esotericism [–] is it so with all the mystics?"[36] Ultimately, of course, Yeats not only chides Nietzsche for his "esotericism", but condemns him for his anti-Christian pessimism; but this can best be considered later.

Let us now turn our attention to the Nietzschean echoes in Yeats' poetry and verse plays. So far as the plays are concerned, the influence of Nietzsche is seen most clearly in the years 1903–10; but there are echoes of Nietzsche right through to 1935. There seems little doubt that Yeats will have had his mind cleared wonderfully by Nietzsche's theory of the Dionysian "mystery doctrine of tragedy". *This* is where "Nietzsche completes Blake" in Yeats' own words, for both Nietzsche and Blake see art as the means, or hope, of restoring the original oneness between man and nature. After referring to the rebirth of Dionysos, whose ritual passion tragedy once celebrated, Nietzsche writes of:

> a profound and mystic philosophy [Orphism] and ... the mystery doctrine of tragedy; a recognition that whatever exists is of a piece, and that individuation is the root of all evil; a conception of art as the sanguine hope that the spell of individuation may yet be broken, as an augury of eventual reintegration.[37]

This Dionysian definition of tragedy appears to have influenced Yeats' *Where There Is Nothing* (see below); it is also reflected in the essay 'Poetry and Tradition' (1907), where Yeats defines tragic emotions in terms of Nietzsche's "Dionysiac rapture":

> Shakespeare's persons, when the last darkness has gathered about them, speak out of an ecstasy that is one-half the self-surrender

> of sorrow, and one-half the last playing and mockery of the victorious sword before the defeated world.[38]

This appears to reflect Nietzsche's view that it was the combination of tragic terror and the *comic* spirit that was the salvation of Greek art. In another essay, 'The Tragic Theatre' (1910), we find Yeats distinguishing between "an art of the flood" or "tragic art", and "an art that we call real". The latter, "the daily mood grown cold and crystalline", evidently derives from Nietzsche's "Apollonian sphere", "that artificially restrained and discreet world of illusion", the world of the (Apolline) art of dream, with which Yeats was so deeply concerned. But it is surely Nietzsche's Dionysos, god of tragic passion, who inspired Yeats' definition of tragic art in 1910: "Tragic art, passionate art, the drowner of dykes, the confounder of understanding, moves us by setting us to reverie, by alluring us almost to the intensity of trance. The persons upon the stage ... greaten until they are humanity itself."[39] His basic view in the same essay, that "tragic ecstasy ... is the best that art – perhaps that life – can give," and that the audience participates in the discovery of a place "where passion ... becomes wisdom", also exactly parallels Nietzsche's view in *The Birth of Tragedy*; it was not for nothing that this was Yeats' favourite work by Nietzsche. And Yeats' essays contain other echoes of Nietzsche, for example, the statement that "the nobleness of the arts is in the mingling of contraries, the extremity of sorrow, the extremity of joy",[40] the reference to Hesiod and Homer as "those pure first artists",[41] and so on. But such echoes and parallels are incidental, as even the Dionysian definition of tragedy is incidental. What matters in the last analysis is that Yeats shares Nietzsche's hatred of "the real world" and his belief in art as the only remaining means of saving an otherwise doomed world. As Erich Heller has pointed out,[42] the "artifice of eternity", of which Yeats writes in 'Sailing to Byzantium' (1927), springs from the same view of art and reality as Nietzsche's definition of art as "the last metaphysical activity within European nihilism" and of the world as an "aesthetic phenomenon". Nietzsche and Yeats are so closely linked because they both believe in the religion of Art and therefore tend to confuse the aesthetic and the moral spheres.

Turning to individual plays, echoes of Nietzsche are first found in *The Hour Glass* (1903), the title of which may derive from

Zarathustra's definition of Eternal Recurrence, where the metaphor of the hour-glass ("sand-glass" in the translation Yeats read) of the universe is used. The theme of *The Hour Glass* is thoroughly Nietzschean, and surely reflects Yeats' reading of *The Birth of Tragedy*: the antinomy of Socratic and Tragic man, named by Yeats the Wise Man and the Fool respectively.

If *Where There Is Nothing* (1903) is based on Nietzsche's Dionysian definition of tragedy, Yeats is no less interested in the Apolline element ("the dream itself", as he calls it in *On Baile's Strand*). *Where There is Nothing* – like *On Baile's Strand* (1903), *The King's Threshold* (1904), and *The Unicorn From the Stars* (1908) – shows Yeats' preoccupation with spiritual heroism of the type embodied in Zarathustra; the Nietzschean hero of the play, Paul Ruttledge, becomes a Zarathustra-like Wanderer searching for "lawless" freedom and Dionysian laughter. Cuchulain in *On Baile's Strand* is "an heroic great man, drawn probably out of an admiration of Nietzsche's theories which were constantly in W. B.'s head at the time";[43] in 1906 Yeats' father found it necessary to criticize "the theory of the overman" as "but a doctrinaire demi-godship", and two years later he wrote of Nietzsche as "malign" (no doubt he was thinking of Nietzsche's influence on W. B. at this time). Yeats was certainly very full of Nietzsche on the occasion of a visit to Edinburgh in 1906; in his Preface to V. K. Narayana Menon's *The Development of W. B. Yeats* (1942), Sir Herbert Grierson recalled: "I had not left the bedroom, to which I conducted him to change, before he had told me of his interest in Nietzsche as a counteractive to the spread of democratic vulgarity." Clearly Yeats' preoccupation with Nietzsche must have been approaching the obsessive at this time; the testimony also confirms that he must have felt an instinctive sympathy with the 'aristocratic' philosopher. *The King's Threshold* opens with the King speaking of "two kinds of Music: the one kind/Being like a woman, the other like a man", which is presumably an echo of the first sentence of *The Birth of Tragedy*, where the "Apollonian-Dionysiac duality" is likened to "the duality of the sexes"; the play ends with the Youngest Pupil echoing *Thus Spake Zarathustra* in a reference to "the great race that is to come".

In some ways there is a very close parallel between Yeats' heroic ideal and that of Nietzsche, between the Yeatsian Hero and the Nietzschean Superman. Indeed, despite the differences between the two writers on this score, Yeats' Hero is more truly akin to Nietzsche's ideal than are the more obviously – and superficially – Nietzschean superman-types of so many other writers (for instance, Jack London). Yeats and Nietzsche both reject "the real world" and its vulgar, democratic ideals; they believe rather in a natural aristocracy of men whose ideals are "not of this world". Both believe in what Nietzsche calls "the eternal second coming" and insist that the heroic personality must respond to tragic knowledge with joy. But having stressed this basic affinity, it must be said that although Yeats accepted the idea that the great individual is the protagonist in the drama of history, he remained critical of Nietzsche's Superman as such; he saw man through Blake's eyes rather than Nietzsche's, as something to be restored to his former estate rather than "surpassed". Though he deeply admired spiritual heroism of the type represented for him by Nietzsche, and shared Nietzsche's ideal of 'nobility' (*Vornehmheit*), he rejected the arrogance of the Superman. He approved Nietzsche's statement that "The noble type of man regards *himself* as the determiner of worth" on an abstract instinctive level, without in any way approving the solipsism that lies behind Nietzsche's words. He therefore disapproved of Nietzsche's "master-morality": "His [Nietzsche's] system seems to lack some reason why the self must give to the selfless or weak or itself perish or suffer diminution".[44]

Certainly Yeats' moral and historical reservations were strongly challenged by the deep aesthetic fascination which the Superman held for him (compare the case of C. F. Meyer); as late as 1919 he suggested that Nietzsche might have taken his conception of the superman in history from Balzac's *Catherine de Medici*, which, although most unlikely, shows his mind still preoccupied by the idea. But he certainly never accepted the Superman idea *in toto*; there is therefore no reason to doubt what F. A. C. Wilson says about *The Unicorn From the Stars*, a revised version of *Where There Is Nothing:* "*The Unicorn From the Stars*, where the hero is made to turn from a life of anarchic action to one of mystical contemplation, seems ... a clear sign of his rejection of the superman theory, and was probably written in his reaction from it";[45] this does not mean, however, that the play was written in reaction against Nietzsche himself, whom – as we have seen – Yeats regarded as a "mystic".*

* G. Wilson Knight has said (in his *Christ and Nietzsche* (1948), 185) that *The King's Threshold*, *The Player Queen*, and *The Unicorn From the*

But by the same token Yeats' next relevant play, *At The Hawk's Well* (1918), does mark something of a temporary reaction against Nietzsche himself. Cuchulain, the hero of the play, belongs to the same phasal type (the twelfth incarnation) as Nietzsche: the so-called "heroic" phase or type. Yeats' comments on this type in *A Vision*, where he says that this type of man wears a "lonely, imperturbable proud Mask" in self-protection because he is "overwhelmed with the thought of his own weakness",[46] can be applied back to Cuchulain and thence to Yeats' view of Nietzsche in 1918. The parallel strongly suggests that by 1918 Yeats was at last seeing Nietzsche pretty objectively. Cuchulain is the would-be Superman who is thwarted by his "all-too-human" limitations and therefore fails to gain the Dionysian Unity of Being for which he quests.

In *The Only Jealousy of Emer* (1918) too, man is seen as "human, all-too-human" in the final chorus which again seems to echo Nietzsche:

> He that has loved the best
> May turn from a statue
> His too human breast.

The last four plays in which the influence of Nietzsche is discernible are all concerned with the Dionysos myth, to which Yeats was introduced by Nietzsche in 1902. At some time between 1903 and 1925 Yeats appears to have studied the Dionysian mysteries in detail, almost certainly via Thomas Taylor's *A Dissertation* (1790). If he read Taylor, and it seems that he did, then it was most likely between 1918 and 1920 since *Calvary* (1920) is the first play in which a fairly detailed knowledge of the Mysteries is in evidence. In general, however, it is difficult to know when Yeats' allusions to the Dionysian mysteries derive from *The Birth of Tragedy*, and when they derive from elsewhere

F. A. C. Wilson, the critic who has examined Yeats' debt to Nietzsche most thoroughly, wrote in his *W. B. Yeats and Tradition* (1958): "The play which owes most to Nietzsche is ... beyond doubt *Calvary*". [47] This I find hard to accept, not only because there is surely more of Nietzsche in *Where There Is Nothing*, but also because in *Calvary* there is very little that seems to come specifically

Stars are "strictly Nietzschean in conception", and has pointed out that Yeats links the unicorn with the Superman; this shows that Yeats understood the talismanic nature of the Superman.

from Nietzsche: the conflict between the objective Christ and his Dionysian antagonists *need* not be Nietzschean. *The Resurrection* (1927), also concerned with the transition between subjective (Dionysian) and objective (Christian) historical cycles, is interesting for the parallels it draws between the Orphic and the Christian mysteries; in asserting the identity of these two myths Yeats seems closer to Hölderlin than to Nietzsche, while the *detailed* symbolism of *The Resurrection* could *not* have come from Nietzsche. The same is true of Yeats' other treatments of the Dionysos-myth, *The King of the Great Clock Tower* (1934) and its revisal *A Full Moon in March* (1935), although the refrain sung by the Severed Head at the end of *The King of the Great Clock Tower* may well be indebted to Zarathustra's 'Drunken Song'. Finally, in *Purgatory* (1939), the old man's final prayer:

Dear God,
How quickly it returns – beat – beat!

Her mind cannot hold up all that dream.
Twice a murderer and all for nothing,
And she must animate that dead night
Not once but many times!
O God,
Release my mother's soul from its dream!
Mankind can do no more. Appease
The misery of the living and the remorse of the dead.

may once again reflect Nietzsche's nightmare vision of the eternal recurrence, though it may equally well reflect the "sorrowful weary Wheel" of Orphism; and besides, this prayer for release is addressed to the *Christian* God. So far as the last five plays are concerned, then, it seems fair to say that while they all centre on the Dionysos-myth in which Nietzsche first interested Yeats, their main sources lie beyond and behind Nietzsche, and are probably to be found in the works of Thomas Taylor ("Sipsop the Pythagorean" as Blake called him), including his translations of Heraclitus and Plotinus.

Nietzsche had less impact on Yeats' poetry than on any other part of his work; but here too there are clear echoes of "that strong enchanter". It was after reading *The Birth of Tragedy*, in which Nietzsche speaks of "Homer the magnificent" as a naïve artist nurtured in the bosom of nature, one of the very rare instances of true naïveté, that Yeats adopted Homer as his own poetic model. His line "Homer is my example and his unchristened heart" in the poem 'Vacillation' (1932) exactly reflects Nietzsche's view of Homer. Similarly Nietzsche's attack on Plato's Socrates as representing "the absolutely perfect man, good, wise, just, a dialectician – in a word, the scarecrow" may be echoed in the line "Old Clothes upon old sticks to scare a bird" in 'Among School Children' (1928); indeed, the bird in question may be the 'Dionysian bird', scared off by 'art-destroying' Socrates.

Yeats instinctively shared Nietzsche's aristocratic morality (his ideal of *Vornehmheit*); as G. S. Fraser has said,

> What may be called his [Yeats'] morality was … a morality of 'style'. It very much resembled (given that Yeats had a more genial and generous temperament) the morality of Nietzsche. Yeats' instinctive sympathies were with the strong and proud, not with the weak and humble; with the brilliant rather than with the stupid, with the exceptional rather than the average.[48]

Confirmation of this is found in the fact that in the volume of Nietzsche selections which he read in 1902, Yeats marked the passage "The noble type of man regards *himself* as the determiner of worth." He was also fond of quoting Zarathustra's "Am I a barrel of memories that I should give you my reasons?" (e.g. in letters to his father in June 1918, and to Mrs Llewellyn Davies in March 1937). The theme of aristocratic morality then becomes the subject of the poem 'To A Friend Whose Work Has Come To Nothing' (1913):

> Now all the truth is out,
> Be secret and take defeat
> From any brazen throat,
> For how long can you compete,
> Being honour bred, with one
> Who, were it proved he lies,
> Were neither shamed in his own
> Nor in his neighbours' eyes?
> Bred to a harder thing
> Than Triumph, turn away
> And like a laughing string
> Whereon mad fingers play

Amid a place of stone,
Be secret and exult,
Because of all things known
That is most difficult.

Yeats will no doubt have sympathized with Nietzsche's Zarathustra – the very embodiment of this secret and exultant morality – because his attitude towards Eternal Recurrence was so similar to Yeats' own attitude towards the cycles; but more generally, Zarathustra's whole philosophy is extraordinarily close to that of Yeats' *aesthetic antiself* (however much his moral self may have disapproved). Zarathustra's 'Dionysiac' attitude – "He who climbeth on the highest mountain laugheth at all tragic plays and tragic realities" – is echoed throughout Yeats' poetry from 1902 onwards (as it is echoed in Eugene O'Neill's plays), e.g. in the line "Who have lived in joy and laughed into the face of Death" in 'Upon a Dying Lady' (1912/13), and is seen particularly clearly in his last poems, e.g. 'Lapis Lazuli' (1936):

All perform their tragic play
...
Gaiety transfiguring all that dread
...
All things fall and are built again,
And those that build them again are gay.
...
There, on the mountain and the sky,
On all the tragic scene they stare.
One asks for mournful melodies;
Accomplished fingers begin to play.
Their eyes mid many wrinkles, their eyes,
Their ancient, glittering eyes, are gay.

For such as these tragic knowledge, the knowledge of eternal recurrence, is indeed a '*gaya scienza*'. The same theme is found in 'The Gyres' ("We that look on but laugh in tragic joy") and in 'A Crazed Girl' and 'News For the Delphic Oracle'. Of course, Yeats was not the first English-language poet to voice this Nietzschean idea of tragic joy, cf. these lines by the American poet Morgan Shephard:

Ye Gods and Men, shall I
Bend low beneath the random soulless hand

Of Fate? Or quail to see the blackened sky?
All these are great, but I will fearless stand
An Atom to defy – a sharp Comparison,
And *laugh* with joy, and wait with teeth close set.

Nor is this the only or even the most significant Nietzschean motif in Yeats' later poetry. It is, for instance, Nietzsche's prophecy of "What is to come" ("I foresee something terrible. Chaos everywhere") that informs the poem 'The Second Coming' (1921):

Things fall apart; the centre cannot hold;
Mere anarchy is loosed upon the world,
The blood-dimmed tide is loosed, and everywhere
The ceremony of innocence is drowned;
The best lack all conviction, while the worst
Are full of passionate intensity.
… I know
That twenty centuries of stony sleep
Were vexed to nightmare by a rocking cradle,
And what rough beast, its hour come round at last,
Slouches towards Bethlehem to be born?

No doubt this "rough beast", slouching its way towards Bethlehem, is Dionysos-as-Antichrist (the selections from Nietzsche which Yeats read in 1902 included passages from *The Antichrist*); it is also reminiscent of the "lion-monster" and the "laughing lions" in *Thus Spake Zarathustra* ("I wait for higher ones … *laughing lions* must come!").[49] In the last of Yeats' 'Supernatural Songs' ('Meru') this same motif is combined with the no less Nietzschean antithesis of thought and life:

Civilization is hooped together, brought
Under a rule, under the semblance of peace
By manifold illusion; but man's life is thought,
And he, despite his terror, cannot cease
Ravening through century after century,
Ravening, raging, and uprooting that he may come
Into the desolation of reality

In the earlier 'Michael Robartes and the Dancer' (1921), Yeats saw thought – with Nietzsche and Bergson (and with Wallace Stevens) – as falsifying reality; now he sees it – again, with Nietzsche, the

Nietzsche of *The Antichrist* – as enabling man to view more or less objectively the "desolation of reality", that same desolation (*Wüste*) which Nietzsche saw as ever growing.

In Yeats' poetry, as in his plays, key-concepts may come from Nietzsche, but the all-important elaborations and symbolic detail as often as not come from elsewhere, as in these lines in the poem 'Byzantium' (1930):

> I hail the superhuman
> I call it death-in-life and life-in-death.

Here "the superhuman" reflects Yeats' aesthetic fascination with the Superman; but the more important second line comes straight from Heraclitus.

Yeats' immediate reaction to Nietzsche's work in August 1902 speaks for itself: the German philosopher's myth-centred tragic aestheticism enthralled him, and it is reasonable to suppose that it was partly the ideas thrown out by Nietzsche, to say nothing of his fervid eloquence, that made the following year – 1903 – a turning-point in Yeats' art. Nietzschean ideas and echoes play an important part in his work from 1903 to 1921, and from 1930 to 1939; there are comparatively few references to Nietzsche in the 1920s. In the first flush of his enthusiasm Yeats would drag in this "strong enchanter's" name on the slightest pretext. The Irish poet Austin Clarke, himself under Nietzsche's spell at that time, has reported that at a meeting commemorating the centenary of Thomas Davis in early 1915,

> he [Yeats] brought in irrelevantly the name of Nietzsche, for the German poet and philosopher of the Superman was regarded with horror in all our pro-British press during the First Great War. I felt annoyed for I had been reading with guilty delight *Thus Spake Zarathustra*, *The Joyful Science* and *The Birth of Tragedy* with its fascinating theory of Dionysiac and Apollonian moods.[50]

In the 'thirties Yeats had a second Nietzsche phase. Jeffares has written of "Nietzsche, to whom Yeats had returned at the end of the nineteen-thirties",[51] but the Nietzschean echoes in his later work suggest that he in fact returned to Nietzsche – if indeed he had ever really left him – at the *beginning* of the 'thirties at the latest. His revived interest in Nietzsche may in fact date from those 'exultant weeks' in Rapallo in spring 1929, when he had decided that "such leisure as he had should be reserved for the study of local memories of Nietzsche".[52] This return to Nietzsche may well have been motivated by nostalgia for his own lost youth. On 7 April 1930 we find him writing to Lady Gregory: "Just outside the gate of the hotel grounds there is a small restaurant and hotel which was once the lodging, or rather tenement house, where Nietzsche lived for some months and boasted to his friends of having found a place where there were eight walks."[53] Nietzsche had stayed in Rapallo in November 1882–February 1883, and it was there that he began writing *Thus Spake Zarathustra*, a book that was written out of despair (compare Yeats' later comment: "My poetry is generally written out of despair."). Some of the mountain-imagery of *Thus Spake Zarathustra* must have been inspired by one or other of those "eight walks".

Even Yeats' thoughts on old age, surely a very personal subject, echo Nietzsche. The middle stanzas of 'An Acre of Grass' (1936/9):

My temptation is quiet.
Here at life's end
Neither loose imagination
Nor the mill of the mind
Consuming its rag and bone
Can make the truth known.

Grant me an old man's frenzy
Myself must I remake
Till I am Timon and Lear
Or that William Blake
Who beat upon the wall
Till Truth obeyed his call;

echo the passage in *Dawn of Day* in which Nietzsche criticizes "the old thinker" for savouring his life's work, infusing into it "a certain amount of fantasy, sweetness, flavour, poetic mists, and mystic lights", rather than continuing to make and test it. John Davidson voiced the same view in his *Fleet Street Eclogues* (1893):

But you are old; the tide of life is low;
No wind can raise a tempest in a cup;
  Easy it is for withered nerves and veins,
  Parched hearts and barren brains
To be serene and give life's question up.

Yet although, as we have seen, Nietzsche had considerable influence on Yeats, he was a minor influence compared with, say, Plotinus. Yeats never really lost his head over Nietzsche, as Edwin Muir was to do in 1912, though he certainly lost his moral judgment in his temporary aesthetic enthusiasm; and it is significant that right from the start he was critical of the Superman-myth which proved to be he headiest of Nietzsche's ideas for other English-language writers. Yeats found many of his own ideas, interests, and even metaphors (e.g. those of birds of prey) rationalized, confirmed, and justified by Nietzsche. He assimilated, criticized, and in several respects went beyond Nietzsche. Thus his view that there are two paths to the spiritual world, the objective (Christian) way and the subjective ('Dionysiac') way, was confirmed by Nietzsche; but his cyclic theory went far beyond Nietzsche's. Nietzsche confirmed Yeats in his view of the Self, of art, of myth, and encouraged him to claim for *A Vision* (in which Nietzsche appears as mythical Hero)* the status of absolute truth. No doubt it was partly because his interests and sources (Plato, Heraclitus, Pythagoras, Goethe, Schopenhauer, Vico, Indian philosophy, etc.) were so extraordinarily close to Yeats' own, that Nietzsche proved to be such a "strong enchanter" for the Irish poet. A. Zwerdling comes to much the same conclusion in his *Yeats and the Heroic Ideal* (1966); he notes that the evidence at first suggests that Nietzsche's influence must have been "overwhelming and decisive", but goes on:

> Yet at the same time we must remember that in almost every case the ideas which we might think were actually derived from the philosopher can in fact be seen in Yeats' own work before 1902. ... What Yeats must have found, then, was a mind which worked in ways very similar to his own, the mind of a man who had already come to some of the conclusions which he had been struggling for years to formulate. As a result, Nietzsche's actual influence lay in providing authority and reassurance for Yeats' somewhat more hesitant and uncertain thinking.[54]

This is a very fair estimate; what Nietzsche gave Yeats was above all the courage of convictions which he already held, or, put it another way, he helped Yeats to be himself.

* Arthur Ransome also saw Nietzsche as a quasi-mythical "hero of thought" in search of the Holy Grail (see his essay 'Friedrich Nietzsche. An Essay in Comprehension', written in 1912, which appeared in his *Portraits and Speculations*, 1913).

It is because Nietzsche held such a strong enchantment for Yeats that it must be stressed that when all is said and done Yeats withheld his assent to Nietzsche's fundamental rejection of Socratic-Christian thought. In Thomas Common's *Nietzsche as Critic, Philosopher, Poet and Prophet* there are a number of passages from *The Genealogy of Morals* denouncing the "Christian infamy". In the margin Yeats wrote the rather 'old-fashioned' comment:

> Did Christianity create commerce by teaching men to live not in the continual present of self-revelation but to deny self and present for future gain, first heaven and then wealth?

And immediately afterwards he added the often-quoted question:

> But why does Nietzsche think that the night has no stars, nothing but bats and owls and the insane moon?[55]

This comment reads very much like an echo of the lines "Night – it was always night/And never a star above" from John Davidson's *New Ballads* of 1897. Nietzsche, of course, is all things to all men; but it is interesting to note that while the Scottish poet was attracted to Nietzsche because he seemed to offer a way out of his own pessimism, the Irish poet ultimately condemned Nietzsche for his pessimism – but only after spending much of his intellectual life in Nietzsche's company.

Chapter Seven

Subjective fantasies: Herbert Read and Edwin Muir

Like W. B. Yeats ten years earlier, Herbert Read came to Nietzsche via William Blake. Retrospectively he wrote that in 1911 he

> had lost his traditional faith ... and all the paths that opened up in the darkness of his soul (signposts that were painted with such names as Ibsen, Strindberg, Shaw, Orage) converged on this tragic German philosopher, whom he pictured (as the philosopher had intended his disciples should) as a lonely mountain spirit, a wanderer, a stargazer, with an eagle and a serpent for his only companions. Zarathustra entered deep into his soul, so deeply that he has never wholly departed.[1]

He discovered Nietzsche in 1912, reading him in English; he only learnt German between 1922 and 1925. While there is no record of which of Nietzsche's books he read in 1912, the reference to Zarathustra makes it fairly certain that he read *Thus Spake Zarathustra*[2] at this time; he certainly read it before 1915 since the title of his first collection of poems, *Songs of Chaos* (1915), is taken from Zarathustra's introductory discourse ("I say unto you; a man must have chaos within him to be able to give birth to a dancing star"). Years later, in an essay entitled 'On First Reading Nietzsche', Herbert Read wrote:

> I cannot remember which volume I read first – I think it was the one I should have read last, his masterpiece, *Thus Spake Zarathustra.* But I read them all, or all that were then available – there were eventually eighteen volumes. Undoubtedly, two volumes of the series produced the deepest effect – two related volumes: the one already mentioned, *Thus Spake Zarathustra*, and the book which comes immediately after it in chronological sequence – *Beyond Good and Evil.* These two volumes contain the essence of Nietzsche's philosophy and the reading of them produced a decisive crisis in my intellectual development.[3]

In 1912 the impact of Nietzsche was both strong and immediate; it can again be described in Read's own words:

> Nietzsche was a new world, and since my discovery of Blake, the most cataclysmic. It was Nietzsche who first introduced me to philosophy … from Nietzsche communications ran in every direction and for at least five years he … was my real teacher … Nietzsche was a starting point and all the circumstances considered, not one that I regret. He gave me vistas that were quite outside the range of formal education; he introduced me to the ferment of contemporary ideas. In his company I knew the excitement of an intellectual adventure.[4]

All this is clear enough. A young man who had "lost his traditional faith" and on whom the poetry of Blake had already descended "like an apocalypse" ("Blake shook me to the depths of my awakening mind, scattered the world of my objective vision, and left me floundering in subjective fantasy"[5]) would naturally be "carried away" by Nietzsche. In retrospect Read confirmed that his first reading of Nietzsche, at the intellectually impressionable age of 19, produced a "crisis" which was "distinct in its impact, decisive in its outcome".[6]

Although he described himself as having been a "Nietzschean" (his word) in 1914, Read qualified this by saying: "My early enthusiasm for Nietzsche ... was purely intellectual: my life was unaffected – I never became a Nietzschean either in thought or deed".[7] In other words, he became a 'Nietzschean' in the technical sense of this study, but not in the contemporary sense whereby a distinction was made between "pious Nietzscheans" and "ordinary human beings".[8] Since he went on to imply[9] that Nietzsche appealed only to his intellect, not to his temperament and instincts, it seems reasonable to conclude that Nietzsche's influence on the young Herbert Read was above all a matter of introducing him to "the ferment of contemporary ideas". This is, I think, confirmed by Read's remark in his diary (28 January 1915) – "I am beginning to suspect that Nietzsche's appeal to me is largely poetical. Nevertheless I think he is a fine stimulus"[10] – which suggests that it was precisely in the field of "subjective fantasy" that Nietzsche provided most stimulus, cf. Read's later comment:

> What I found in Nietzsche, of course, was the complete destruction of all my ancestral gods, the deriding of all my cherished illusions, an iconoclasm verging on blasphemy. All of that I might have found elsewhere – there were plenty of strident atheists and persuasive rationalists about in those days. But I found something more in Nietzsche – a poetic force ... an imagination that soared into the future, a mind of apparently universal comprehension. Something still more: something which I can only call prophetic fire.[11]

There are few better descriptions of Nietzsche's impact on a young intellectual than Herbert Read's.

Yet for all his enthusiasm, Read's attitude towards Nietzsche remains remarkably objective: he sees clearly, for instance, that Nietzsche's attack on democracy, with which he *sympathizes*, is a matter of "divine rage rather than ... reasoned argument".[12] But he evidently accepted Nietzsche's basic argument: "The great task of humanity, now that 'God is dead', is, as Nietzsche was the first to realize, the conquest of nihilism".[13] His diary entry for 6 March 1915 shows that he also accepted many of Nietzsche's other basic ideas at this time:

> I don't think I am satisfied with the tendency of modern Democracy ... it offers no encouragement to the development of the personality of the individual. It will ensure happiness, but

> scarcely nobility. It will be fatal to even a spiritual superman ... in ethics I think I am an individualist ... What would be the virtue of the super-race to which I wish democracy to aspire? ... I can't even decide what Virtue is. We Atheists must get away from the salvation-or-damnation test of Christianity. We must find a new test – a religion of human perfectability. My own ideal is aesthetic rather than ethical.[14]

This entry, uncertain, groping, even muddled, as it is, reflects a reading of several of Nietzsche's earlier works, including *The Birth of Tragedy* and *Thoughts Out of Season*; a later diary-entry echoes Read's favourite work by Nietzsche, *Thus Spake Zarathustra*:

> Now for a philosophy of Evolution. This is where I think Nietzsche comes in. He had a philosphy of Evolution, and for that reason I think we must hesitate before we reject him as a mere prophet of brutality and force ... Some idea of the Superman I believe to be the essential Idea of any evolutionary attitude towards Life.[15]

However, it is not Nietzsche's view of human evolution (Read's comment on which could have been written almost 20 years earlier, in the Darwinian 'nineties) or his view of democracy that is so significant in the present context. What really matters is his view of the State as such. In *The Tenth Muse* Herbert Read quoted from Zarathustra's discourse 'Of the New Idol' ("The State is the coldest of all cold monsters ... the State lieth in all the languages of good and evil ... False is it wholly") and said that this discourse, which he still had by heart some 35 years after first reading it, contained "the seeds of my philosophy of anarchism".[16] So Herbert Read's little-known but important and characteristic political anarchism had its origin in *Thus Spake Zarathustra*! For Read, Nietzsche was the prophet not of evolution, but of revolution. This helps to explain why he retained his enthusiasm for Nietzsche in the post-1918 world when so many others were to reject Nietzsche and all his works in favour of the post-war prophet, Karl Marx. What the aristocratic philosopher would have made of Read's later enthusiasm for Maoist China is better not even imagined.

But however important his political anarchism, Herbert Read was essentially artist and critic, and it was to the essential Read that the following passage from *Beyond Good and Evil*[17] appealed so powerfully:

> Everything in the nature of freedom, elegance, boldness, dance, and masterly certainty, which exists or has existed, whether it be in thought itself, or in administration, or in speaking and persuading, in art as in conduct, has only developed by means of the tyranny of arbitrary law ... Every artist knows how different from the state of letting oneself go, is his 'most natural' condition, the free arranging, locating, disposing, and constructing in the moments of 'inspiration' – and how strictly and delicately he then obeys a thousand laws, which by their very rigidness and precision, defy all formulation by means of ideas ... The essential thing 'in heaven and in earth' is, apparently ... that there should be long *obedience* in the same direction; and thereby results, and always has resulted in the long run, something which has made life worth living; for instance, virtue, art, music, dancing, reason, spirituality – anything whatever that is transfiguring, refined, foolish or divine.

This passage, which Herbert Read marked in his copy of *Beyond Good and Evil*, impressed him so deeply that he wrote many years later: "I would like to think that it has never, since then, been absent from my consciousness".[18] This, for him, was "the essential message of Nietzsche's philosophy"[19] – that art (and everything else that matters in life) is above all else a matter of discipline and self-discipline. What made Herbert Read tick was the mixture of anarchism and formal self-discipline and the tension between the two. And both came from Nietzsche.

That Nietzsche influenced Read in his basic philosophy between 1911 and 1915 is indisputable; this influence is reflected in the early verse (*Songs of Chaos*) which Read later disavowed and then rather regretted disavowing; in the *Collected Poems* (1946) there is virtually no sign of this early influence. The immediate effect of his early reading of Nietzsche was a necessary disillusionment, that opening of the mind which, however painful for the man, is necessary for the artist within. In the long term it is true to say that Nietzsche permanently widened Herbert Read's horizons, gave him the basis of his philosophy of art and of his political philosophy, and – above all, perhaps – confirmed him in his own basic individualism. Read's extraordinary objectivity ensured that the influence was beneficial;

the very fact that Nietzsche helped him to overcome his own youthful nihilism, shows that *he* at least understood Nietzsche.

It was at the time of his intellectual crisis in summer 1912 ("feeling that my illusive world was beginning to crumble around me") that Edwin Muir wrote to A. R. Orage for advice. Orage advised him to study the work of one writer in depth. Muir chose the then fashionable work of Nietzsche: he bought the volumes of the Levy edition one by one, and began a systematic study of the philosopher which lasted, initially, for more than a year. The extent to which Nietzsche held Muir's attention is shown by the fact that in 1918 he was in the habit of retiring to the lavatory at work to read Nietzsche (whether the irony of his most un-Supermanly posture struck him, I don't know), while in 1919 he was still carrying around a volume of Nietzsche in his pocket.

In 1912 Muir became, in a short time, a Nietzschean; he succumbed to Nietzsche more completely than any other British writer. There were three main reasons for this. In the first place, Nietzsche – like Heine – will have represented a powerful compensation for the squalid circumstances in which he was living at the time. Secondly, Nietzsche's ideas will have had a special, personal appeal for someone who had lost his Christian faith but felt the need for some kind of surrogate; for Muir God had died with his brother Johnnie in 1905; years later we still find him treading the Nietzschean *via negativa*:

> If I could hold complete
> The reverse side of the pattern,
> The wrong side of Heaven,
> O then I should know in not knowing
> My truth in my error.[20]

And Nietzsche's language, his use of metaphor and myth, will have impressed the young would-be poet, just as it impressed the more experienced Scottish poet, John Davidson, 20 years earlier. More generally, "In Nietzsche, especially in *Thus Spake Zarathustra*, he found the poetic content and the wide cosmic sweep ... he wanted".[21] Nietzsche is a powerful writer at any time; for the young Muir he was irresistible, a "drastic stimulus":

> The idea of a transvaluation of all values intoxicated me ... I had

> no ability and no wish to criticize Nietzsche's ideas, since they gave me exactly what I wanted: a last desperate foothold on my dying dream of the future. My heart swelled when I read, 'Become what thou art,' and 'Man is something that must be surpassed,' and 'What does not kill me strengthens me.' Yet it swelled coldly; my brain was on fire, but my natural happiness was slipping away from me as I advanced into colder and colder regions and found myself confronted with the forbidding thought of the Eternal Recurrence ... I ... remained intellectually a Nietzschean ... Actually, although I did not know it, my Nietzscheanism was ... a 'compensation.' I could not face my life as it was, and so I took refuge in the fantasy of the Superman.[22]

If Muir in 1912 lacked Herbert Read's objectivity, this passage shows that he later achieved a very clear understanding of his own early Nietzscheanism. In 1912 he was obsessed by "images of the Superman"[23] in particular, for his Nietzscheanism centred around his "belief in personality": the thought of Eternal Recurrence may have been particularly forbidding for Muir, but it was also – as for Nietzsche himself – a necessity; this is no doubt why it, of all things Nietzschean, was to remain essential to his view of life. His compulsive study of Nietzsche in the Levy translation also had an important side-effect: his feeling for good English was impaired, so that when he began to write in earnest some years later, he produced what he himself called "a sort of pinchbeck Nietzschean prose".[24] I am thinking here of *We Moderns* (1918), and not of the early verse (1913–16) which, although written in Muir's most Nietzschean period, was mostly written in imitation of *Heine*; this very early verse, published (like *We Moderns*) under the pseudonym 'Edward Moore', was a false start – Muir's real poetry began with *First Poems* (1925).

Edwin Muir's youthful "infatuation" with Heine lasted from 1908 to 1914. He delighted in Heine's wit and irreverence and charm"[25] and in his "ironical paganism",[26] although in retrospect he recognized that "There is, as well as exquisite wit, a sickly, graveyard strain in Heine's poetry".[27] Be this as it may, in 1913 Muir "steeped [himself] in that sweet poison, and began to write lonely ironic, slightly corpse-like poems"[28] which Orage printed in *The New Age* in the section appropriately entitled 'Pastiche'. Although

Muir said that from Heine he got the "habit of speaking about everything ironically", and "became ruthless towards sentimentality",[29] his early poems in fact attempt to combine irony and sentiment in the manner of Heine, and – like some of Heine's own earlier poems – tend to be rather sickly nostalgic. No doubt the ironical pose, like the later Superman pose, was essentially a mask to disguise the naïve young writer's emotional reticence. In *An Autobiography* Muir leaves the reader in little doubt that on balance both Heine and Nietzsche (who had himself so much admired Heine's irony) were pernicious influences. This they probably were, though Muir's enthusiasm for Heine was shared by Ezra Pound and William Carlos Williams: in his *Literary Essays* Pound several times lists Heine as one of the few post-Classical poets of importance, and indeed mentions Goethe (much admired by Yeats) only to say that his lyrics are "as good as Heine's"; William Carlos Williams, for his part, read Heine avidly in Leipzig in 1909/10 and referred to the poems of the *Buch der Lieder*, some of which he learnt by heart, as "beautiful things".

When Edwin Muir began to take up writing, he was, as he says, "still under the influence of Nietzsche".[30] The literary product of his early Nietzscheanism was the book of aphorisms *We Moderns* (1918). The Nietzscheanism is evident in both the style and the content of these texts which Herbert Read for one found "full of acceptable suggestions",[31] though Muir himself later rejected them as immature, written "in excited ignorance".[32] In *We Moderns* the excitement, deriving from Nietzsche, is certainly much in evidence; the emphasis is on the Will-to-Power, the most central of all Nietzsche's themes; the Superman ideal is there ("The fall from innocence – that was the fall from the Superman into Man. And how, then is Man to be redeemed? By the return of the Superman!"),[33] as are Nietzsche's view of ancient Greek civilization ("There is something enigmatical … behind the Greek clearness of representation, something unexplained; in short, a problem"[34]), his conception of Dionysian or Tragic man, his Dionysian morality including the cult of 'hardness', his view of tragedy as the supreme affirmation of life, the doctrine of eternal Becoming, and the opposition of the Christian and the Dionysian with the repudiation of Christ in favour of Dionysos. The section on Nietzsche, whose ideas are scattered throughout the book, conveniently summarizes Muir's view in 1918:

> What was Nietzsche, that subtlest of modern riddles? First, a great tragic poet: it was by a divine accident that he was at the same time a profound thinker and the deepest psychologist. But his tragic affirmative was the core of his work, of which thought and analysis were but outgrowths. Without it, his subtlety might have made him another Pascal. The Will to Power, which makes suffering integral in Life; the Order of Rank whereby the bulk of mankind are doomed to slavery; the Superman himself, that most sublime child of Tragedy; and the last affirmation, the Eternal Recurrence: these are the conceptions of a tragic poet. It is, indeed, by virtue of his tragic view of Life that Nietzsche is for us a force of such value. For only by means of it could modern existence, sunk in scepticism, pessimism and the greatest happiness of the greatest number, be re-created.[35]

When *We Moderns* appeared, Muir's mentor, A. R. Orage, while noting that Muir inhabited a "world shared mainly by himself and Nietzsche, a world of his intellectual imagination", praised the work highly:

> Mr. Edward Moore has published a notebook under the title of *We Moderns*. If you regard it as an imitation of Nietzsche, you must admit that it is, as a tour de force, parody of the very highest order, parody amounting to originality almost equal to Nietzsche's own ... to my mind no writer and thinker that ever lived is so lacking in common sense as Nietzsche ... Mr. Moore is a romantic to whom it is fatal to apply the criterion of common sense. The world in which his discoveries are made is not the world in which the jury of mankind sits: it is a world shared mainly by himself and Nietzsche, a world of his intellectual imagination.[36]

In truth *We Moderns* was imitation rather than parody of Nietzsche. Willa Muir, for her part, reports that she was "put off Edwin Muir" – whom she had not met at that stage – by the "extreme admiration for Nietzsche" running through *We Moderns*.[37] When she first met her future husband, later in 1918, he appeared with a volume of Nietzsche stuffed in each side-pocket.

Edwin Muir himself later came to repudiate the intellectual arrogance displayed in *We Moderns*, just as he was at this time soon to reject the arrogance of the Superman-idea. In the following year (1919) already there began a reaction against Nietzsche which – like his Nietzsche cult – took some years to be more or less complete. He now began to distrust the Superman and to discard the mannered Nietzschean rhetoric of *We Moderns*. As Willa Muir has said, "Edwin's reaction from Nietzsche, which was bringing a new sobriety into his style, was part of a general reaction against what he felt to be the false personality he had hidden behind in Glasgow".[38] As we shall see, this parting-of-the-ways was accompanied by a breakdown.

By the time of his next prose work, *Latitudes* (1924), which includes a chapter on Nietzsche, Muir had achieved a rather more detached attitude to his former master. The rejection of absolute values and assertion of Life as eternal Becoming, which underlies the book, may be essentially Nietzschean; but the fact remains that Muir has by this time regained his objectivity. He quotes Nietzsche in support of his own ideas, rather than as a prophet to whom he has lost his judgment and to whom he therefore owes blind acceptance. In other words, Muir has come to terms with Nietzsche, who has fallen into place as part of his intellectual heritage. The Nietzscheanism as such has gone.

In 1924 Muir still held to that "joyous affirmation of life even at moments when everything threatens to go to pieces, and an enormous strengthening of will-power", in which Nietzsche's influence on his followers was said[39] to consist. By 1926, however, he finally achieved a positively critical attitude towards his one-time idol. In *Transition* (1926), he wrote that Nietzsche "rarely reached past a will-to-acceptance to acceptance itself", which strikes at the very roots of Nietzsche's philosophy, and is confirmed by Nietzsche's own diary-entry: "I have tried to affirm life myself – but ah!" In the last analysis this is true of Muir himself, who came to see that his "belief in the ideas of Nietzsche was a willed belief".[40]

Right from the beginning, Muir's social and Christian idealism had been basically incompatible with his Nietzscheanism, although at first he had deliberately refused to recognize the fact. A friend later reported that Muir "quite literally drove himself ill trying to reconcile the intellectual appeal of Nietzsche with his latent Christian idealism".[41] There seems in fact to be little doubt that the emotional disturbance which he underwent in about 1919 was the direct result – like Nietzsche's insanity – of trying to reconcile irreconcilable opposites (a problem which others less honest than

Muir and Nietzsche have solved by pretending that the opposites in question were not irreconcilable). As a young man Muir suffered a conflict between self and antiself – there was a very deep antagonism between Edwin Muir and his Nietzschean alter ego, 'Edward Moore' – and therefore took a long time to find his true self. Nietzsche *seemed* to help, and certainly kept him going for a time; but in the long run Nietzsche led him further and further away from his true self, hence the inevitable breakdown when his mind began to reject the intellectual foreign body. As Willa Muir has said,

> It was no wonder that Nietzsche … came to him as a great light in his darkness: the poetic imagination in *Thus Spake Zarathustra* encouraged his inner self to go on, although in the wrong directions. The Will to Power strengthened but imprisoned him. The Superman flickered brightly on his horizon for a while, yet his true self finally recognized that the Superman was a mirage.[42]

The truth of this seems to be confirmed by the fact that he was restored, and Nietzsche's stranglehold on him broken, after an extraordinary dream in 1919 *about Nietzsche*, a dream

> which contained a curious criticism of him and my infatuation with him. I dreamt that I was in a crowd watching a crucifixion. I expected the crucified man to be bearded like Christ, but saw with surprise that he was clean-shaven except for a heavy moustache. It was undoubtedly Nietzsche; he looked as if he had usurped the Cross, though like many a usurper he appeared simultaneously to be perfectly at home on it. He stared round him with an air of defiant possession, as if this were the place he had always been seeking, and had now, with deep astonishment, found – or, rather, conquered – at last; for he was like a man who had violently seized a position which belonged to some one else. His temples were so racked with pain that I could see the nerves twitching and jangling under the thin skin; his thick eyebrows were drawn down in a scowl, but in his eyes there was a look of triumph. I was bewildered by this dream, which seemed at such odds with Nietzsche's philosophy; yet it had the profound naturalness of a dream, the cross seemed to fit the man and the man the cross; and I slowly began to realize that *Nietzsche's life had been a curious kind of self-crucifixion, out of pride, not of love.*[43]

This remarkable dream may well have been prompted by Nietzsche's well-known letter to Peter Gast in which he signed himself "The Crucified One". It shows just how deeply Muir had understood Nietzsche, and how very deeply Nietzsche had wormed his way into Muir's soul; some years earlier Muir had even experienced a dream of Nietzsche's! The present dream marks the point in time when Muir first saw Nietzsche objectively, first realized that Nietzsche had usurped the place that belonged to his own basic Christian idealism; it was soon after this that he dropped his "Nietzschean affectations of super-manhood".[44]

We have already seen that *Latitudes* (1924) was still essentially Nietzschean in its basic attitudes, and Michael Hamburger has stressed "how much of Nietzsche's doctrine Muir retained to the end".[45] In particular it was the "forbidding thought of the Eternal Recurrence" which continued to haunt Muir:

All things return, Nietzsche said,
The ancient wheel revolves again,
Rise, take up your numbered fate;
The cradle and the bridal bed,
Life and the coffin wait.
All has been that ever can be,
And this sole eternity
Cannot cancel, cannot add
One to your delights or tears,
Or a million million years
Tear the nightmare from the mad.

Have no fear then. You will miss
Achievement by the self-same inch,
When the great occasion comes
And they watch you, you will flinch,
Lose the moment, be for bliss
A footlength short. All done before.

Though "the heart makes reply" in this particular poem ('The Recurrence', from *The Narrow Place*, 1941), it is clear that the "idea of Nietzsche's eternal return to the union which is at the heart of every mystic's vision"[46] remained at the heart of Edwin Muir's vision:

Nothing yet was ever done
Till it was done again,

And no man was ever one
Except through dead men.[47]

The depth of Nietzsche's impact on Edwin Muir is shown not only by his remarkable dream of the Crucified Anti-Christ, but by the fact that his dying words were quintessentially Nietzschean: "There are no absolutes, no absolutes."

Chapter Eight

The pagan Infinite: D. H. Lawrence and J. C. Powys

There seems to be some confusion in D. H. Lawrence criticism as to whether or not Lawrence was 'influenced' by Nietzsche. E. W. Tedlock, Jr, for instance, has written: "Another influence was Nietzsche, and here the resemblance between Lawrence's values and the philosopher's ideas is much clearer".[1] That such a 'resemblance' exists cannot be denied; the real question is whether or not it is the result of Lawrence being 'influenced' by Nietzsche.

According to Jessie Chambers, Lawrence "found" Nietzsche in the public library at Croydon: "He never mentioned him [Nietzsche] directly to me, nor suggested that I should read him, but I began to hear about the 'Will to Power', and perceived that he had come upon something new and engrossing".[2] Which of Nietzsche's works Lawrence read at this time (*c.* 1908/9) is not recorded, but it will very likely have been *Beyond Good and Evil: Prelude to a Philosophy of the Future*,[3] which was added to the stock of Croydon

Central Library in 1908;* not only would a recent accession be likely to catch the eye, but Jessie Chambers' reference to the Will-to-Power points in the same direction. However, in 1908 Croydon Central Library also possessed *The Case of Wagner*,[4] *The Dawn of Day*,[5] *A Genealogy of Morals*,[6] *Poems*,[7] and *Thus Spake Zarathustra*,[8] all of which were added to stock in 1903, at the beginning of the real Nietzsche vogue in England. Be this as it may, in *Paul Morel*, one of the early drafts of *Sons and Lovers*, Lawrence later wrote that Paul (= himself) and Miriam (= Jessie Chambers), at 17 and 16 respectively, read Schopenhauer and Nietzsche, "authors who hurt her inexpressibly, and delighted him"; he subsequently omitted this reference. Now although Lawrence's imagination has clearly been at work here – in reality he did not encourage Jessie to read Nietzsche – it seems reasonable to suppose that he himself was not only "engrossed", but positively "delighted" by Nietzsche's work when he first discovered it.

Lawrence's reading of Nietzsche in 1908/9 is reflected in his work from 1912 onwards, beginning with *The Trespasser* (1912); the way in which Helena carries a volume of Nietzsche around with her suggests that Lawrence may be alluding to Nietzsche's contrast between Dionysian and domestic tragedy, while Siegmund's and Helena's responses to the Christian symbols strongly suggest Nietzsche's vitalistic concept of Christianity as a slave-religion. It is to Nietzsche the Antichrist that Lawrence – despite his Christian humility – is attracted at this time: "Now we say that the Christian Infinite is not infinite. We are tempted, like Nietzsche, to return back to the old pagan Infinite, to say that is supreme".[9] Though this may not be Lawrence's position in the long run, his review 'Georgian Poetry: 1911–1912' confirms his early admiration for Nietzsche as fellow artist and iconoclast: "The last years have been years of demolition. Because faith and belief were getting pot-bound ... therefore faith and belief and the Temple must be broken. This time art fought the battle, rather than science or any new religious faction. And art has been demolishing for us: Nietzsche, the Christian religion as it stood".[10] The implication is unmistakable: Lawrence is on Nietzsche's side. In the same review he writes that "The great liberation gives us an overwhelming sense of joy, *joie d'être, joie de vivre*", which parallels what Nietzsche said in

* For this information I am indebted to the Chief Librarian of Croydon Central Library, Mr A. O. Meakin.

Human, All Too Human about the "great liberation" (*grosse Loslösung*) from the trammels of the past.

The 'Study of Thomas Hardy', also dating from this early period, shows that Lawrence is not only attracted towards the "pagan Infinite", but shares Nietzsche's preference for the pagan-aristocratic mode generally. Lawrence finds the Greek attitude to the female reflected in Nietzsche, and writes of this attitude which "belongs to passion, makes a man feel proud, splendid ... He feels full of blood, He walks the earth like a Lord. And it is to this state Nietzsche aspires in his *Wille zur Macht*".[11] The attitude ascribed to the Greeks, whereby the female is "administered unto" the male, surely echoes Zarathustra's notorious dictum "Thou goest to women? Remember thy whip!" There is another, similar reference to the *Wille zur Macht* in *Women in Love*.[12] More important is Lawrence's apparent advocacy of the Will-to-Power in general; but it should also be noted that in the Hardy study he adds that "The Wille zur Macht is a spurious feeling".[13]

In addition to the apparent references to *Beyond Good and Evil*, *Thus Spake Zarathustra*, and *The Will to Power* already noted, there are also apparent references in Lawrence's letters of this period to *The Dawn of Day* ("Today [in 1915] I have begun again my philosophy – *Morgenrot* is my new name for it".[14] This is surely a reference to *The Dawn of Day* – *Morgenröte* in the original German title – the book which Nietzsche described as beginning his campaign against morality), and to *Human, All Too Human* ("Allzu Menschliches"[15]).

In Lawrence's third period (1920–25) the Will-to-Power looms large in *Aaron's Rod* (1922), and indeed in all his leadership novels. Lilly in *Aaron's Rod* – it is generally agreed that she acts as Lawrence's mouthpiece – speaks at length about the "power motive", appropriating Nietzsche's term for it, but defining the "will-to-power" in an apparently very different sense:

> We've exhausted the love-urge, for the moment ... We've got to accept the power motive ... It is a great life-motive ... Power – the power-urge. The will-to-power – but not in Nietzsche's sense. Not intellectual power. Not mental power. Not conscious will power. Not even wisdom. But dark, living, fructifying power ... That's where Nietzsche was wrong. His was the conscious and benevolent will, in fact the love will.[16]

In fact this suggests that Lawrence had misunderstood Nietzsche and taken his Will-to-Power too narrowly as referring to "intellectual power", for Lilly's view of power is very close to Nietzsche (and to Schopenhauer, whom Lawrence had read before he came to Nietzsche). The urge-to-dominate, to which Nietzsche devoted not a little of his psychological acumen, as well as not a little of his tendency to over-generalize, is much more a question of "dark, living ... power" than of anything more cerebral; to identify it with the "love will" is nonsense. Lawrence is here far closer to Nietzsche than he realized.

Closely connected with the leadership novels are Lawrence's essays of the period such as 'Aristocracy' (in *Reflections on the Death of a Porcupine*, 1925), 'Education of the People' (in *Phoenix*, 1936), and *Fantasia of the Unconscious* (1922). C. B. O'Hare has written that in these essays Lawrence "makes plain his belief, in this period, in a world of peacocks and sparrows. His *leaders* were to be supermen of a sort, but not, perhaps, in the Nietzschean sense. What he envisioned ... was an aristocracy of leaders who would lead by virtue of the fact that they would make it possible for more life to come into being".[17] That Lawrence did envision such an aristocracy is beyond argument; but here too he is far closer to Nietzsche than has been realized, for the second part of O'Hare's comment is tantamount to a summary of Nietzsche's views: more life, superabundant life – this was very much Nietzsche's goal, despite his aristocratic Darwinism. There are other allusions to Nietzsche in Lawrence's work of the 'twenties, e.g. in *Kangaroo*,[18] 'The Borderline'[19] and 'Bottom Dogs',[20] though none is intrinsically important.

So much, then, for explicit and apparent references to Nietzsche and his work. To these we have to add some of Lawrence's frequent references to Apollo and Dionysos (references to Dionysos/Bacchus/Iacchus are second only to references to Venus in terms of frequency in his work), though here we really come to the parallels between Lawrence and Nietzsche.

An outline of these parallels may appropriately begin with the Dionysian element in the work of both writers, for Lawrence – like Nietzsche – celebrates

> the *ego sum* of Dionysus
> The sono io of perfect drunkenness
> Intoxication of final loneliness.[21]

Although the anarchic Dionysian tendency of Lawrence's imagination is counteracted by his respect for human limitations, Eugene Goodheart was surely right to insist that "Nevertheless, Lawrence is *essentially* like Blake and Nietzsche in his address to the untapped powers of man and his hatred of the rules and forms that curb those powers".[22] Like Zarathustra, Lawrence celebrates nature in its Dionysian aspect. It is surely no chance that the nationalist movement in *The Plumed Serpent* (1926) has as its emblem Zarathustra's eagle and serpent; the conflict in this novel between Christianity and the Zarathustran religion of Quetzalcoatl is *entirely* Nietzschean, hence Hugh Kingsmill's suggestion that *The Plumed Serpent* is basically a mixture of *Thus Spake Zarathustra* and Rider Haggard's *She*. More generally, Nietzsche's Dionysian "yea-saying to life ... the will to life" prefigures much of Lawrence's work. Both writers advocate surrender to life and celebrate unbridled instinct. In *Twilight in Italy*, Lawrence wrote of Dionysos: "Man knows satisfaction when he surpasses all conditions and becomes, to himself, consummate in the Infinite, when he reaches a state of infinity. In the supreme ecstasy of the flesh, the Dionysian ecstasy, he reaches this state".[23] Though the context ("the supreme ecstasy of the flesh") is admittedly different, this is basically Nietzsche's 'self-overcoming'; Lawrence clearly shares Nietzsche's belief that man is something to be surpassed and is surpassed in Dionysian ecstasy. But Lawrence's picture is perhaps more balanced than Nietzsche's, for he also writes: "When Northern Europe, whether it hates Nietzsche or not, is crying out for the Dionysiac ecstasy, practising on itself the Dionysiac ecstasy, Southern Europe is breaking free from Dionysos, from the triumphal affirmation of life over death".[24] The fact remains, however, that Lawrence is at root an a-moralist in the Nietzschean sense of rejecting morality-in-itself, morality-as-a-matter-of-habit. His emphasis on and praise of the knowledge of the blood or "blood consciousness" parallels and echoes Nietzsche's distinction between tragic and theoretical man in *The Birth of Tragedy*. Indeed, so many of the parallels point back to *The Birth of Tragedy* that it is reasonable to conclude that Lawrence was much impressed by it. The Dionysian ecstasy of which Nietzsche wrote is nowhere featured more recognizably than in Lawrence's work. The belief in self-transcendence is central in the work of both writers. Lawrence was as much aware of the "death of God" as Nietzsche was, although his religious nature prevented him from employing the phrase which Nietzsche's religious nature had impelled him to use. Like Nietzsche, Lawrence tended to see Christianity as the enemy of life; late essays such as 'Aristocracy' and 'Blessed are the Powerful' (both in *Reflections on the Death of a Porcupine*, 1925) are similar in their basic attitude to Nietzsche's *A Genealogy of Morals** – one of Nietzsche's works which Lawrence is likely to have read. *Apocalypse* (1931) closely parallels Nietzsche's *Antichrist*: both books attack Christianity for much the same reasons, and in much the same ambiguous spirit. But – unlike a number of other British writers – Lawrence did not accept the doctrine of Eternal Recurrence; in his 'Study of Thomas Hardy' he wrote: "Nietzsche talks about the *Ewige Wiederkehr*. It is like Botticelli singing cycles. But each cycle is different. There is no real recurrence".[25]

In view of parallels such as these, we may safely conclude that Lawrence was not only "engrossed" (Jessie Chambers) by Nietzsche's work when he discovered it in 1908, but will have been positively "delighted" (*pace* Paul Morel) by many of Nietzsche's attitudes, which held his attention. It is clear that Nietzsche did in fact 'influence' Lawrence, although on balance it seems more appropriate to speak of strong resemblances between his and Nietzsche's ethics, for Lawrence normally only goes so far with Nietzsche before turning back. When all is said and done, Lawrence lacked Nietzsche's nerve, hence his admiration for Nietzsche's awful daring; his Christianity lay a good deal nearer the surface than Nietzsche's.

Like Yeats, John Cowper Powys began to fall under Nietzsche's spell shortly after the turn of the century. His "second little book of imitative poems", as he called the *Poems* of 1899, already pointed forward to the influence of Nietzsche:

> These lonely heights
> Were not for parrots made.
> I would not leave my eagle flights
> To learn to be afraid!

Shortly after this he began to write a "monstrous epic poem" entitled 'The Death of God'; published in 1956 in a much-revised

* I quote the title of Wm Haussmann's 1899 version, which is the one that Lawrence is likely to have read; the later version by H. B. Samuel, which appeared in the Levy edition, was entitled *The Genealogy of Morals*.

version under the title of *Lucifer*, the poem reflects his early reading of Nietzsche – Nietzsche, whose work belonged, for Powys, among the "great dramatic philosophies".[26] In the decade before the First World War, Powys spent much time reading Nietzsche and discussing "that German's" work with his friends; he later wrote that Nietzsche's work held a "fatal intoxication" for him. While in Florence he read *Ecce Homo*, "this nobly-maniacal book", and "pretended to myself that I too ... would be a proclaimer of planetary secrets".[27] On Nietzschean ground in Switzerland, his head "full of the hyperborean breath of Nietzsche's imaginations",[28] Powys again dallied with the notion that "it would be my destiny one day to give to the world a philosophy as startling and new as that of the author of *Ecce Homo*".[29]

Unlike any of the other writers under discussion except Huneker and Levy, Powys even made a pilgrimage to the Nietzsche household in Weimar:

> by my cousin's influence I actually was invited by Frau Foster [sic] Nietzsche to take tea with her in Nietzsche's own house. Imagine what I felt when this devoted lady showed me the dead man's books, his editions of those 'Great Latins' he so ridiculously overrated, De Maupassant, Mérimée and so forth! There was, I remember, a certain modern French idealist among these books, an author I had never heard of; but against some eloquent passage of his, in praise of 'the resolute pursuit of the higher truth,' Nietzsche had written in pencil in the margin, several times over, the words: 'in vain' ... 'in vain' ... 'in vain'.[30]

But for all his devotion to Nietzsche, the appearance of Powys' *The War and Culture* (N.Y., 1914; English title, *The Menace of German Culture*, 1915) showed that he "had ... for some years been hostile, as an individualist, to the authoritarian and monopolistic views ... current in the Germany of his beloved Goethe and Nietzsche".[31]

In 1915 the first of Powys' two essays on Nietzsche appeared, in his *Visions and Revisions*. The idea that Nietzsche was at heart a "true Christian", asserted by John Davidson, has rarely been argued with more conviction and force than by Powys in *Visions and Revisions*. Here he variously describes Nietzsche as "a saint and a martyr" and as "an intellectual sadist"; but his basic view is that Nietzsche "seized upon Greek tragedy and made it dance to Christian cymbals", that "Even ... in the sort of wickedness he evokes,

Nietzsche remains Christ-ridden and Christ-mastered".[32] He describes Nietzsche's "spiritual contest" as "a deliberate self-inflicted Crucifixion of the Christ in him".[33] If this characterizes his view of Nietzsche, the suggested antidote to Nietzsche is highly characteristic of Powys himself; arguing that Nietzsche "smote whom he went out to smite", he adds: "But one thing he could not smite; he could neither smite it, or unmask it, or 'transvalue' it. I mean the Earth itself – the great, shrewd, wise, all-enduring Mother of us all ... The antidote to Nietzsche is ... to be found ... in burying your face in rough moist earth".[34]

In his second essay on Nietzsche, in *The Pleasures of Literature* (1938), Powys declared that what underlies Nietzsche's work is a "loathing for average humanity and for average humanity's moral values",[35] and repeated the view, already expressed in *Visions and Revisions*, that Nietzsche's "secret soul was riddled with religion",[36] and that his writings "reveal ... the translunar vein of purely spiritual sadism".[37] But here too, more clearly than anywhere else, he spelt out what Nietzsche meant to him personally: Nietzsche is "the most prophetic voice since Blake"[38] – a juxtaposition which is by now familiar to us; he is unique:

> There is no one in the remotest degree like Nietzsche, as far as I know, in the whole history of literature ... What we get from Nietzsche's book [*Thus Spake Zarathustra*] is the greatest of all gifts that any writer can give us – namely, a heightening of our dramatic interest in life ... I cannot see a volume of Nietzsche on any shelf without opening it, and it is like the Tree of Knowledge of Good and Evil – you cannot open it without feeling, just as you did at first, the old fatal intoxication.[39]

For all his intoxication, however, Powys did not hesitate to criticize Nietzsche's ideas in detail, viz.:

> Every epoch of human history, for each epoch incarnates some imperishable aspect of human nature, returns sooner or later in a great historic curve; though it never returns, as Nietzsche in his self-crucifying *amor fati* forced himself to imagine, with the same identical repetition of man and things.
>
> It returns; but with a difference: and in that difference lies the whole secret of human progress.[40]

Although he was fascinated by some of Nietzsche's ideas, chief among them the idea of Eternal Recurrence (as modified above), and although he said that his own philosophy "amounted to a vivid Nietzschean recognition of the 'pathos of difference' in the world",[41] it was not in fact particular ideas that attracted him so powerfully to Nietzsche; indeed, he remained critical of many of Nietzsche's ideas. Thus for him the Superman is "a great and terrible idea", Eternal Recurrence a "horrible closed circle", a "frightful dogma". But no matter, for

> It is not essential that we should accept a single one of all the Nietzschean *doctrines*. What *is* essential, if we are not ... to stop our ears to the most prophetic voice since Blake, is that we should apply to the spiritual drama of our own life the searching psychology Nietzsche applied to his, and let the arctic wind of his relentless purification blow free upon us.[42]

In Powys' own philosophy magic replaces the Nietzschean myths as a substitute for belief in God. No, it was something deeper and vaguer that attracted Powys: he recognized in Nietzsche a fellow-"romanticist of ideas" who shared his own delight in indulging in "half-poetic, half-philosophic generalizations about the history of human ideas".[43] In other words, it was essentially a temperamental attraction. But for all that, Powys' *Autobiography* in particular is an important monument to British Nietzscheanism, and when his work is again available, so that a proper study can be made of his philosophy, the full extent of the parallels between his philosophy and Nietzsche's will no doubt be made clear. After all, Powys, more than anyone else, obeyed Zarathustra's injunction to "remain true to the Earth". In the meantime, let us recall Powys' words in *Visions and Revisions* (1915):

> It is not the hour in which to say much about Nietzsche. The dissentient voices are silent. The crowd has stopped howling. But a worse thing is happening to him, the thing of all others he dreaded most; – he is becoming 'accepted' – the preachers are quoting him and the theologians are explaining him.
>
> What he would himself pray for now are Enemies – fierce, irreconcilable Enemies – but our age cannot produce such. It can only produce sneering disparagement; or frightened conventional approbation.[44]

In 1915 this was rather an odd comment, for the patriotic crowd was then howling at its loudest, baying for Nietzsche's blood. Powys' comment confirms how close he himself was to his own image of Nietzsche: "For the final impression one carries away after reading Nietzsche, is the impression of 'distinction', of remoteness from 'vulgar brutality', from 'sensual baseness', from the clumsy compromises of the world".[45] The words could stand, with little modification, as an epitaph to John Cowper Powys himself. By 1955, however, when *Visions and Revisions* was reprinted, his comment had become true: the crowd had stopped howling, Nietzsche had become accepted, and the theologians were indeed explaining him (Father Copleston's *Friedrich Nietzsche, Philosopher of Culture*, appeared in 1942, his *St. Thomas and Nietzsche* in 1944). But before Nietzsche could pop up alongside Thomas Aquinas, he had first to face those 'Enemies' lurking implacably behind their Georgian turn-down collars.

Chapter Nine

"A very dangerous experiment" (Nietzsche in Georgian England)

The idea of Nietzsche taken into what Edward Thomas called the "tender bosoms and charming parlours" of Georgian England inevitably calls to mind the proverbial bull in a china shop, although in fact Nietzsche did relatively little damage in circles that are here called 'Georgian' partly as a matter of convenience. While the 'advanced' writers, the 'men of 1914' (discussed in the next Chapter) tended to take Nietzsche very seriously indeed, the 'Georgians' tended to take a vicarious delight in his 'wickedness'. Reading of Harold Monro's "very dangerous experiment" – his plan to write a Nietzschean poem – one cannot help thinking of J. Alfred Prufrock's "Do I dare/Disturb the universe?" There is, similarly, something determinedly with-it and daring about Rupert Brooke's first reference to Nietzsche. What I wish to consider at this point, then, is Nietzsche's impact on some contributors to *Georgian Poetry* (Lascelles Abercrombie, Rupert Brooke, Harold Monro), on other writers who can properly be called 'Georgians' (Edward Thomas), including the 'Georgian war-poets' (Charles Sorley and Isaac Rosenberg), and on several other writers who in the present context can best be brought together under the Georgian umbrella (Wilfred Scawen Blunt, John Middleton Murry *et al.*). Although it emanated from conservative rather than advanced literary circles, the reaction against Nietzsche in August 1914 will be discussed in the next Chapter, for this reaction was to mark the beginning of the end of his influence in England.

Edward Thomas began reading Nietzsche in 1907, and was at once deeply impressed. On 26 December 1907 he wrote to Gordon Bottomley: "Isn't Nietzsche magnificent? and so necessary these days? Yet he damns me to deeper perdition than I had yet bestowed on myself".[1] It seems that Thomas began his reading of Nietzsche with *The Genealogy of Morals*, for on 15 January 1908 he again wrote to Gordon Bottomley: "Nietzsche will have to come in later. *The Genealogy of Morals* is a very great book. But I kick at his too completely aristocratic view".[2] Since Thomas apparently read Nietzsche in preparation for his *Richard Jefferies. His Life and Work* (1909), it is hardly surprising to find him there quoting from *The Genealogy of Morals*[3] and attributing to Richard Jefferies his own criticism of Nietzsche's élitism:

> In 'Nature and Eternity' [in Longman's Magazine, 1895], he [Jefferies] says: 'It is necessary that some far-seeing master-mind, some giant intellect, should arise and sketch out in bold, unmistakable outlines the grand and noble future which the human race should labour for.' This dream of a master-mind ... recalls the words: 'This man of the future who will redeem us from the old ideal ... as also from what had to grow out of this ideal; ... this bell of noonday and the great decision which restores freedom to the will, which restores to the earth its goal and to man his hope ... he must come some day.' But Jefferies would not have made the mistake of so admiring the unfettered great man's prowess as not to see the beauty of the conquered and all the other forms of life which the powerful would destroy if they might.[4]

As we have seen, Thomas here voices a common English criticism of Nietzsche's anti-democratic philosophy. In addition to *The Genealogy of Morals*, he also read *Thoughts Out of Season* (2 volumes), *The Birth of Tragedy*, and *Beyond Good and Evil*, as well as M. A. Mügge, *Friedrich Nietzsche. His Life and Work* (1908) and A. R. Orage, *Friedrich Nietzsche: The Dionysian Spirit of the Age* (1906; listed in the Bibliography of his *Richard Jefferies*). These additional titles (with the exception of Orage's book) are the subject of Thomas's review 'Nietzsche' in *The Bookman* (June 1909),[5] an enthusiastic, well-informed review which shows that he found in Nietzsche much to admire and not a little to criticize. The review is worth quoting at length because it is so characteristic of the 'Georgian' reaction to Nietzsche:

> Everybody who has not read Nietzsche's work knows that he was very wicked ... But they also know that he was punished by madness as other offenders were punished by hemlock and cross. Justice is satisfied, and since we know that only the good can prevail, we may begin to handle the abomination with security. Even if it were not harmless we are so used to poisons that one more will not affect the mixture which we drain so devoutly, though without growing perceptibly happier or wiser or more amusing. Let us enjoy him disinterestedly, knowing that our souls are safe. Let us take a dilettante's joy in him. He is worthy of it. For there are few spirits of a more godlike fury and colour than Nietzsche, and the godlike spirits are made for men, not men for the godlike, as he insolently thought. We shall disagree with him, but we need not be angry, since we are certain that we shall conquer, and that he, like other great men, will only be great when he is popularized and our grandchildren pillory men for denying him. He will colour and change us, but we need not fear ... Perhaps it will make our claim that he is not dangerous more convincing if we point out that he is a poet and prove it by a few delectable quotations ... He is a Greek, but what a romantic Greek ... this exquisitely sensitive poet and man of culture ... Unless we of the middle classes take him into our tender bosoms and charming parlours and stifle him there, it will perhaps be not with the aristocracy so-called [,] which is dead or dying, but with the brutal unspoilt multitude that his hope of life or resurrection will lie.

It is interesting to compare this with Lascelles Abercrombie's review of the same books (see below). Edward Thomas's reaction to Nietzsche is not only enthusiastically ironical; it is also quintessentially 'Georgian'. There is complacency as well as irony in his opening sentences; he may be mocking himself for saying it, but he *is* saying that this mad bull can do no harm in the Georgian china-shop, that "we may ... handle the abomination with security." Within five years it was to be a very different story indeed.

Another Georgian poet who fell under Nietzsche's spell for a time – also in about 1907 – was Harold Monro, the eclectic proprietor of the Poetry Bookshop. In June 1909 Monro stated that, under the influence of Nietzsche and Victor Hugo, he had begun "a very dangerous experiment"; he was referring to his attempts to write an epic poem about the 'death of God', attempts which lasted, on and off, until 1923. The influence of Nietzsche is apparent in Monro's conviction that "The real action of the spirit of Man is to break the fetters of Good and Evil and smash the idea of absolute Godhead".[6] In 1913 Nietzsche seems to have been still in the forefront of Monro's mind, cf. his comment on Ezra Pound: "Mr. Pound is a stern dictator. He hates dogma ... Nevertheless, Nietzsche-like, he is himself dogmatist".[7] His definition of "The first principles of *our* Futurism" as being:

> i. To forget God, Heaven, Hell, Personal Immortality, and to remember, always, the earth.
> ii. To lift the eyes from a sentimental contemplation of the past, and though dwelling in the present, nevertheless, always, to *live* in the future of the earth.[8]

is certainly 'Nietzschean' enough, too, though there is no evidence that it necessarily derives from Zarathustra's "Remain true to the earth!" In fact it is more likely to derive from a parallel source, Edward Carpenter's *Civilization: its Cause and Cure* (1889).

Lascelles Abercrombie was another Georgian poet to respond enthusiastically to Nietzsche, on whom he first wrote in the *Liverpool Daily Courier* ('The Thought-Shaker', 20 November 1908; 'Nietzsche Again', 22 January 1909; 'Nietzsche's Work', 23 July 1909); more important than these reviews, however, is Abercrombie's *Romanticism* (1926), in which he made a brilliant analysis of Nietzsche's romanticism in terms which do much to explain the kinship which Hart Crane must have felt with the Dionysian philosopher (see Chapter Eleven below).

Abercrombie's first writing on Nietzsche, 'The Thought-Shaker', took the form of a review of H. L. Mencken's *The Philosophy of*

Friedrich Nietzsche (1908), and showed that he already knew something of the "astonishing" works of this "bewildering" writer who set "European thought shaking and startling under the impact of his tidal speech." For Abercrombie in 1908 Nietzsche was "a soldier, a mercenary of ideas", a "noble and great-hearted man" whose books contain "a species of energising which is eminently needed by the general thought of to-day." In particular, he finds "the notion of the Overman" to be "so sublime and yet so natural ... that nowadays nobody's thought can help acknowledging its dominance" (cf. Arthur Symons' comment, made two years earlier, that "No one can think, and escape Nietzsche").

Two months later Abercrombie is again found reviewing Nietzscheana: his 'Nietzsche Again' takes the form of a review of M. A. Mügge's *Friedrich Nietzsche: His Life and Work* and A. M. Ludovici's *Who is to be Master of the World?* Whether he had spent the interval reading Nietzsche, I do not know; but his enthusiasm has, if anything, increased. He now writes that "Nietzsche was a man; a prodigiously great man, if you will"; he criticizes him – "Nietzsche was far too much of a mental anchorite to be as profound in political as he is in ethical philosophy" – but then draws back, for:

> we must not range ourselves with the contemners of Nietzsche; that would be infinitely worse than swallowing him whole. Like it or not, his Transvaluation of all Values is the word now; and no one with any reverence for the vital nobilities could read 'Zarathustra' without feeling that it is one of the greatest of modern books. His magnificent praise of life with his glorious belief that man can be surpassed, have given half the world a new conception of destiny. He is the greatest and noblest affirmer, or yes-sayer, of modern Europe, with the exception of Goethe.[9]

Though he does not reckon himself a Nietzschean – Abercrombie criticizes Nietzscheans for taking themselves altogether too seriously – his own enthusiasm for "the modern Heraclitus" only just stops short this side of idolatry. But how much of Nietzsche's work did he in fact know?

'Nietzsche's Work', a review of the first volumes of *The Complete Works of Friedrich Nietzsche*, shows that Abercrombie knew, in addition to *Thus Spake Zarathustra* (mentioned in 'The Thought-Shaker', and quoted here), *Thoughts Out Of Season*, *The Birth of*

Tragedy, and *Beyond Good and Evil*. This is the most confident and personal of his early reviews of Nietzsche. He now writes (in July 1909) that he himself is "not of those who swallow his doctrines whole"; but he nonetheless finds much to admire in the work of this "Archilochus of philosophy" who was "so nearly a poet", this "divine rhapsodist, amphibious in the two worlds of poetry and philosophy." He singles out for particular praise *The Birth of Tragedy*, "that marvellous analysis of the Hellenic spirit and the aesthetic instinct." Remarking that Nietzsche's philosophy is popularly supposed to be "an even more subtle poison than those vast boluses concocted by Zola", Abercrombie stresses his positive importance:

> Nietzsche's philosophy is not altogether a dangerous abomination; it is even, if you take it aright, extraordinarily health-giving and stimulative towards righteousness ... there are many blinding flashes of truth ... The grand importance of Nietzsche is ... that he is the most ruthless foe that pessimism could have. The most notable effect of his writing is that, like poetry, it infects us with a mood ... It pours into us a Titanic exultation in being alive.[10]

Although he regarded Nietzsche as "so nearly a poet" and described his work as poetry-like, in the long run it was as critic rather than poet that Abercrombie reacted to Nietzsche, whom he came to see as exemplifying romantic egoism and pessimism. For Abercrombie Nietzsche remained "the thought-shaker," a "great spirit" whose self-importance contained grandeur; but by 1926 he came to see Nietzsche's philosophy as "the essence of romantic pessimism: the utter disvaluation of the apparent world by belief in the reality of the mere unpurposed energy of existence – the inner life in its purest abstraction".[11] He is still clearly fascinated by *Thus Spake Zarathustra*, which he describes as a "remarkable" book, and more especially by Nietzsche's "openly defiant romanticism":

> But what an astonishing piece of romanticism, so sublimely to ignore all logic, that Eternal Recurrence – symbol of man's absolute and helpless fate in one universal whole of unending circular destiny – is to be accepted as the condition of deliberate aspiration towards the Overman – symbol of man's triumphantly free will to transcend himself and to create his own destiny![12]

Like so many of his contemporaries, Abercrombie is both fascinated and appalled by "Nietzsche's formidable ideas of Overman and Eternal Recurrence";[13] he points out that these ideas are "directly contradictory", and goes on:

> But Nietzsche's self-importance had grandeur in it. Belief in man's perfectibility is, after all, a very handsome delusion; and only a great spirit could enjoy the intellectual splendour of that appalling idea, Eternal Recurrence ... Life as a whole and life in itself – that is the only metaphysic classicism allows. – It was ... precisely this immediate *life-delighting value* which gave their talismanic property to Nietzsche's formidable ideas of Overman and Eternal Recurrence. But in him romanticism claims them rather than classicism, because they led him into Dionysiac notions of value transcending appearance.[14]

Abercrombie's penetrating analysis of "the talismanic metaphysics of Nietzsche" is based, above all, on his reading of *Thus Spake Zarathustra.* His own romantic fascination is evident when he writes of Eternal Recurrence as "one of philosophy's pure romances",[15] and it is this "pure romance" which provides the most obvious echo of Nietzsche in his own poetry. The lines in 'Zagreus':

> the slow world's weight,
> Eternally disturbed in circular fate,
> ...
> Thus in perpetual vision I must see
> Man's life enact itself.[16]

echo the phrase "man's absolute and helpless fate in one universal whole of unending circular destiny" used to describe Eternal Recurrence in *Romanticism*; 'Zagreus' first appeared just two years later, in *Twelve Idyls* (1928).

Apart from this one clear echo, we find in Abercrombie's *Poems* what mostly appear to be parallels, but which are probably fainter echoes of Nietzsche. Such parallels appear, significantly, in *Interludes and Poems* (1908) and in *Twelve Idyls* (1928), that is, in precisely those collections which coincide with Abercrombie's preoccupation with Nietzsche. Some of the subject-matter, situations, and imagery in, for instance, 'The New God' and 'The Fool's Adventure'[17] parallel Nietzsche; in 'The New God' Abercrombie, writes of the "ending of the Gods" (thus anticipating the later, more truly Nietzschean 'The Olympians'), "the Power that makes", writes that "Evil o'ertakes Good"; in 'The Fool's Adventure', with its Zarathustran setting of a dialogue between Seeker and Hermit, he alludes to the Heraclitan-Nietzschean flux of Becoming in the phrase "All's flowing" (again elaborated in 'The Olympians'), while the Seeker's view that

> the white flame
> Called Consciousness ousts from its habitation
> All but its own delusion

is as romantic or 'Dionysian' as the World's image of the waters "Whose surface is Appearance". Even the words spoken by God – "I am Thy Self" – appear to carry the Nietzschean connotation of man as his own God.

There are many parallels between Abercrombie's analysis of Nietzsche's Dionysos in his *Romanticism*, and his 'The Olympians".[18] A memorable metaphor – "Multitudinous atoms of passionate will/Seething in separate purposes"[19] – describes the life of man in terms reminiscent of Schopenhauer and Nietzsche, while into this era of dying Olympians comes Dionysos who "can die/A thousand times and still be living god".[20] Dionysos is made to describe himself in precisely the same terms which Abercrombie had used in *Romanticism* to describe Nietzsche's Dionysos:

> A dream dreamt by the world I am indeed:
> But yet a dream of what is not the world.
> I am the rapture of the measureless force
> For ever passing into and beyond
> The measured form of the world. ...
> I am the dream of that unchanging energy,
> You [Apollo] of the eddying pattern of the world.[21]

We need hardly remind ourselves that for Abercrombie Nietzsche's philosophy was marked by "the utter disvaluation of the apparent world by belief in the reality of the mere unpurposed energy of existence";[22] that this reading of Nietzsche is echoed in 'The Olympians' is self-evident. Dionysos' dream with its alternations of "Unseizable joy and unendurable woe" is "the dream that triumphs now";[23] even Apollo makes Dionysos say:

> I am your rescue from the seeming world;
> Follow me out of seeming, and I will give you
> Inconceivable things.[24]

He adds: "This is the god/Henceforth".[25]

Although there are faint echoes of Nietzsche in two of Abercrombie's earlier dramatic poems ('The New God' and 'The Fool's Adventure') dating from 1907/8, when he first discovered Nietzsche, and much clearer echoes of his reading of Nietzsche's 'talismanic metaphysics' in the later 'The Olympians' and 'Zagreus', written shortly after his work on Nietzsche in 1925/6, it must be stressed that there is no sign in any of his collections as such of substantial indebtedness to Nietzsche.

Nietzsche features in a very different way in the work of another contributor to *Georgian Poetry 1911–1912* – Robert Calverley Trevelyan (author of *The Bride of Dionysus*, 1912). In Trevelyan's *The New Parsifal. An Operatic Fable* (1914), Nietzsche is – for once – not taken seriously. In the 'Induction' Wagner speaks of "this abhorred Nietzschean impostor", and in Act II the Chorus proclaims:

> He [Ghost of Wagner] planteth a punishing blow in the
> belly of Nietzsche.
> But aloof, surveying the fight in Olympian grandeur,
> Stands Goethe detached and serene. Now Nietzsche is done
> for.[26]

Among Georgian men of letters who read Nietzsche but rejected many of his pronouncements was Wilfred Scawen Blunt, who wrote to Maude Petre on 13 November 1908:

> I am most grateful to you for sending me the articles. Those about Nietsche [sic] are what have interested me most. I knew little of Nietsche at first hand, except Zarathustra, which, taken apart from his other writings, seemed to me somewhat chaotic, and you have explained him to me. I should have liked to have had the rest of the series.
>
> Though accepting the general facts of existence much as Nietsche does, I agree with very few of his pronouncements – I am on the whole an optimist about the Universe, considering Man, especially civilized Man, an unfortunate but not very important exception, whose sorrows are mainly of his own making. Nietzsche, like all the rest of philosophers and religious teachers, exaggerated Man's importance in the Universe, and therein lies his flaw. Also, like all men of genius, he exaggerates

> his own importance, or rather the importance of his intellect. He admires strength because he is physically a weakling. He despises women because he does not know them.[27]

Though both his letter and his continued misspelling of Nietzsche's name show that his knowledge of the philosopher's work was very limited, Blunt's rather blasé attitude is again typical of the time.

Another member of the same generation to reject Nietzsche – in the long run – was Eric Gill. On 9 March 1907 Gill heard A. R. Orage speak on 'Nietzsche versus Socialism at the Reform Club, and it seems likely that Nietzsche was the subject of discussion in the Arts and Philosophical Group of the Fabian Society at this time, for Eric Gill was given a copy of *Thus Spake Zarathustra* by a girl he met at the Fabian Society; his biographer reports that "Other new influences were making themselves felt, and the most important of these was Nietzsche. Eric would read *Zarathustra* by the hour".[28] However, in the long run Gill's enthusiasm for Nietzsche was only a passing phase: his *The Necessity of Belief* (1936), which appeared six years after he had drawn a portrait of Frau Foerster-Nietzsche during a stay at Naumburg, was a flat rejection of Nietzsche's philosophy.

Stephen Graham, on the other hand, was in the habit of reading *The Genealogy of Morals* to a colleague at Somerset House in the early years of the century. In about 1910, in Baron Knoop's library, he came across a complete set of the works of Nietzsche in the original German editions and noticed that only one volume seemed to have been read:

> It was *Also Sprach Zarathustra*. The rest were uncut. Being an addict of that dynamic volume of poetic prose, I pulled it out from the shelf. Maya [Baroness Knoop] ... said it was curious that I had seized upon it, because it was the only book in that immense library which meant much to her. When ... she had found herself in great distress, *Thus Spake Zarathustra* had saved her. It had taught her to abjure slavishness, to get a hold on herself, and become what she was intended to be.[29]

He goes on to quote Baroness Knoop as saying: "One day I discovered Nietzsche and his philosophy was an inspiration ... The German philosopher said, 'Be hard as a diamond'. I could not get as hard as that, but hard enough to begin again to live my own life".[30]

There must have been many who read Nietzsche seeking to ameliorate their own lives and their own attitudes to life; perhaps even the majority of his English readers did so. Another case in point is that of W. N. P. Barbellion, author of *The Journal of a Disappointed Man* (1919). Although he wrote in his journal on 11 October 1914 that "Nietzsche is no consolation to a man who has once been weak enough to be brought to his knees",[31] the entry for 23 November 1914 contains this note: "Reading Nietzsche. What splendid physic he is to Pomeranian puppies like myself! I am a hopeless coward ... But Nietzsche makes me feel a perfect mastiff".[32] Many other British readers clearly derived the same mastiff-feeling from Nietzsche; Barbellion is merely more honest than most.

A few years later John Middleton Murry was giving *his* approval to Zarathustra's "Be hard!" On 28 June 1918 he wrote of Rousseau's *Confessions*: "He is totally without some hard aristocratic stuff which is necessary to the ideal composition." In his autobiography, *Between Two Worlds* (1935), he commented: "Maybe the demand for the 'hard aristocratic stuff' came from my reading of Nietzsche at this moment. It was now (1918) that I conceived a great admiration for the critical power of Nietzsche which, unlike my disapproval of Rousseau, has endured".[33] Middleton Murry then goes on to quote his own criticism of Nietzsche, which presumably also dates from *c.* 1918:

> The memorable and true thing in Nietzsche's criticism is its incessant and fundamental humanism. It is the never-failing sympathy with the torments of the creative soul, and an almost unique understanding of them. He is therefore essentially self-guarded against the boorish insensitiveness of *soi-disant* disciples, Nietzscheans and *hoc genus omne*, for he has given us the touchstone to try his own achievements. His absolutes are as personal to him as they are to any great artist. Doubtless he knew it; he cannot not have known it. Therefore he is doubly great in that, having a conscious understanding of his own creative soul, he yet could so well wear the mask he knew was necessary, that at times, even many times, looking in the glass, he straightway forgot what manner of man he was.[34]

But it is time that we left these literary by-ways and returned to the Georgians in the persons of the 'Georgian war-poets' Rupert Brooke and Isaac Rosenberg. First, however, Charles Sorley.

Charles Sorley, whose father (W. R. Sorley) occupied the Chair of Philosophy at Cambridge and mentioned Nietzsche in his writings,[35] attended lectures in philosophy at the University of Jena in the summer semester of 1914. On the face of it, it would therefore seem likely that he should have come across Nietzsche's work some time before he left Germany, the more so in view of his great admiration for many things German. In fact he does not appear to have read Nietzsche until November 1914. In a letter to the Master of Marlborough dated 28 November 1914 Sorley wrote: "You ask me … what I … think of Nietzsche now? I have only now begun to read the man. I was never one of those advanced intellectuals who quoted him at debates".[36] The only other reference to Nietzsche occurs in another letter to the Master of Marlborough dated 27 (?) December 1914, where Sorley mentions "the stomach (which Nietzsche calls the Father of Melancholy)",[37] which suggests that he may have been reading *Beyond Good and Evil.*

It appears, then, that Charles Sorley only began to read Nietzsche in November 1914, possibly prompted by the controversy then raging around Nietzsche's name; there is no evidence to suggest that he reacted strongly to what he read. This is not really surprising, for if the outward circumstances of his life might lead one to expect Sorley to have come across Nietzsche well before November 1914, the fact remains that he was never "one of those advanced intellectuals who quoted him at debate".

Rupert Brooke, however, was precisely that. It seems that Rupert Brooke became familiar with some of Nietzsche's ideas, or at least with Nietzsche's name, while still at Rugby. On 4 October 1906, a few days before going up to Cambridge, he wrote to Geoffrey Keynes about the life he planned to lead there:

> I shall read all day and all night – philosophy or science – nothing beautiful any more. Indeed I have forsworn art and things beautiful; they are but chance manifestations of Life. All art rests on the sexual emotions which are merely the instruments of the Life-force – of Nature – for the propagation of life. That is all we live for, to further Nature's purpose. Sentiment, poetry, romance, religion, are but mists of our own fancies, too weak for

> the great nature-forces of individuality and sexual emotion. They only obscure the issue. Our duty is but to propagate the species successfully and then to wait quietly for the disintegration of our bodies, brains, and 'souls' in the grave; heeding as little as possible the selfish and foolish greed for personal immortality ... This is the teaching of all our highest and clearest thinkers, Shaw, Meredith, Wells, Nietzsche ... It is rather grey, but quite logical and scientific.[38]

What is immediately apparent here is that although Brooke counts him among "our highest and clearest thinkers", he has very little idea of Nietzsche's philosophy. Nietzsche is merely a name. The teaching that is ascribed to him is a typical late nineteenth-century materialism; and this philosophy is but a temporary phase – or pose even – for the young Rupert Brooke. There is no reason to suppose that Brooke, in 1906, was particularly impressed by Nietzsche, or even that he had read any of Nietzsche's works, though he may have read the series on 'Human Evolution' in *Natural Science* (1897). And within four years even this hear-said Nietzsche was 'dead' for him.

Addressing the Cambridge Fabian Society as President for the last time on 10 December 1910, Rupert Brooke made a passionate plea for living art and financial assistance to living artists, asking:

> Do you think this unnecessary, slightly insulting? Is anyone muttering 'But we *are* modern and up to date. Nietzsche is our Bible, Van Gogh our idol. We drink in the lessons of Meredith and Ibsen and Swinburne and Tolstoy ... ' They are dead, my friends, all dead. Beware, for the generations slip imperceptibly into one another, and it is so much easier for you to accept standards that are prepared for you. Beware of the dead.[39]

Now whatever one thinks about Brooke's ostensible acceptance of Nietzsche four years previously, this is an unambiguous rejection of the then highly fashionable philosopher in the name of Fabianism, though the emphasis on not accepting pre-formulated standards could be said to be 'Nietzschean'. In view of this it may seem surprising that Brooke should be found referring to and indeed reading Nietzsche in 1912. In March 1912 he wrote to Katherine Cox: "I was suddenly ferocious and talked of Nietzsche",[40] and in mid-June 1912 he was (again?) reading *Thus Spake Zarathustra*, marking passages in 'On War and Warriors' such as "War and courage have done more things than charity." There can be no doubt, however, that he was at this time merely seeking an antidote to his own depression ("syphilis of the soul", he called it); there is no question of any deep or abiding interest in Nietzsche on Brooke's part. Had he been really interested in Nietzsche, his letters from Germany in 1911–12 would surely have revealed the fact; as it is, they reveal only his antipathy to German culture ("I have sampled and sought out German culture. It has changed all my political views. I am wildly in favour of nineteen new Dreadnoughts. German culture must never, never prevail"[41]), although he did, for a time, persevere in his attempts to translate Swinburne's early poetry into German – probably at the suggestion of Karl Wolfskehl – and in his plans to translate Wedekind. Brooke met Wolfskehl at one of the latter's Thursday evening receptions in Munich in 1911; to Frances Cornford he wrote of "Dr Wolfskehl who is shy and repeats Swinburne in large quantities with a villainous German accent, but otherwise knows no English".[42]

One can only speculate as to whether in August 1914 Brooke remembered the passages he had marked two years before in Nietzsche's 'On War and Warriors'; the heroic view of war, of which Brooke's 1914 sonnets are the apotheosis, does, however, parallel Zarathustra's view ("What warrior wisheth to be spared?").

In the first of his essays on Nietzsche in *The Savoy*, Havelock Ellis wrote of Nietzsche that "He is the modern incarnation of that image of intellectual pride which Marlowe created in Faustus." Some 16 years later, in his essay 'The Slade and Modern Culture' (*c.* 1912) Isaac Rosenberg similarly made the point that "Marlowe foreshadows Nietzsche":

> Hidden in air, in nature, are unexplored powers which the earlier masters had no hint of. We are immeasurably in advance of them in range and scope of subject. The spirit of inquiry wrestled with superstition; Luther brought to bear upon the moral world what Darwin has upon the physical world. Marlowe foreshadows Nietzsche. Tamburlaine, the towering colossus, symbolizes the subjection of matter to will – the huge blind forces of nature shrink terrorised before this indomitable energy of purpose, clay for some colossal plastic shaping.
>
> We of this age stand in the same relation to things as they, but

> with a sharpened curiosity. Religious freedom, freedom of thought have prepared the way for heights of daring and speculation.[43]

This is the only reference to Nietzsche in Rosenberg's collected works; it is quoted in its full context because it is important as showing that Rosenberg knew something of Nietzsche, and as implying that he found Nietzsche sympathetic (cf. the influence on Rosenberg of Blake and Marlowe, and his admiration for Emerson). Quite apart from the compliment Rosenberg is paying Nietzsche by associating him with his admired Marlowe, the passage *implies* that Rosenberg saw Nietzsche as a modern master, an explorer of the human spirit, and connected him with "energy of purpose", "freedom of thought", and "speculation"; in other words, he appears – quite rightly – to have seen Nietzsche in Marlovian, Faustian terms. This in turn suggests some knowledge of *Thus Spake Zarathustra*. Now Marlowe was associated with Blake in Rosenberg's mind, and what he admired in Blake was not so much the "antithetical wisdom" (Yeats) and rejection of conventional moralities (which he would have found paralleled in Nietzsche's *Beyond Good and Evil*), as the sheer strength of imagination; in 'Art' Rosenberg wrote: "I hold Blake to be the highest artist England has ever had ... No other artist that ever lived possessed in so high a degree that inspired quality; that unimpaired divinity that shines from all things mortal when looked at through the eye of imagination."[44] Since *Thus Spake Zarathustra* is Nietzsche's most imaginative work and is couched in the same kind of vigorous, Biblically-inspired imagery that runs through all Rosenberg's own work, it is likely that he would have been attracted to this work of Nietzsche's. But in view of the "ecstasy in form" which was Rosenberg's aim, his interest in art history, and his admiration for Dionysian "energy of purpose", *The Birth of Tragedy* would also have been likely to appeal to him.

Given, then, that Rosenberg knew Nietzsche's work and seems to have found it sympathetic, it would be a fair deduction that he is most likely to have read *The Birth of Tragedy* and *Thus Spake Zarathustra*. And since he was only 22 in 1912, the year when he probably read Nietzsche, it would also seem reasonable to look for possible signs of the impact of Nietzsche on his work. Are there any echoes of *The Birth of Tragedy* and *Thus Spake Zarathustra* in Rosenberg's work? This is a natural question to ask in view of the

Biblical-prophetic tone of his work, his admiration for "ecstasy in form", and the Faustianism of *Moses*, *The Amulet* and *The Unicorn*.

As Siegfried Sassoon wrote in his foreword to *The Collected Works of Isaac Rosenberg*, Rosenberg "*modelled* words with fierce energy and aspiration, finding ecstasy in form, dreaming in grandeurs of superb light and deep shadow".[45] This is a comment which applies equally to Nietzsche and more especially to the imagery of *Thus Spake Zarathustra*, a work which, as we have seen, Rosenberg may well have read in about 1912, the year in which he published his first collection, *Night and Day*. 'Night and Day' – the very title recalls Zarathustra's successive 'The Shadow' and 'Noontide', and the imagery of Rosenberg's poem in fact parallels that of Nietzsche's prose-poem at many points. Thus the phrase "a tragic jest"[46] recalls Zarathustra's "He who climbeth on the highest mountains, laugheth at all tragic plays and tragic realities".[47] Does not "A bruten lust of living their life's leave"[48] exactly parallel the Dionysian attitude to life of the Superman? The point where man becomes superman appears to be described by Rosenberg in the words:

I am grown wise
And big with new life – eager and divine.

Last night I stripped my soul of all alloy
Of earth that did ensphere and fetter it.[49]

This is "Dionysian wisdom", so well described by Lascelles Abercrombie. Again, Rosenberg's lines:

Mingles man's song of pride
With the divine
Song of the day's great star
Struck from the noon-day heat
...
A song that throbs and glows
Through all the noon-day heat.[50]

might be taken to refer to a song sung at the "secret, solemn hour" of "hot noontide" when the sun stood exactly over Zarathustra's head; for both poets it is at noontide and midnight that "the Eternal rhythm" (Rosenberg[51]), the very "perfume and odour of eternity" (Zarathustra's 'Drunken Song') is revealed.

At this time Rosenberg even voiced his own 'Aspiration' in 'Zarathustran' terms:

> For I would see with mine own eyes the glory and the gold.
> With a strange and fervid vision see the glamour and the dream –
> And chant an incantation in a measure new and bold,
> And enaureole a glory round an unawakened theme.[52]

In another poem he continues:

> I'd shape one impulse through the contraries
> Of vain ambitious men, selfish and callous,
> And frail life-drifters, reticent and delicate.[53]

The contraries here are those of what Nietzsche called "Masters" and "Slaves".

The Faustian theme – "We are grown God"[54] – occurs early in Rosenberg's work and may be linked with another theme, that of the "miasma of a rotting god";[55] the themes are linked in *Thus Spake Zarathustra*,[56] where Zarathustra proclaims that it is "better to be God oneself" and that "that old God liveth no more", while the motif of the "rotting God" appears in the parable of the Mad Man in *The Joyful Wisdom*; but even Nietzsche does not elaborate as consequentially as Rosenberg:

> In his malodorous brain what slugs and mire,
> Lanthorned in his oblique eyes, guttering burned!
> ...
> Ah! this miasma of a rotting God![57]

The Faustian/Marlovian theme – man as overreacher, overweener – of 'Moses', 'The Amulet', and 'The Unicorn' parallels Nietzsche's view of man as something that must be overcome. More specifically, the consciousness that is described at the end of 'Moses' is surely a 'Dionysian' consciousness in Nietzsche's sense:

> So grandly fashion these rude elements
> Into some newer nature, a consciousness
> Like naked light seizing the all-eyed soul,
> Oppressing with its gorgeous tyranny
> Until they take it thus – or die.[58]

No less 'Dionysian' is the description of this same consciousness in 'The Unicorn':

What is this ecstasy in form,
This lightning
That found the lightning in my blood
Searing my spirit's lips aghast and naked?[59]

And the same theme recurs in a more general context in 'Bacchanal':

If life would come to me
... with music and with laughter
We would scare black death away.[60]

The idea here is a fundamentally Nietzschean, and more specifically a Zarathustran one.

But the poetic context of the passage from 'The Unicorn' is important too because "ecstasy in form" is an exact parallel to Nietzsche's "Dionysian art" as defined in *The Birth of Tragedy*, where the major theme is the clash between Apollo and Dionysos, form and chaos, or, as Rosenberg put it, "Chaos that coincides, form that refutes all sway".[61] The tension of chaos and form in Rosenberg (cf. the strength of conception but relative weakness of execution in his plays) points straight back to *The Birth of Tragedy*, as do the clashing and counterbalancing elements of "dream" and "ecstasy" of which all his work is composed.

Enough has perhaps been said to make it seem more than likely that Isaac Rosenberg did read both *The Birth of Tragedy* and *Thus Spake Zarathustra*, and did indeed draw on them in his own work. But while the parallels between Rosenberg and Nietzsche are many and close, there is no evidence to enable us to say categorically that Rosenberg is 'echoing' Nietzsche at any given point. Besides, however close Rosenberg may be to Nietzsche at times, he is often at least as close to the Song of Songs, and the parallels between the two writers may be partly explained by the influence of the Old Testament on both. Two final points remain to be made: that it would be pedantic to pursue such parallels any further in the case of a poet as original as Isaac Rosenberg, and that there is a striking parallel between Rosenberg's all-important imagery and that of another poet who was unquestionably influenced by Nietzsche: John Gould Fletcher (see Chapter Thirteen below).

Chapter Ten

The "men of 1914" and Nietzsche

One of the most revealing aspects of Nietzsche's reception in Anglo-saxony centres around the year 1914. In this chapter I wish to consider this aspect from the point of view of the reaction to his writings of the so-called 'men of 1914' (the avantgarde of the immediate pre-war years: Wyndham Lewis, T. E. Hulme, T. S. Eliot, James Joyce, Ezra Pound, and A. R. Orage), and of the reaction against Nietzsche of the literary warriors of August 1914, who, led by Thomas Hardy, mounted a campaign of vilification which in the long run put an end to his influence in Britain, though not in the United States.

In the 'Editorial' in *Blast*, no. 2 (July 1915), Wyndham Lewis declared that "unofficial Germany has done more for the movement that this paper was founded to propagate, and for all branches of contemporary Science and Art, than any other country." That Nietzsche was one of the "unofficial Germans" that Lewis had in mind, is suggested by an earlier comment in the same 'Editorial': "Art and culture have been more in people's mouths in England than they have ever been before, during the last six months. Nietzsche has had an English sale such as he could hardly have anticipated in his most ecstatic and morose moments." This is, of course, rather dubious evidence; there were probably several reasons for this dramatic increase in Nietzsche's English sales in 1914/15, and some readers may well have wished to satisfy themselves that he was indeed "the execrable 'Neech'" that he was popularly supposed to be.[1]

Be this as it may, Wyndham Lewis clearly strikes a personal note when he writes that "his [Nietzsche's] 'aristocratism' ... raises doubts in the mind of the most enthusiastic student",[2] for there are obvious parallels between Vorticism and Nietzsche's view of art, and between Lewis's "Enemy of the Stars" and *Thus Spake Zarathustra* (it is partly the Nietzschean allusions that make the conversation between Hanp and Arghol so "strangely recondite" in E. W. F. Tomlin's words). We know from his letters that Wyndham Lewis was acquainted with Nietzsche's work by 1908 at the latest.

In 'Long Live the Vortex', 'Manifesto – I', and 'Manifesto – II' in the first number of *Blast*, in which the Vorticist aesthetic is summarized, there are many parallels with Nietzsche. Wyndham Lewis writes there that "Blast presents an art of individuals", which is in line with Nietzsche's view that art celebrates the individual, and indeed with the whole individualist trend of his work. While Nietzsche continually stressed the need to overcome the past, to live for the present, Lewis wrote "We stand for the reality of the present." Lewis's statement that "We only want the world to live" recalls Nietzsche's view of art as affirmation of life, as a matter of teaching people how to live. The way in which Lewis links Humour and Tragedy recalls Nietzsche's statements on the union of Apollo and Dionysos, and indeed Vorticism sought to combine the principles of Apollo and Dionysos, although in practice the Dionysian element is more in evidence than the Apolline. On the one hand Lewis wrote that "The art-instinct is permanently primitive", "The artist of the modern movement is a savage", and "Any great Northern Art will partake of this insidious and volcanic chaos", all of which recalls Nietzsche's view that there is something fantastic and irrational in all art; Nietzsche stressed the irrational basis of *all* art, which he defined as "a kind of elemental force in man". On the other hand, Lewis advocated "bareness and hardness", cf. Nietzsche's remarks on the necessity of making a virtue of hardness; as we have seen, the cult of 'hardness' loomed large in contemporary British Nietzscheanism. The Vorticists were opposed to "a narrow and pedantic realism", while Nietzsche for his part had stressed that artistic integrity has nothing to do with realism. Vorticism, then, combines "volcanic chaos" ('Dionysos') with "bareness and hardness" ('Apollo'). And so on. The parallels could be continued, but it would be unwise to press the case too far, because enough has already been said to establish that there *are* parallels, and because there is more to Vorticism than a secondhand Nietzschean aesthetic (for all the noisy antagonism to futurism, for instance, there is not a little of the futurist adulation of the machine in Vorticism, to say nothing of futurist savagery). And besides, by quoting Nietzsche's wide-ranging remarks out of context almost anything can be – and often has been – 'Nietzschefied'. But certainly these parallels are reinforced by the many apparent echoes of *Thus Spake Zarathustra* in 'Enemy of the Stars'.[3]

However, since Wyndham Lewis was nothing if not original, it will be more interesting and profitable to examine the references to Nietzsche in his other (theoretical) works, for it is a fact that references to Nietzsche are scattered throughout Lewis's critical writings of the 'twenties and 'thirties, and especially in *The Art of Being Ruled* (1926), *Paleface* (1929), and *Men Without Art* (1934). The natural starting-point is the section on 'Nietzsche as a Vulgarizer' in *The Art of Being Ruled*,[4] which shows beyond question that for all his enthusiasm for Nietzsche, Lewis was emphatically no uncritical Nietzschean; characteristically, he retained an astringent independence of mind. Though he speaks of Nietzsche as a "very great writer", a "fine artist" and "the greatest popular success of any philosopher of modern times", he has many eloquent reservations about this "vociferous showman" (Nietzsche's own criticism of Wagner!), this "death-snob" and "madness-snob" with his "intellectual opportunism." While conceding that Nietzsche sometimes wrote "with very great wisdom" – praise indeed – Lewis attacks him for writing as he did while realizing that he was addressing a non-existent audience, with the result that his message got into the wrong hands and therefore had the opposite effect to that intended:

> The influence of Nietzsche was similar to that of Bergson, James, Croce, etc. He provided a sanction and licence, as the others did, for LIFE – the very life that he never ceased himself to objurgate against; the life of the second-rate and shoddily emotional, for the person, very unfortunately, smart and rich enough to be able to regard himself as an 'aristocrat', a man 'beyond good and evil', a destroying angel and cultivated Mephistopheles.[5]

Despite the fact that 'Nietzscheans' tended to be 'smart' (in the intellectual sense) rather than 'rich', there is much truth in this. Certainly "the doctrine of aristocracy arranged by Dr. Nietzsche, for Tom, Dick and Harry, was a snobbish pill very violent in its action"[6] – the case of one minor Nietzschean after another confirms it.

But Wyndham Lewis's central criticism – and it is one which again shows his real knowledge of Nietzsche's work – comes when he is discussing the Will-to-Power:

> In reality the will to enjoy was dead in Nietzsche ... He had plenty of Will left: only, it was the Will to struggle merely, not the Will to live. Fine artist as he was, he passed his life in a nightmare, and was, I think, unable to benefit by his own falsification theory. Schopenhauer probably was a wiser man, and came to better terms with life than Nietzsche did.[7]

In the present context Wyndham Lewis's criticism of Nietzsche is important mainly as confirming how well he knew the philosopher's work, though there is certainly much truth in his basic thesis that Nietzsche, as a "great vulgarizer", wrote in such a way as to appeal to those whose ears he was not concerned to reach (including many if not most 'Nietzscheans'). Lewis was unquestionably 'influenced' by Nietzsche in a general sense in that Nietzsche became an essential and permanent part of his extensive literary heritage. Quite apart from the evidence dating from the days of *Blast*, this is shown, *inter alia*, by the very fact that he wrote about Nietzsche and continued to use Nietzschean terminology at a time when British Nietzscheanism as such was a thing of the past.

More long-lived and more widely influential than *Blast* was *The New Age*. Both Herbert Read and Edwin Muir were among the many young writers of the time who benefited from the intellectual stimulus of A. R. Orage and his *The New Age*. Muir was, of course, a contributor, and Herbert Read later wrote to Michael Hamburger:

"I was ... a Nietzschean in my time, one of the circle around Orage. If only we had known how the Master had been betrayed by those nearest to him, we might have remained more faithful!"[8] *The New Age* championed Nietzsche no less than Bergson. Most of the translators of the Levy edition of Nietzsche's works were contributors to *The New Age*, including the editor and greatest Nietzschean of them all, Oscar Levy, who in his *The Revival of Aristocracy* (1906) welcomed Nietzsche as a new Messiah; J. M. Kennedy and A. M. Ludovici in particular contributed historically important early articles on Nietzsche's philosophy to *The New Age*, and were both authors of hagiographical works on Nietzsche (J. M. Kennedy, *The Quintessence of Nietzsche*, 1909; A. M. Ludovici, *Who is to be Master of the World? An Introduction to the Philosophy of Friedrich Nietzsche*, 1909; *Nietzsche, His Life and Works*, 1910 – in Constable's influential 'Philosophies Ancient & Modern' series; and *Nietzsche and Art*, 1911).

A. R. Orage himself was introduced to Nietzsche's works, which were to influence his thought decisively, by Holbrook Jackson at their first meeting in 1900. By 1906 Nietzsche was for him "the greatest European event since Goethe":

> From one end of Europe to the other ... discussion in the most intellectual and aristocratically-minded circles turns on the problems raised by him. In Germany and in France his name is the warcry of opposing factions, and before very long his name will be familiar in England. Already half a dozen well-known English writers might be named who owe, if not half their ideas, at least half the courage of their ideas to Nietzsche ... Nobody is more representative of the spirit of the age. In sum, he was his age; he comprehended the mind of Europe ... There has been nobody more moving in literature. There are books that appeal to sentiment, books that appeal to the mind, and books that appeal to the will. Nietzsche's belong to this last small but immortal section. Nobody can read his books without receiving a powerful stimulus in one direction or another ... Nietzsche was the tragedian in the spiritual drama of Mansoul.[9]

Orage himself certainly received a "powerful stimulus" from Nietzsche's works which he spent seven years (1900–7)* studying

* It was from 1907 to 1910 that *The New Age* made something of a cult of Nietzsche. During this period contributions on Nietzsche appeared as follows:

and then propagating in books, articles, and lectures; and we have seen that Yeats, Read, and Muir were no less powerfully affected. It was *Thus Spake Zarathustra* that led Orage to conclude that "ideas were meaningful only in relation to action".[10] Once again we see the vitalism so characteristic of the time; Herbert Read too got from his reading of Nietzsche "that highest exaltation which only comes when truth is conceived as a fleeting quarry in whose pursuit the whole mind must be engaged".[11] Since he was intellectual intermediary and man-of-letters rather than poet, Orage's ideas are not immediately relevant here, though it is worth noting his view that "Human consciousness in itself is no more than the antenatal condition of Superman".[12] Two further points should also be noted: that this influential figure, whose *The New Age* struck Edwin Muir at least for its intellectual exclusivity (Nietzsche's *Vornehmheit*), was the author of two books on Nietzsche (*Friedrich Nietzsche: The Dionysian Spirit of the Age*, 1906; *Nietzsche in Outline and Aphorism*, 1907), and that when Anglo-German literary relations turned to literary warfare in 1914, *The New Age* – unlike many other magazines – did *not* suddenly turn against Nietzsche.

T. E. Hulme was a regular contributor to *The New Age*, although he had little time for the Nietzscheans on the staff (Levy, Kennedy, and Ludovici); indeed, he denounced the Nietzschean philosophizing of A. M. Ludovici because he considered him a charlatan. What, then, is Hulme's own position vis-à vis Nietzsche?

In the well-known essay on 'Romanticism and Classicism',[13] Hulme has recourse to Nietzsche's distinction between the "classical static" (Apollonian) and the "classical Dynamic" (Dionysian), and claims that Shakespeare, "the classic of motion", belongs to Nietzsche's latter category. In other words, as Alun R. Jones has remarked, "Hulme falls back on Nietzsche in order to refute those who consider the difference between classic and romantic to be one between restraint and exuberance, and, also, in order to claim both Shakespeare and Racine as classical".[14] So Hulme is here making use of one of Nietzsche's best-known points, and is – to say the least – somewhat blurring the distinction made by Nietzsche; in *The Birth of Tragedy* Apollo stands for restraint, and Dionysos for lack of restraint.

1907 (17 October); 1908 (20 June; 12 September; 24 October); 1909 (20 May; 27 May; 30 December); 1910 (27 January; 3 February; 14 April; 7 July; 28 July).

In 'A Tory Philosophy', Hulme quotes Nietzsche's "Philosophy is autobiography", summarizes what he calls "the 'classical' point of view", and comments:

> Most people have been in the habit of associating these kinds of views with Nietzsche. It is true that they do occur in him, but he made them so frightfully vulgar that no classic would acknowledge them. In him you have the spectacle of a romantic seizing on the classic point of view because it attracted him purely as a theory, and who, being a romantic, in taking up this theory, passed his slimy fingers over every detail of it. Everything loses its value. The same idea of the necessary hierarchy of classes, with their varying capacities and duties, gets turned into the romantic nonsense of the two kinds of morality, the slave and the master morality, and every other element of the classic position gets transmuted in a similar way into something ridiculous.[15]

Hulme was evidently conversant with some of Nietzsche's ideas on a superficial level, and was not above making use of them when it suited his purposes to do so; thus the statement that "There is no such thing as an absolute truth to be discovered. All general statements about truth, etc. are in the end only amplifications of man's appetites"[16] presumbly reflects his reading of *Human, All Too Human*. But he remained critical of Nietzsche. In his 'Notes on Language and Style'[17] he criticized Nietzsche for his (undeniable) tendency toward meaningless generalization, for "his ambition to say everything in a paragraph". But it is 'A Tory Philosophy' in particular which makes it abundantly plain that Hulme regarded Nietzsche's treatment of ideas that were in part close to his own as "frightfully vulgar", with the result that Nietzsche's work is dismissed as "romantic nonsense". That something like Nietzsche's dual morality is a logical consequence of his own "hierarchy of classes" does not seem to occur to him. One recalls H. G. Wells' comment in 1897 accusing Nietzsche of "the glorification of blackguardism"; in Wells and Hulme we are faced with what might be termed "a Tory view of Nietzsche". Hulme's view of Nietzsche clearly represents the conservative backlash against Dionysian romanticism in all its artistic, political, and ethical manifestations; thus Hulme said, in 1911, that he was very much in sympathy with the anti-romanticism of Pierre Laserre's *La Morale de Nietzsche* (1902). In some ways, of course, it is rather odd that the Tory view of Nietzsche should be so much more hostile than, say the Fabian view. Certainly there seems to be no valid reason to continue to speak of Hulme as being influenced by Nietzsche in any real sense,* though he was undoubtedly deeply indebted to Wilhelm Worringer: in *Speculations*[18] he admitted that his views on art – so much more important than his political views – were "practically an abstract of Worringer's views".

At a time when all around were falling under Nietzsche's spell in one way or another, what about the arch-poet of the age, T. S. Eliot, newly arrived in England as a Harvard graduate in philosophy? At Harvard Eliot may well have attended the very popular lectures by Josiah Royce in the 1913–14 session; it would be very surprising if he did not do so. Josiah Royce (1855–1916), outstanding among American idealist philosophers at the time, was certainly no Nietzschean; but he did lecture on Nietzsche (cf. the paper on 'Nietzsche' found among his posthumous papers and published in *Atlantic Monthly*[19]), in whom he found much "matter for the strengthening of hearts"; in his objective but sympathetic essay Royce concludes that "Nietzsche's ... individualism has ... its place in the history of Christian doctrine".[20] Although there is no evidence that this was the case, Eliot could well have first heard of Nietzsche from Royce. That Eliot was familiar with Nietzsche's work before 1916 is certain (see below).

Now in an interesting note on 'T. S. Eliot and Nietzsche',[21] F. N. Lees has pointed out that in *The Waste Land* Eliot makes clear his interest in matters to which Nietzsche devoted attention in *The Birth of Tragedy*. Thus Nietzsche's proclamation of the death of the gods is paralleled by the words "you know only/A heap of broken images." More particularly, Lees points to two possible echoes of *The Birth of Tragedy* in Eliot's work. Thus Nietzsche quotes the line "Oed' und leer das Meer" from Wagner's *Tristan und Isolde*, which Eliot also quotes in the first section of *The Waste Land*. In each case the context is similar. In *The Birth of*

* Further confirmation of this is found in Hulme's 'German Chronicle' (*Poetry and Drama*, June 1914, 221–8), in which Nietzsche is mentioned several times; Hulme refers to Nietzsche's 'What the Germans lack', which implies that he had read *Twilight of the Idols*; but there is no suggestion of any interest in Nietzsche on Hulme's part. The chronicle is interesting, however, as a contemporary record of the activities of the avantgarde in German poetry in 1914 and as showing Hulme's sympathetic reaction to the German variety of imagism.

Tragedy the relevant passage, in Haussmann's translation of 1909, reads:

> 'waste and void is the sea.' And when, breathless, we thought to expire ... and only a slender tie bound us to our present existence, we now hear and see only the hero wounded to death and still not dying, with his despairing cry: 'Longing! Longing! In dying still longing! For longing not dying ...'

This may be compared with these lines from *The Waste Land*:

> I was neither
> Living nor dead, and I knew nothing,
> Looking into the heart of silence,
> *Oed' und leer das Meer.*

However, since Eliot in his Notes to the poem refers directly to Wagner, whom he, unlike Haussmann, quotes in German, this cannot be regarded as a likely echo of Nietzsche, for all the contextual similarity.

Lees also suggests that the now-famous term "objective correlative", which Eliot first formulated in *The Sacred Wood* (1920), in the essay 'Hamlet and other Problems', may derive from Nietzsche. In *The Birth of Tragedy* Nietzsche uses the term "adäquate Objectivation" ("adequate objectification" in Haussmann's version), and immediately goes on to write about Hamlet.

Another parallel, not noted by Lees, is that between a passage in the first of the *Thoughts Out Of Season*, where Nietzsche writes: "woe unto ... the whole aesthetic kingdom of heaven, when once the young tiger ... rises to seek his prey!" and Eliot's lines in 'Gerontion':

> In the juvescence of the year
> Came Christ the tiger
>
> In depraved May

We have already seen that Nietzsche, in *Thus Spake Zarathustra*, associates the lion (cf. tiger) with Dionysos-as-Antichrist. G. Wilson Knight, in his *Christ and Nietzsche* (1948), also referred to a number of parallels between *Thus Spake Zarathustra* and Eliot's earlier poetry, though without drawing specific attention to them. However, such parallels in no way suggest any actual indebtedness to Nietzsche, of whom Eliot does not seem to have had a particularly high opinion.

Neither Lees nor Knight gave any sign of being aware that Eliot wrote about Nietzsche in 1916 in a review of A. Wolf, *The Philosophy of Nietzsche* (1915). Wolf's book consisted of a series of lectures, on Nietzsche and the War, Nietzsche's Method, The Motive of Nietzsche's Philosophy, Nietzsche's Theory of Knowledge, Nietzsche's Theory of the Universe, and Nietzsche's Theory of Life and Conduct; lucidly written, the book was well received, and was indeed one of the best books on the subject at that time. T. S. Eliot had by 1915 had two opportunities to get to know Nietzsche's work: from the Harvard course in philosophy, notably Royce's lectures, and from his stay in Germany, where he went on a travelling scholarship in 1914. In April 1916 he reviewed Wolf's book in the *International Journal of Ethics*,[22] writing as the graduate philosopher "T. Stearns Eliot". The most interesting part of his review is the characteristically magisterial first paragraph:

> Nietzsche is one of those writers whose philosophy evaporates when detached from its literary qualities, and whose literature owes its charm not alone to the personality and wisdom of the man, but to a claim to scientific truth. Such authors have always a peculiar influence over the large semi-philosophical public, who are spared the austere effort of criticism required by either metaphysics or literature, by either Spinoza or Stendhal; who enjoy the luxury of confounding, and avoid the task of combining, different interests.

Eliot evidently tends to disapprove of Nietzsche as "a philosopher of this hybrid kind", and this despite the "charm" which he imputes to his writings. Most of the rest of his review consists of detailed criticism of Wolf's book; there is little in it to help us to judge the extent of Eliot's knowledge of Nietzsche's work or his personal opinion of it. He ends, somewhat inscrutably, by regretting the "omission of any account of Nietzsche's views on art, with the interesting pessimism with respect to the future of art evinced in Human, All-too-Human." Since Wolf does not mention this subject at all, Eliot's prior knowledge of Nietzsche's work (though not the extent of that knowledge) is confirmed; but he does not seem to have been familiar with contemporary Nietzsche literature (cf. Ludovici's *Nietzsche and Art*, 1911), and at no point does he link Nietzsche with his own "interesting pessimism with respect to the future" which was to be shown in *The Waste Land* (1922).

This review, then, does not throw any light at all on the parallels that have been suggested between Eliot's work and Nietzsche's. Wolf's book is simply an academic treatment of Nietzsche's philosophy, of interest no doubt to the former student of philosophy, but with nothing whatsoever in it that would have been likely to attract the *poet's eye*. As a possible source-book, it must be ruled out, as must any question of T. S. Eliot being in any real sense indebted to Nietzsche: his review notwithstanding, Eliot could hardly have taken *less* interest in the most fashionable philosopher of his student years.

If W. B. Yeats' interest in Nietzsche ran deep for more than a decade and caused rather more than a tremor in his work, James Joyce's interest in the "strong enchanter", whose work he discovered in 1903, remained superficial. As Richard Ellmann has written, "it was probably upon Nietzsche that Joyce drew when he expounded to his friends [in 1903/4] a neo-paganism that glorified selfishness, licentiousness, and pitilessness, and denounced gratitude and other 'domestic virtues' ".[23] Nietzsche was in fact the prophet of the neo-pagan cult practised half-seriously by James Joyce and Oliver St John Gogarty in the Martello Tower at Sandycove in 1904 – until, that is, Joyce was frightened off by a third member of the group (Samuel Chenevix Trench) firing a revolver at an imaginary black panther in the middle of the night! This incident may have made Joyce decide that there was something to be said for the 'domestic virtues' after all; he certainly showed a most un-Zarathustran alarm. In the long run, certainly, Joyce's interests and sympathies were contrary to any sustained interest in Nietzsche, and only relatively unimportant echoes of Nietzsche are found in his work; but in 1903/4, when he was rather in the doldrums, he found it satisfying to think of himself as a Nietzschean Superman, "James Overman" as he ironically styled himself. Ten years later, however, Joyce was arguing against Schopenhauer and Nietzsche in favour of Thomas Aquinas; Nietzsche had been little more than a passing whim.

From the avantgarde 'men of 1914' we now pass to the literary warriors of August 1914 who were mainly, though not entirely, literary backwoodsmen. Although there had been a Nietzsche-cult in certain literary and intellectual circles ever since the first translations of his work began to appear in the mid-'nineties, and although at the turn of the century there were at least two journals devoted to propagating Nietzschean ideas (*The Eagle and the Serpent*, ed. Erwin McCall, 1898–1902; *Notes for Good Europeans*, ed. Thomas Common, 1903–9), to say nothing of a Nietzsche Society, there was little *general* interest in the philosopher until August 1914. In August 1914 interest in Nietzsche entered a totally new stage with the declaration of war, for which he was posthumously made scapegoat by a whole string of public and literary figures including Robert Bridges and Thomas Hardy, as is shown by the following anonymous comment in *The Literary Digest* for 7 November 1914: "Something of a subsidiary war is just now raging among the ranks of the Allied sympathizers over the responsibilities of Nietzsche in the present imbroglio ... the worst offender from the point of view of the Nietzschean ranks is Mr. Thomas Hardy". Indeed, the First World War was actually dubbed the 'Euro-Nietzschean' war by a bookseller in the Strand!

Now Thomas Hardy, who was deeply impressed by Schopenhauer, also knew Nietzsche's work, some of which he had read when the first English translations appeared, though there is no reason to suppose that he knew it particularly well. In a letter to the *Manchester Guardian* dated 13 October 1914, Hardy wrote: "He [Nietzsche] used to seem to me (I have not looked into his works for years) to be an incoherent rhapsodist who jumps from Machiavelli to Isaiah as the mood seizes him, and whom it is impossible to take seriously as a mentor." It is impossible to judge the extent of Hardy's knowledge – or former knowledge – of Nietzsche's work from this perceptive generalization, or from his reply a few months earlier, in June/July 1914, to a rather untimely invitation to honour Nietzsche's memory on the seventieth anniversary of his birth:

> It is a question whether Nietzsche's philosophy is sufficiently coherent to be of great ultimate value, and whether those views of his which seem so novel and striking appear thus only because they have been rejected for so many centuries as inadmissible under human rule.
>
> A continuity of consciousness through the human race would be the only justification of his proposed measures.
>
> He assumes throughout the great worth intrinsically of human masterfulness. The universe is to him a perfect machine which only requires thorough handling to work wonders. He forgets

> that the universe is an imperfect machine, and that to do good with an ill-working instrument requires endless adjustments and compromises.[24]

His comments suggest that by this time Hardy's knowledge of Nietzsche's work was in fact sketchy and largely confined to memories of the Superman-idea.

Returning to the First World War, in letters to the *Daily Mail* (27 September 1914) and *Manchester Guardian* (7 October 1914) Hardy referred to the bombardment of Rheims Cathedral and went on to state his view that the German leaders had been corrupted by the 'Will-to-Power':

> Should it turn out to be a predetermined destruction ... it will strongly suggest what a disastrous blight upon the glory and nobility of that great nation has been brought by the writings of Nietzsche, with his followers Treitschke, Bernhardi, etc. I should think there is no instance since history began of a country being so demoralized by a single writer, the irony being that he was a megalomaniac and not truly a philosopher at all.
>
> What puzzles one is to understand how the profounder thinkers in Germany, and to some extent elsewhere, can have been so dazzled by the writer's bombastic poetry – for it is a sort of prose-poetry – as to be blinded to the fallacy of his arguments ... Yet he and his school seem to have eclipsed for the time being in Germany the close-reasoned philosophies of such men as Kant and Schopenhauer.[25]

Hardy's letter blaming the long-dead Nietzsche for the German atrocities at Rheims provoked several other correspondents to rush to Nietzsche's defence (see below). In a further, slightly conciliatory letter to the *Manchester Guardian*, headed 'A Reply to Critics' (13 October 1914), Hardy pointed to the inflammatory nature of some of Nietzsche's writings, e.g. "Ye shall love peace as a means to new wars, and the short peace better than the long ... I do not counsel you to conclude peace but to conquer ... Beware of pity".[26] It was in this same letter that Hardy said that he had not looked into Nietzsche's work for years, which means that unless he 'looked into' *Thus Spake Zarathustra* to discover Zarathustra's views on 'War and Warriors', he must have had Nietzsche by heart! The former seems far more likely; but in either case Hardy was evidently disclaiming knowledge of Nietzsche's work for patriotic reasons. He concluded his letter:

> Nietzsche used to seem to me (I have not looked into his works for years) to be an incoherent rhapsodist who jumps from Machiavelli to Isaiah, as the mood seizes him, and whom it is impossible to take seriously as a mentor. I may have been wrong, but he impresses me in the long run, owing to the preternatural absence of any overt sign of levity in him, with a curious suspicion (no doubt groundless) of his being a first-class Swiftian in disguise.
>
> I need hardly add that with many of his sayings I have always heartily agreed; but I feel that few men who have lived long enough to see the real colour of life, and who have suffered, can believe in Nietzsche as a thinker.[27]

Views similar to those expressed by Thomas Hardy appeared in many other sections of the press; in August/September 1914 all too many literary gentlemen on both sides were anxious to do their bit;[28] in a letter to *The Times* (9 September 1914), Robert Bridges similarly described Germany as having been corrupted by Nietzsche's ideas. Lesser poets naturally joined in too, cf. the anti-Nietzschean sentiments expressed in Bertram Dobell's 'little book of verse' *Sonnets and Lyrics on the Present War* (1915). It was because some of this mud, thrown by men who had little or no knowledge of his work, stuck, that Nietzsche became known as "the execrable 'Neech'" (as reported by Wyndham Lewis).

In America the situation was similar: before the war there had been talk of a 'Nietzsche-invasion', so fast were his ideas gaining ground, and now, when the war came, an American professor (who shall be nameless) continued the military metaphor by referring to the war – not entirely inaccurately – as "Nietzsche in action"; the *Harvard Graduates* magazine joined in the demand that the Nietzschean colossus be struck down, while H. L. Mencken, America's foremost Nietzschean, was actually arrested after being denounced as an agent of "the German monster, Nietzsky". Mencken later wrote of this war-hysteria in the Introduction to his translation of *The Antichrist* (N.Y., 1923):

> The thing went to unbelievable lengths. On the strength of the fact that I had published a book on Nietzsche in 1906, six years

> after his death, I was called upon by agents of the Department of Justice, elaborately outfitted with badges, to meet the charge that I was an intimate associate and agent of 'the German monster, Nietzsky.' I quote the official procès verbal, an indignant but often misspelled document. Alas, poor Nietzsche![29]

Like so many other things, the Committee for Un-American Activities appears to have its roots in 1914. In March 1915 Mencken understandably wrote in *The Smart Set* of the "imbecile Nietzsche legend" and its part in the war-hysteria of the time:

> Of ... Nietzsche ... one hears a lot of startling gabble in these days of war, chiefly from the larynxes of freshwater college professors, prima donna preachers, English novelists, newspaper editorial writers, Chautauqua yap-yankers and other such hawkers of piffle. He is depicted as an intellectual pestilence, a universal fee-faw-fum, a high priest of diabolism ... It is solemnly and indignantly argued, not only that he plotted and hatched the burning of Louvain (as if a special devil were needed to account for so commonplace an act of war!), but also that he left behind him detailed plans and specifications for the blowing up of all the churches of Christendom, the butchery of all their rectors and curates, and the sale into levantine bondage of all their communicants, without regard to age, virtue or sex. It is more than hinted that the Turks have adopted him as their god, vice Allah, resigned in disgust. His hand is seen in at least forty or fifty massacres of Armenians, the *pogrom* of Kishinev, the *Titanic* disaster, the cruise of the *Emden*, the eruption of Mount Pelée, the Claflin failure, the assassination of King Carlos, the defeat of the Prohibition amendment, the torpedoing of the *Audacious*, the shelling of Rheims and the Italian earthquake. He is credited with advocating a war of extermination upon all right-thinking and forward-looking men, especially his fellow Germans. He is hailed as the patron and apologist of all crimes of violence and chicane, from mayhem to simony, and from piracy on the high seas to seduction under promise of marriage.

On both sides of the Atlantic Nietzsche was therefore, within 14 years of his death, transmogrified into a mythical monster (Neech-Nietzsky).

There were, of course, many other people in 1914 who objected to the wholesale linking of Nietzsche with German nationalist thinkers, cf. Thomas (later Sir Thomas) Beecham's letter to the *Manchester Guardian* of 9 October 1914, in which he condemned Thomas Hardy for his "light-minded and ill-considered attack on a writer with whose works he is very slightly acquainted", and continued: "To me, an old student of Nietzsche, it is only too evident that Mr. Hardy's criticisms of this remarkable man are founded on the most superficial basis of knowledge, and provide a deplorable example of that ignorance which has prevailed for over a generation in this country of matters concerning real German life and thought." He ended by pointing to Nietzsche's bitter criticism of modern Germany, and expressed the fully justifiable view that Nietzsche – "this gladiator of real culture" – must be turning in his grave at being daily placed in the same category as men like Treitschke and Bernhardi. Elsewhere in the contemporary press Nietzsche's criticism of nineteenth-century Germany was taken as justifying England's moral position in the war.

The extent to which Nietzsche was posthumously involved in the wholly deplorable literary warfare of 1914 had one ironical result: the first edition of the Levy translation sold out rapidly (it was reprinted in 1924), and borrowings of Nietzsche's works from public libraries also soared. In view of this it is interesting to find H. W. Nevinson writing in his *Changes and Chances* (1923): "When first I was in Germany, Nietzsche was still almost unknown, and my German friend urged me to translate and comment upon him. I wish I had done so, for then perhaps we should have heard less nonsense talked about that remarkable man as the cause of the war".[30] This comment is either extremely naïve, for few writers have been so copiously translated and commented upon within a few years of their death, or Nevinson is implying that those who did translate and comment upon Nietzsche did him something of a disservice. There is some truth in this, for it is precisely the 'Nietzscheans' (in the popular sense) who have caused most misunderstanding of his work; and besides the British reader at least does not take particularly kindly to proselytizing.

Wyndham Lewis gave some idea of the reaction against Nietzsche in 1914 when he wrote:

> This contempt of law, regulation and 'humanity' is popularly supposed to be the outcome of the teachings of the execrable

> 'Neech', and to be a portion of aristocratic 'haughtiness.' Nietzsche was much too explicit a gentleman to be a very typical one. And his 'aristocratism', so gushing and desperate athwart his innumerable prefaces, raises doubts in the mind of the most enthusiastic student.[31]

With this reaction the tide of British Nietzscheanism had in fact turned. The prophet of the post-war world was to be not Nietzsche, but Karl Marx, although there were nonetheless those writers who viewed the crises of the 1918–39 world in Nietzschean terms, cf. the aesthetic élitism of Clive Bell's *Civilization* (1928) and – more importantly – the work of Norman Douglas (1869–1952). Douglas's *How about Europe?* (1930; American title, *Goodbye to Western Culture*, N.Y., 1930) shows clearly the Nietzschean basis of his idiosyncratic attitude to life. Half-German by birth and bilingual in English and German, Douglas was a 'Dionysian' humanist who shared Nietzsche's pet aversions (Christianity, socialism, democracy, etc.). It was not for nothing that he was a friend of Oscar Levy, to whom *How About Europe?* was dedicated.

In the meantime we must turn our attention to the United States, where the reaction against the "German monster" in 1914–18 was no less fierce, but where his influence lasted longer.

Chapter Eleven

Nietzsche and American literature

Nietzsche was himself not only influenced by Emerson (cf. the studies by Stanley Hubbard and Eduard Baumgarten); his thought also paralleled that of Walt Whitman in a number of important particulars, although, as C. N. Stavrou has written:

> So far as is known, there is no evidence which claims Walt Whitman (1819–1892) directly influenced the thought of Friedrich Nietzsche (1844–1900). Since Whitman had virtually finished his life and life's work before Nietzsche had hardly commenced his, it is within the realm of possibility that the precocious Nietzsche, who admired Emerson though he detested Carlyle, had read the perfervid disciple of the Great Brahmin. But nothing can be produced to support this intriguing speculation. Although both Whitman and Nietzsche freely admit their respective debts to Emerson, Nietzsche never mentions or alludes to Whitman.[1]

In fact it is hardly 'within the realm of possibility' that Nietzsche read Whitman. Despite Freiligrath's enthusiastic account of the Rosetti edition of Whitman's *Poems* in the *Augsburger Allgemeine Zeitung* (24 April 1868) and his subsequent very weak translations, which attracted hardly any attention, Whitman was virtually ignored in Germany during Nietzsche's creative lifetime. The beginning of the Whitman cult in Germany dates from J. V. Widmann's acceptance of Whitman as the prophet of a new natural religion in 1889, a matter of months before the onset of Nietzsche's insanity. These facts only serve to underline that however much Nietzsche *might* have appreciated Walt Whitman's work, it is *most* unlikely that he knew it.

Leaving aside the question of the influence of American writers on Nietzsche, which is interesting but irrelevant, Nietzsche's own first impact in America was on literary criticism, and more especially on critics who were themselves of part-German origin (Huneker, Mencken, Nathan). Walt Whitman continues to be relevant only insofar as Nietzsche rode in on the wave of Whitman-inspired vitalism.

The American public's first introduction to Nietzsche's philosophy was inauspicious, coming, as in England, in Max Nordau's best-selling *Degeneration* (N.Y., 1895), which savagely attacked Nietzsche and all his works. Despite the controversy which raged around *Degeneration*, it was not until the following year, 1896, that critical interest in Nietzsche really began in America; 1896, the year of Havelock Ellis's articles on Nietzsche in *The Savoy*, also saw the publication of the first full and sympathetic review of Nietzsche's philosophy in the United States, in an article (by W. F. Barry) entitled 'The Ideals of Anarchy' in *Littell's Living Age*.[2] True, most of the reviews of Nietzsche's work (newly translated in Britain, but already crossing the Atlantic) in 1896 were hostile, but by 1897 Camillo von Klenze was writing that Nietzsche was bound to *continue* to appeal to a generation suffering from a lack of vitality.[3] By 1903 the critic of the *Athenaeum* was stating that "Nietzsche for good or evil speaks with a formidable voice ... he cannot be disregarded".[4] Five years later another critic wrote that "Friedrich Nietzsche was until recently almost unknown in America; but nowadays his name constantly appears in all sorts of connexions".[5] In 1910 the "slow but persistent growth of Nietzsche's fame" was stated to be "one of the intellectual romances of our time",[6] which makes nonsense of Thomas Common's article 'Will Nietzsche come into vogue in America?'[7] By 1912 H. L. Mencken's Nietzsche-shelf, once so small, was five feet long. Nietzsche as a phenomenon had finally arrived; as Paul Elmer More commented in his *The Drift of Romanticism* (1913), "if the number of books written about a subject is any proof of interest in it, Nietzsche must have become the most popular of authors among Englishmen and Americans".[8] Among the books in question was Paul Elmer More's own *Nietzsche* (Boston and N.Y., 1912), claiming to present "an independent opinion on a much ventilated subject".

Within a short time of arriving in this sense, Nietzsche finally assumed mythical stature as "the German monster, Nietzsky". Most of the credit for arousing this degree of American interest in Nietzsche must go to the critics Huneker and Mencken, one of whom (Mencken) was to be the official victim of this myth.

In the first three decades of the present century the two most influential critics in America were probably those 'playboys of the arts', James G. Huneker and H. L. Mencken, both of whom championed Nietzsche. In 1932 Ludwig Lewisohn wrote that "the entire modern period of American culture is scarcely thinkable without the long energetic and fruitful activity of James Huneker".[9] Hunekers' basic critical approach was anti-Philistine, an attitude in which he will doubtless have been confirmed by Nietzsche's *Thoughts Out Of Season*. When he came to write his autobiography, Huneker expressed his credo in a parody of *Thus Spake Zarathustra*:

> And now when the Great Noon had come Steeplejack touched the top of the spire where instead of a cross he found a vane which swung as the wind listeth. Thereat he marvelled and rejoiced. 'Behold!' he cried, 'thou glowing symbol of the New Man. A weathercock and a mighty twirling. This then shall be the sign set in the sky for Immortalists: A cool brain and a wicked heart. Nothing is true. All is permitted, for all is necessary!'[10]

At the same time Huneker claimed that he corresponded with Nietzsche as early as 1884–5.[11] Be this as it may, his real enthusiasm for Nietzsche seems to date from *c.* 1888; H. L. Mencken later wrote that Huneker perceived the rising star of Nietzsche as early as 1888: "Before the rev. professors had come to Schopenhauer, he was hauling ashore the devil-fish, Nietzsche".[12] From then on Huneker himself was hooked and became the champion of Nietzsche, as is shown by the chapters on Nietzsche in his *Overtones: A Book of Temperaments* (1904; the chapter in question was written in "1896 or 1897"[13]) and *Egoists: A Book of Supermen* (1909), to say nothing of the references to Nietzsche scattered throughout Huneker's other works of the period. In 1903 he duly visited Frau Foerster-Nietzsche in Weimar.

Huneker's *Overtones: A Book of Temperaments* (N.Y. and London, 1904) included the essay 'Nietzsche the Rhapsodist'. The opening of the essay – "A sane and complete estimate of the life and philosophical writings of Friedrich Nietzsche has yet to be made in English"[14] – was hardly fair to Havelock Ellis, whose essay Huneker knew and admired. Huneker's own essay is less 'complete' than Ellis's; it is, however, brilliantly written in his characteristic aphoristic style. For Huneker in 1904 Nietzsche is "a stimulus to thought, an antiseptic critic of all philosophies, religions, theologies, and moral systems, an intellectual rebel, a very Lucifer among ancient and modern thinkers".[15] His admiration for this "magnificent dialectician" who "dared to be naked and natural, though a philosopher"[16] is evident. He refutes the vicious argument that "a man in a madhouse could only produce a mad philosophy", pointing out that Nietzsche's mind was turned by the "very intensity of [his] mental vision ... his hopeless attempt to square the circle of things human".[17] Praising the "thunder-march of his ideas, the brilliancy ... of his style",[18] Huneker agrees with Havelock Ellis that Nietzsche is "a great aboriginal force" whose immortality – "as immortality goes among world thinkers: fifty years of quotation and then – the biographical dictionaries"[19] – is assured. This was not a bad estimate.

In 'Nietzsche the Rhapsodist' Huneker was mainly concerned to introduce Nietzsche to his readers; the real criticism – and it is often incisive criticism – was reserved for his second major essay on Nietzsche, 'Phases of Nietzsche', which appeared in *Egoists: A Book of Supermen* (1909). But however much valid criticism this latter essay contained, what is perhaps even more important in the present context is that Nietzsche is again presented in an *heroic* light; indeed, Huneker at one point calls him "the great culture-hero of his days". The reader is left with the impression of an intellectual tragic hero:

> Nietzsche is the most dynamically emotional writer of his times. He sums up an epoch. He is the expiring voice of the old nineteenth-century romanticism in philosophy. His message to unborn generations we may easily leave to those unborn, and enjoy the wit, the profound criticisms of life, the bewildering gamut of his ideas; above all, pity the tragic blotting out of such a vivid intellectual life.[20]

It seems reasonable to say with LeRoy C. Kauffmann that "Huneker and [Percival] Pollard discovered Nietzsche for America ... With Huneker and Pollard the spirit of Nietzsche came to America".[21] Percival Pollard, who rallied to the Nietzschean cause in his *Masks and Minstrels of New Germany* (Boston, 1911), was to the fore among the many intellectuals influenced by Huneker; his book is of no more than marginal importance in the present story. Huneker was, of course, revered by a number of younger critics, among them H. L. Mencken, George Jean Nathan, and Benjamin De Casseres – all of them 'Nietzscheans'; it was Benjamin De Casseres, author of some rather peculiar Nietzscheana (see Bibliography), who was to introduce Eugene O'Neill to Nietzsche's work. In its golden years (1913–24) the magazine *The Smart Set* was run by genial Nietzscheans: Willard H. Wright (author of *What Nietzsche Taught*, N.Y., 1915), Nathan, and Mencken (cf. *The New Age* in England, with which the foremost British 'Nietzscheans' were associated). This fact is reflected in *The Smart Set's* policy of "enlightened skepticism" aimed at "the civilized minority". From 1924 Nietzsche's philosophy was taken no less seriously by the *American Mercury* group; but then the *American Mercury* was also edited by Mencken.

The dawn of Nietzscheanism in America has been well summarized by Brom Weber

> by the second decade of this century his [Nietzsche's] ideas and personality had begun to permeate many writers and intellectuals, among them Lewis, Pound, Margaret Anderson, and John Gould Fletcher, who reacted antagonistically to the genteel dogmatism of the nineteenth century and the aimless brutality of the twentieth. In page after page of their work and in the magazines they edited – *The New Freewoman, The Egoist, Blast* ... the emancipating message of Nietzsche was directly and indirectly stressed in ringing tones.[22]

This is true; but no one did more to propagate Nietzsche's ideas than H. L. Mencken.

As reviewer for and later co-editor of *The Smart Set*, H. L. Mencken became "America's most influential literary critic" (William H. Nolte); in the late 1920s, when he was editor of the *American Mercury*, he was referred to as "the most powerful private citizen in America" (*The New York Times*), "the most powerful personal influence on this whole generation of educated people" (Walter Lippmann). And Mencken, born iconoclast, author of that "Nietzschean Gemara in the vulgate", *The Philosophy of Friedrich Nietzsche* (Boston and London, 1908; 3rd edn, 1913, repr. 1967), "arranger" of *The Gist of Nietzsche* (Boston, 1910), and translator of *The Antichrist* (N.Y., 1923), was above all a tireless propagator of Nietzsche's ideas in *The Smart Set*[23] and elsewhere; indeed, he has long been considered America's foremost Nietzschean – an accolade (if that is the word) which now properly belongs to Eugene O'Neill.

Mencken's most recent biographer, William H. Nolte, has written of Nietzsche as one of the two writers who exercised "the most enormous influence" on Mencken's thought; his influence on Mencken's style was scarcely less. The many parallels between Nietzsche's and Mencken's ideas and styles have been very adequately examined by Edward Stone. Here let it suffice to say that Mencken's own remark that "In my own mind, my debt to Nietzsche seems very slight"[24] is not borne out by the facts. Notwithstanding Mencken's statement that 'I seldom quote the men I admire most, for example, Nietzsche",[25] his work in fact contains *extensive* quotation from Nietzsche, as well as numerous references and allusions to Nietzsche. It seems indisputable that Mencken *both* obtained many of his basic ideas from Nietzsche, *and* was in the habit of quoting Nietzsche in support of his own ideas. His critical premiss comes straight from Nietzsche: that art is not a matter of morality, that the artist operates in an aesthetic sphere 'beyond good and evil'. And over and above this general 'Dionysian' standpoint, he continually quotes Nietzsche on specific points to back up his own views, as indeed he had done in his *The Philosophy of Friedrich Nietzsche*, the subject of which was "Mencken's Nietzsche, not Nietzsche's Nietzsche" (William Manchester). His views on Christianity, democracy, morality, art, truth, evolution, *amor fati*, etc., closely follow Nietzsche's. And the style in which he writes is the "explosively alive" style of which Nietzsche gave him the perfect example.[26]

Nietzsche was first introduced into American literature, as opposed to literary criticism, in the novels of Jack London, although H. L. Mencken had no part in arousing London's interest in Nietzsche's philosophy. Among the writers whom Mencken did try to interest in Nietzsche, however, was one to whom he owed his position as literary critic of *The Smart Set*: Theodore Dreiser. The novels of London and Dreiser are discussed in the next chapter. Other writers whose interest in Nietzsche was almost certainly aroused by Mencken are Conrad Aiken and Hart Crane. Crane's knowledge of Nietzsche (see below) and his enthusiasm for the German philosopher in the early 1920s, probably reflect his reading of Mencken's writings in *The Smart Set* and elsewhere. These writers apart, it is an ironical fact that the (sub-) literary fruits of Mencken's enthusiasm for Nietzsche are chiefly to be seen in the second-rate novel of the period, e.g. Floyd Dell's *The Moon-Calf* (1920), and Ben Hecht's *Erik Dorn* (1921) and *Humpty Dumpty* (1924). At first sight it may seem strange that Mencken, and Huneker, should have failed to arouse more enthusiasm for Nietzsche among major writers. In fact it is hardly surprising, for major writers are far more likely to be stimulated by other writers than by hot-gospelling critics, however gifted. Besides, Nietzsche is arguably far more alien to mainstream modern American literature than to its British equivalent.

The other major American writers who were, or who have been said to be, influenced by Nietzsche – John Gould Fletcher, Robinson Jeffers, Eugene O'Neill, and Wallace Stevens – all came across Nietzsche elsewhere. John Gould Fletcher had his attention drawn to Nietzsche by a Harvard friend. Robinson Jeffers, who strongly denied being influenced by Nietzsche at all, came across the philosopher's work when he was himself in Switzerland. Eugene O'Neill was introduced to Nietzsche's work by Benjamin De Casseres, although George Jean Nathan also played a part, and Mencken gave O'Neill his most important recognition to date when he published three of O'Neill's fo'c'sle plays (*Ile*, *Long Voyage Home*, and *Moon of the Caribbees*) in *The Smart Set* in 1917–18. Whether Nietzsche was mentioned in the Mencken-O'Neill correspondence is not known, although it is likely that he was. And Wallace Stevens – probably the most surprising name to find in this context for many readers – appears to have come across Nietzsche at second-hand, in Hans Vaihinger's *The Philosophy of 'As If'*. Fletcher, O'Neill and Stevens must be considered separately; but first let us return to Hart Crane and Robinson Jeffers.

Hart Crane was one of the many writers who defended Nietzsche against the abuse hurled at him in 1914–18 (see his first piece of published prose, 'The Case Against Nietzsche', published in *The Pagan*, April/May 1918). In his masterly study *Hart Crane* (1948), Brom Weber wrote: "To Friedrich Nietzsche must unquestionably be assigned a considerable share in the development of Hart Crane".[27] But although Crane's essay on Nietzsche presupposes some knowledge of *Human, All-Too-Human* and *Ecce Homo*, he is known to have read only *The Birth of Tragedy*, and it seems most likely that he obtained his knowledge of Nietzsche from the writings of H. L. Mencken (one of his early idols) in *The Smart Set*; he may well also have read George Burman Foster's essay 'The Prophet of a New Culture' which appeared in the first number of *The Little Review* in March 1914.[28]

Exactly when Hart Crane came across Nietzsche is not known, although it was probably in 1917–18, perhaps when looking through back numbers of *The Smart Set*. In 1917 he wrote to his mother: 'I am beginning to see the hope of standing entirely alone and to fathom Ibsen's statement that translated is, 'The strongest man in the world is he who stands entirely alone!' "[29] This comment probably reflects a mind ready for the discovery of Nietzsche. His defence of Nietzsche appeared a year later; in it he wrote of Nietzsche as "so elusive ... a mystery", but showed quite a good general knowledge of his work. By October 1921 Nietzsche ranked as one of his favourite authors (see his letter of 6 October 1921 to Gorham Munson[30]), and Crane had taken to using the epithet 'Nietzschean' as an accolade of approval; thus in autumn 1922 he wrote to Munson that Joyce's *Ulysses* had "a strong ethical and Nietzschean basis".[31] Crane appears to use the word in the sense of 'individualistic', though presumably it had both a wider and a more particularized connotation for him.

In support of his contention that Nietzsche had "a considerable share in the development of Hart Crane", Brom Weber wrote:

> That Nietzsche's aesthetic and philosophical ideas, particularly as expressed in *The Birth of Tragedy*, received an opportunity

> to display themselves concretely in Crane's career is evident. Crane's faith in the myth, his desire to transmute music into his poetry, his disregard for cause and effect logic, his affirmation of life's joy coupled with an affirmation of suffering and tragedy, his belief in metaphysical inquiry as the artist's task – the entire Dionysian complex of dance, ecstasy and triumph of the will which Nietzsche portrayed [,] formed the backbone of Crane's life. It is even possible that Nietzsche's call for 'a rising generation ... with bold vision ... to desire a new art, the art of metaphysical comfort ... to claim it as Helen, and exclaim with Faust' in *The Birth of Tragedy* contributed to the genesis of 'Faustus and Helen'.[32]

In a general way this is true enough; but implicitly the statement only bears out the impression one obtains from Crane's work and letters – that while he undoubtedly enthused over Nietzsche in the early 1920s, there is simply no evidence that he knew Nietzsche's work well enough for the German philosopher to have had a 'considerable' share in his development. It is more a question of admiration for a writer many of whose ideas closely matched his own, than of 'influence' as such; compare Crane's letter to William Wright dated 29 November 1930: "By ascribing my almost chronic indigence to so Nietzschean a program as the attitude of 'living life dangerously' infers, you make me blink a little. For my exposures to rawness and to risk have been far too inadvertent, I fear, to deserve any such honorable connotations".[33]

Nietzsche's 'influence' on Hart Crane was in fact general rather than specific. Above all, Nietzsche powerfully reinforced Crane in his basic romanticism, in his belief in the poet as visionary superman and redemptive hero. Increasingly Crane found self-respect and 'metaphysical consolation' in the status of élitist outsider, and in psychological terms this represents his main debt to Nietzsche. In his early poetry, when Nietzsche is on the surface of his mind, a frequent theme is that of the need for the poet-superman to soar, eagle-like, to the peaks of ecstasy; Nietzsche's concept of Dionysian art, and the example of Zarathustra, are unobtrusively present in the background. It was to Nietzsche that Hart Crane owed much of his contempt for material reality; it was Nietzsche who taught him to transcend such reality and cling desperately to his own absolute vision of a higher reality "more real than life". In effect the best description of Crane's position and of his closeness to Nietzsche is provided in Lascelles Abercrombie's analysis of Nietzsche's Dionysian romanticism, which points straight to the heart of Crane's work.

More specifically, one can see in Hart Crane's early poetry the juxtaposition of and constant tension between the Apollonian and Dionysian impulses. From these two contrary impulses come two different concepts of beauty: 'Apollonian' as in "The Bathers" ("Two ivory women by a milky sea ... A dreamer might see these"), and 'Dionysian' as in 'Carmen de Bohème' ('There is a sweep, – a shattering, – a choir/Disquieting of barbarous fantasy"). Apollo and Dionysos, the art of the dreamer and barbarous fantasy, are first united in 'To Portapovitch' (1919):

> Release, – dismiss the passion from your arms.
> More real than life, the gestures you have spun
> Haunt the blank stage with lingering alarms,
> Though silent as your sandals, danced undone.[34]

The most obviously Nietzschean poem by Crane is 'For the Marriage of Faustus and Helen',[35] of which L. S. Dembo has written: "In 'For the Marriage of Faustus and Helen' (1923), Crane made his first attempt to reconcile through tragedy Apollonian dejection with Dionysian ecstasy, and the three parts of the poem seem to have been arranged according to a clearly Nietzschean logic".[36] This is true, and is in line with Crane's expressed intentions in the poem.[37] But when all is said and done, what really matters is that "The imagination spans beyond despair,/Outpacing bargain, vocable and prayer." It is the ability of the poetic imagination to transcend itself that is important to Crane:

> it seems evident that certain aesthetic experience ... can be called absolute ... It is my hope to go *through* the combined materials of the poem, using our 'real' world somewhat as a spring-board, and to give the poem *as a whole* an orbit or predetermined direction of its own ... Its evocation will ... be ... toward a [new] state of consciousness ... [38]

His ultimate commitment is not to either of the two worlds which he contrasts in 'For the Marriage of Faustus and Helen' and in *The Bridge*, but to the "third world" of imaginative ecstasy symbolized by Zarathustra's eagle. The lines in *The Bridge* – "Time like a serpent down her shoulder, dark,/And space, an eaglet's wing, laid on her hair"[39] – appear to be one of the "dead echoes" of the poem, involving an allusion to the American past in the person of the Aztec god Quetzalcóatl (whose name means 'feathered serpent' in Mayan, as D. H. Lawrence also knew). The lines may also, as L. S. Dembo has noted, involve an allusion to Blake's 'America: A Prophecy' in which Orc envisions eagle, lion, and serpent; but a more obvious allusion is to Zarathustra's symbolical companions.

The more one reads Hart Crane's poetry, however, the clearer does it become that it is not the faint specific echoes that matter; on the surface his work is far removed from Nietzsche – his diction, for instance, is quite un-Nietzschean. What does matter is that Crane's work rests on a wholly Nietzschean view of poetry as "more real than life". Otherwise Nietzsche may well have given Crane his general belief in the poet as a type of redemptive hero; but that is about all that he actually did give him. The critic would do well, in fact, to remember Blake's lines quoted by Crane:

> We are led to believe in a lie
> When we see *with* not *through* the eye.

Conrad Aiken went through a phase of immature Nietzscheanism which he later rejected and indeed condemned as an aberration. His first collection of poems, *Earth Triumphant and Other Tales in Verse* (1914), contained much imitation of *Thus Spake Zarathustra*, understood via Mencken; the title alludes to Zarathustra's doctrine of obedience to the earth. But Aiken reprinted nothing from *Earth Triumphant* in his *Selected Poems* (1929) and *Collected Poems* (1953) as he considered nothing in that first collection to be "even remotely salvageable". By the time of the next collection, *Turns and Movies and Other Tales in Verse* (1916), the Nietzscheanism as such has gone, though the vigour of Nietzsche's style has left its mark.

Aiken later returned to the subject of his own early Nietzscheanism in that "queer book" (his own words), the pseudopsychological novel *King Coffin* (1935). The hero of the novel, Jasper Ammen (his name echoes Aiken's), is by no means a Nietzschean Superman; he merely plays "the part of the ... Zarathustran prophet",[40] keeps a mask of Nietzsche somewhat selfconsciously on his mantelpiece, and is fond of quoting from *Thus Spake Zarathustra* ("O my brethren, am I then cruel? Everything of today – it falleth, it decayeth; who would preserve it! But I – I wish also to push it!"[41]), and from *Beyond Good and Evil* ("Egoism is the essence of the noble soul, every star is a similar egoist. I revolve like Nietzsche proudly amongst my proud equals".[42] Jasper Ammen's crazy morality is based on the idea that "one must value one's capacity for hate"; he follows Zarathustra in deriding pity. As the "tree of his vision" grows, so do his misgivings, but "You must expect to have misgivings, that is the penalty of the solitary spirit. The one who dwells in the abyss."[43]

Enough has been said to make it clear that Jasper Ammen imagines himself to be a Nietzschean Superman. But the whole point of the novel is that he is not; he is merely a "megalomaniac" who "thinks he's God Almighty". At the end of the novel he is cured of his inflation. In short, *King Coffin* is a highly personal work in which Conrad Aiken retrospectively condemns his own early Nietzscheanism (which produced no poetry worth reprinting) as a temporary aberration.

In the Foreword to his *Selected Poetry* (n.d.), Robinson Jeffers – rather unwisely – wrote: "Another formative principle came to me from a phrase of Nietzsche's: 'The poets? The poets lie too much.' " Years earlier he had quoted the same phrase in a review of James Rorty's *The Children of the Sun* (1927) in *Advance* (1 April 1927). On the strength of such allusions, many of Jeffers' earlier critics sought to turn him into a Nietzschean; Eric Bentley, for instance, in *The Cult of the Superman* (1947), placed Jeffers among those 'Heroic Vitalists' who had followed Nietzsche in the "quest for a new immortality".[44] This is both to exaggerate the significance of the ostensibly 'Nietzschean' elements in his work, and – more especially – to ignore the fact that Jeffers himself wrote of Nietzsche as "somebody that local people accuse me quite falsely of deriving from".[45] In their book *A History of American Poetry 1900–1940* (N.Y., n.d.), Horace Gregory and Marya Zaturenska wrote of "a measurable influence of ... Nietzsche upon his [Jeffers'] imagination",[46] and of "Jeffers' affinity with the teachings of Nietzsche";[47] they figured that "It was a Nietzschean 'reality' that Jeffers perceived",[48] for "The great poet in him cannot get clear of Nietzsche's philosophy",[49] so that "His last answer is always a return to Nietzsche".[50] But while it may be true that "Jeffers ... long held Nietzsche's writings in high regard",[51] Gregory and Zaturenska adduce no conclusive evidence that he was influenced by Nietzsche in any significant way or degree.

Robinson Jeffers attended school and university in Switzerland, and is known to have read *Thus Spake Zarathustra* in 1906, hence his use of the phrase "transvaluing values" in *The Women at Point Sur.* Nietzsche was, however, a far less 'measurable' influence on his work than Schopenhauer and Spengler. In general, it seems true to say that what we find in Jeffers' work are not so much echoes of Nietzsche, as occasional parallels with some of Nietzsche's – mainly incidental – ideas; basically his view of life is totally different from Nietzsche's. Such a view is confirmed by Radcliffe Squires, who has written: "When Jeffers and Nietzsche touch, it is the accident of their both feeling for bearings in the same dark room".[52] Indeed, Squires argues convincingly that Jeffers and Nietzsche represent two opposed responses to Schopenhauer's philosophy, with Jeffers closer to Schopenhauer than Nietzsche is. It is, in fact, time to stop perpetuating the local gossip of which Robinson Jeffers complained, for there is no more evidence that he was measurably influenced by Nietzsche, than there is that Theodore Roosevelt had Nietzsche in mind when he praised the virtues of 'hardness' in a speech at the Hamilton Club in Chicago in 1899.

Surprisingly, Theodore Roosevelt's name has more than once been linked with that of Nietzsche. In his *The Philosophy of Friedrich Nietzsche* (1908), H. L. Mencken wrote: "in all things fundamental the Rooseveltian philosophy and the Nietzschean philosophy are identical … It is inconceivable that Mr. Roosevelt should have formulated his present confession of faith independently of Nietzsche".[53] Mencken is here referring to Theodore Roosevelt's *The Strenuous Life* (N.Y., 1902), which contains ideas first voiced in his speech at the Hamilton Club:

> I wish to preach, not the doctrine of ignoble ease, but the doctrine of the strenuous life, the life of toil and effort, of labor and strife; to preach the highest form of success which comes to the man who does not shrink from danger, from hardship, or from bitter toil, and who out of these wins the splendid ultimate triumph.[54]

Mencken's irresponsible assertion that Roosevelt is here echoing Nietzsche has often been reiterated. Although there was, admittedly, a Nietzschean cult of 'hardness' at the time, this assertion is surely quite mistaken, for the fact is that Roosevelt never mentions Nietzsche's name, preaches an individualism which need not have any connexion with the German philosopher's ideas, and combines this with a basic Puritanism that is entirely un-Nietzschean. It seems, in fact, that Mencken was unable to distinguish between Puritanism and stoicism.

Chapter Twelve
Fictional Supermen: Jack London and Theodore Dreiser

The Nietzschean Superman was introduced into American literature in the novels of Jack London who read Nietzsche in *c.* 1903 and was fascinated by his philosophy; evidence of this is to be found in the novels *The Sea-Wolf* (1904), *The Iron Heel* (1907), and *Martin Eden* (1909), while less important evidence is also to be found in *Burning Daylight* (1910), *John Barleycorn* (1913), and in some of the short stories.

Jack London's interest in Nietzsche was fired by his friend Frank Strawn-Hamilton, whom he described, shortly after their meeting in (?) 1903 as "a remarkable man ... spilling over with the minutest details of every world-philosophy from Zeno to Nietzsche ... in short, a genius of extraordinary caliber".[1] Strawn-Hamilton appears in *Martin Eden*, both under his own name as one of the radical intellectuals whom Martin meets through Russ Brissenden, and also in the person of Brissenden.

Joan London has written that on hearing of Nietzsche from Strawn-Hamilton, Jack London "promptly became intoxicated":

> The situation was even more serious in regard to Nietzsche. Temperate by reason of his greater knowledge, Hamilton could take both philosophers [Spencer and Nietzsche] in stride without losing his perspective; Jack promptly became intoxicated. While Hamilton was tolerant of Nietzsche, weighing his worth very precisely, every prejudice, and what today might be termed 'complex' in Jack responded violently to the Nietzschean doctrines. In time ... he might have read himself back to sobriety. But success came too soon, and with it the end of time for studying.[2]

But not only did London respond violently to the Nietzschean doctrines of the Superman complex; he also delighted in the phrases in which these doctrines were couched:

> His knowledge of Nietzsche was derived largely from listening to Strawn-Hamilton, and when he did turn to Nietzsche's own pages he was so enchanted by the philosopher's vocabulary and slogans that he noted little else. 'The blond beasts,' 'the glad perishers,' 'the Superman,' 'Live dangerously!' – these were more potent than wine.[3]

Two points are to be noted in this connexion: that London will have been confirmed by Nietzsche in the ideal of "strength of style" or "strength of utterance" which he sought, for this is what he admired in Nietzsche and what he both practised and preached himself. And, secondly, that his enchantment with Nietzsche was primarily *aesthetic*; rationally he may have been increasingly an advocate of the Socialism so detested by Nietzsche, but aesthetically he was totally captivated by the Superman-idea. Besides, London came to believe that mankind was unable to achieve its own salvation without superhuman leaders; and, as his disenchantment with Socialism grew, he came to concentrate his hopes more and more on the great individual. Even Joan London admits that he was "more impressed by Nietzsche than by Marx".[4]

Shortly after his discovery of Nietzsche, Jack London wrote to his wife that he had read *The Genealogy of Morals*, *The Case of Wagner*, *The Antichrist*, and *Thus Spake Zarathustra*, among others of Nietzsche's works, and that he "ate them up" enthusiastically.

His main enthusiasm was reserved for the Superman-idea, for reasons well explained by Richard O'Connor:

> it was … Nietzsche's deep dark well of pessimism at which he drank the most copiously. The … German philosopher … seemed to confirm and enlarge upon so much of what he had learned from experience. 'I teach you the Superman. Man is something to be surpassed … ' From his early teens Jack had secretly regarded himself as a superior creature, one born to dominate his fellows because he was stronger and wiser. This belief existed side by side … with a fervent dedication to Socialism, which was supposed to protect the weaker and more ignorant.
>
> His own antireligious beliefs … were given substance by Nietzsche's tirade against Christianity …[5]

In other words, Jack London was attracted to Nietzsche by that same sense of affinity between the Superman and his own secret super-ego which accounts for so many other writers' Nietzschean proclivities and which was foreseen by Havelock Ellis when he wrote in the third of his articles on Nietzsche in *The Savoy*: "So the 'master-morality' it is that your true Nietzschean is most likely to close his fist over." The influence of Nietzsche is seen in the supermanhood of characters like Wolf Larssen, Ernest Everhard, Martin Eden, and Burning Daylight. But this is *not* to say that Jack London simply took over Nietzsche's conception of the Superman lock, stock and barrel. He was fascinated by the Superman; but he was never (in writing) uncritical of Nietzsche's philosophy, about which he always had his reservations. His basic attitude to Nietzsche is in fact well illustrated by his remark to Frederick Bamford that "Personally I like Nietzsche tremendously, but I cannot go all the way with him".[6] More specifically, "London accepted the basic orientation of Schopenhauer and Nietzsche, but he was never able to follow Nietzsche's search for values. He converted the *Übermensch* into a biological Superman".[7]

When considering his novels, we shall see that London did indeed convert the *Übermensch* into a merely biological Superman, with the result that a character like Wolf Larssen is close to the popular misconception of the Superman, but far indeed from embodying Nietzsche's essentially spiritual ideal. Theodore Dreiser's Frank Cowperwood is closer to Nietzsche than any of London's characters; but it is Yeats' Heroes – so far removed from both London and

Dreiser – who come closest to Nietzsche's ideal of aristocratic supermanhood. That this is so, is a further confirmation of what we have already seen: that what matters in this context is how various writers used or abused more or less understood Nietzschean ideas; historical truth is of secondary importance. Jack London did not follow Nietzsche's 'search for values' because – like the otherwise so very different Edwin Muir – his values were given by the Socialism to which he was dedicated.

London's Superman-characters are both the most important and the least understood aspect of his Nietzscheanism. Thus Wolf Larssen is neither projection nor perversion of the Nietzschean Superman. Philip S. Foner has argued (in the Introduction to his *Jack London, American Rebel*, 1958) that Wolf Larssen is a perfect specimen of the Nietzschean superman, although his brutality and ruthlessness is really a mask for his inner weakness. Now while it is true that Wolf Larssen's brute strength masks an ultimate inner weakness, it is certainly not true to say that he is a "perfect specimen of the Nietzschean superman". But Lewis Mumford is also wrong in seeing Larssen as a mere perversion of Nietzsche's ideal:

> The career of the Superman in America is an instructive spectacle. He sprang, this overman, out of the pages of Emerson ... caught up by Nietzsche, and colored by the dark natural theology Darwin had inherited from Malthus, the Superman became the highest possibility of natural selection: he served as a symbol of contrast with the ... 'slave morality' of Christianity. The point to notice is that in both Emerson and Nietzsche the Superman is a higher type ... London ... seized the suggestion of the Superman and attempted to turn it into a reality. And what did he become? Nothing less than a preposterous bully, like Larssen, the Sea-Wolf, like Burning Daylight, the miner and adventurer, like his whole gallery of brutal and brawny men – creatures blessed with nothing more than the gift of a magnificent animality, and the absence of a social code which would prevent them from inflicting this gift upon their neighbours. In short, London's Superman was little more than the infantile dream of the messenger boy or the barroom tough or the nice, respectable clerk whose muscles will never quite stand up under strain. He was the social platitude of the Old West, translated into literary epigram.[8]

This is brilliantly destructive criticism, and is reminiscent of G. K.

Chesterton's identification of the Superman with "the tall man with curling moustaches and Herculean bodily power". It is easy to sneer at "the numerous biographic projections he [London] called novels",[9] but many novels could be dismissed by the same token; and besides, the critic should stop to consider whether in *The Sea-Wolf* at least London may not have achieved his aim.

In fact *The Sea-Wolf*, written in 1903–4, when Jack London was in the first flush of his intoxicated enthusiasm for Nietzsche, was intended as an *attack* on "Nietzsche and his super-man idea"; in a letter to Mary Austin of 5 November 1915 London wrote: "I have again and again written books that failed to get across. Long years ago, at the very beginning of my writing career, I attacked Nietzsche and his super-man idea. This was in *The Sea-Wolf*. Lots of people read *The Sea-Wolf*, no one discovered that it was an attack upon the super-man philosophy."[10] *The Sea-Wolf* opens with an ironical reference to a friend of the narrator who "loafed through the winter months and read Nietzsche and Schopenhauer to rest his brain." This mocking reference not only shows that London is not in danger of taking Nietzsche over-seriously; it also confirms that the novel is to be a confrontation with the philosophy of Nietzsche and (less obviously) Schopenhauer. It is clear that the narrator, Humphrey Van Weyden, is London's *alter ego*. Wolf Larssen, for his part, *is* a would-be Nietzschean Superman, though certainly not "a perfect specimen of the Nietzschean super-man"; rather he is a caricature and an embodiment of the popular misconception. It is obvious that both author and narrator are deeply fascinated by Larssen; but it is also clear that London ultimately *is* attacking his superman-hero, for

> The true significance of *The Sea-Wolf*, to its author, was that the Nietzschean hero was doomed by his inevitable imperfections ... Wolf Larssen was no epic hero but a fatally flawed brute. No more forceful way could be found to demonstrate, as Jack did in the last chapters of his novel, that Supermanship was folly, that it was bound to end in raging futility.[11]

Wolf Larssen is in fact 'tragic man' both in the sense defined in *The Birth of Tragedy*, and in the sense that his very supermanship represents a fatal flaw in his character by which he is ultimately destroyed. Later, in defending himself against the ridiculous charge that he was propagating the Nietzschean ethic, London claimed that *The Sea-Wolf* was intended to prove that "the Superman cannot be successful in modern life".[12] In her biography of her father, *Jack London and His Times* (1939, repr. 1968), Joan London goes even further and claims that *The Sea-Wolf* is an attempt to prove that "the strength of the strong individual was intrinsically worthless, that individualism itself was an anachronism and would disappear ... when a capitalist society was replaced by a socialist".[13] However, this comment goes too far, and, like Jack London's own protestations that his novel was "an attack upon the super-man philosophy", ignores the fact that in 1904 Nietzsche's philosophy – the polar opposite to his socialism – held a deep aesthetic fascination for him. On a rational level London implicitly condemned the Superman; but on an irrational level he was captivated. That this aesthetic fascination continued for some years is shown by his subsequent novels.

Ernest Everhard, hero of *The Iron Heel* (1907), is described in Nietzschean terms in the opening chapter of the novel: "He was a natural aristocrat – and this in spite of the fact that he was in the camp of the non-aristocrats. He was a superman, a blond beast such as Nietzsche has described, and in addition he was aflame with democracy." A footnote amplifies the reference to Nietzsche for the reader's benefit: "Friedrich Nietzsche, the mad philosopher of the nineteenth century of the Christian Era, who caught wild glimpses of truth, but who before he was done, reasoned himself around the great circle of human thought and off into madness." Evidently Ernest Everhard – whose very name echoes Zarathustra's commandment "Be hard!" – is another autobiographical projection, for London's description of this "natural aristocrat" who was "in the camp of the non-aristocrats", is echoed in his letter to George P. Brett of 21 February 1912, in which he wrote: "Benjamin De Casseres ... is really and truly the American Nietzsche. I, as you know, am in the opposite intellectual camp from that of Nietzsche. Yet no man in my own camp stirs me as does Nietzsche or as does De Casseres".[14] The juxtaposition of these two passages shows that Ernest Everhard is a projection of London as Nietzschean "natural aristocrat" in the Socialist camp.

The hero of *Martin Eden* (1909) is another Ernest Everhard and another (more literary) Wolf Larssen; he is also another Jack London, for London wrote in *John Barleycorn* (1913): "I was Martin Eden." But above all Martin Eden is again a Nietzschean who shows London still fascinated by the Superman-idea. Eden himself says:

> I look only to the strong man, the man on horseback, to save the state from its own rotten futility.
>
> Nietzsche was right ... The world belongs to the strong – to the strong who are noble as well ... the world belongs to the true noblemen, to the great blond beasts, to the non-compromisers, to the 'yes-sayers'.

But Jack London's condemnation of his hero is also more explicit than it was in *The Sea-Wolf*. In the letter to Mary Austin in which he said that *The Sea-Wolf* was "an attack upon the super-man philosophy", he went on: "Later on, not mentioning my shorter efforts, I wrote another novel that was an attack upon the super-man idea, namely my *Martin Eden*. Nobody discovered that this was such an attack."[15] He obviously felt particularly strongly about *Martin Eden* being misinterpreted, for in the copy of the novel which he inscribed for Upton Sinclair, he wrote: "One of my motifs, in this book, was an attack on individualism (in the person of the hero). I must have bungled it, for not a single reviewer has discovered it".[16] He returned to the subject in one of the last notes he made before his death: "Socialist biography. *Martin Eden* and *Sea-Wolf*, attacks on Nietzschean philosophy, which even the socialists missed the point of".[17]

The attack on 'Nietzschean philosophy' is, however, obvious enough. Not only does London write of Martin Eden that "this burning, blazing man ... from outer darkness was evil"; he makes Brissenden tell Eden: "You are antediluvian, anyway, with your Nietzsche ideas. The past is past, and the man who says history repeats itself is a liar." And Martin Eden is obliged to tell himself: "you're a damn poor Nietzsche-man." Besides, Eden's fate speaks for itself: his hard-won and very doubtful success gets him nowhere. *His* apparently superhuman strength certainly conceals a tragic weakness; his life ends in self-willed death, which both clearly reflects Schopenhauer's Nirvana and prefigures Jack London's own suicide.

The hero of *Burning Daylight* (1910) starts as a rugged frontiersman-superman:

> He, who was one of the few that made the Law in that far land, who set the ethical pace, and by conduct gave the standard of right and wrong, was nevertheless above the Law. ... Deep in his life-processes ... was the urge of Life healthy and strong, unaware

> of frailty and decay, drunken with sublime complacence, ego-mad, enchanted by its own mighty optimism.

Having achieved great material success, Daylight "pre-empted for himself the position and vocation of a twentieth-century superman." But in this novel too the superman-idea is criticized and condemned, for London makes his hero return to nature from the economic jungle of the cities; in the Valley of the Moon Daylight matures to a joyous acceptance of life which may sound 'Nietzschean' in theory, but which is emphatically not seen or presented in Nietzschean terms. So once again London is seen to have travelled much of the way with (his misconception of) Nietzsche only to part company with him at the end.

For all the difference in their backgrounds, styles, personalities, and reputations, Jack London and Theodore Dreiser have much in common. Both see life in terms of a Darwinian jungle governed by the principles of natural selection, a jungle in which some men are supermen and women love them for it. There is something antediluvian not only about Martin Eden, but about most of London's he-men; and Lewis Mumford has written of Theodore Dreiser's heroes in similar terms: "they wander about, these Cowperwoods and Witlas, like dinosaurs in the ooze of industrialism".[18]

Although H. L. Mencken had no part in arousing Jack London's interest in Nietzsche, Theodore Dreiser *was* one of the writers whom Mencken tried to interest in his favourite author. Mencken sent Dreiser a copy of his *The Philosophy of Friedrich Nietzsche* shortly after it appeared. On 6 December 1909 Dreiser wrote to Mencken: "I have received *The Philosophy of Friedrich Nietzsche*, by one H. L. Mencken ... If the outline of Mr. Nietzsche's philosophy in the introduction is correct, he and myself are hale [sic] fellows well met".[19] On 16 December 1909, however, Dreiser wrote again: "I am deep in Nietzsche, but I can't say I greatly admire him. He seems to [me] Schopenhauer confused and warmed over".[20] This somewhat discouraging comment did not prevent Mencken from greeting Dreiser's *The Titan*(1914) as "a great Nietzschean document".[21] Is there any truth in this claim? To what extent *is* Dreiser's reading of Nietzsche reflected in Frank Cowperwood, hero of the trilogy *The Financier* (1912), *The Titan* (1914), and *The Stoic* (1947)?

In the case of *The Financier*, written shortly after Dreiser read

Mencken's book on Nietzsche, there is virtually no sign of any Nietzschean influence. True, Frank Cowperwood is presented right from the beginning as the outstanding individual; but it is only when he comes into his own in *The Titan* that he is seen in 'Nietzschean' terms. Dreiser's reading of Nietzsche appears in fact to be reflected in *The Titan*. In this second volume of the trilogy Frank Cowperwood is presented as an "exceptional man";[22] "individualistic and even anarchistic in character, and without a shred of true democracy",[23] he "subscribed to nothing ... and did as he pleased".[24] He "believed in himself, and himself only":[25] "*I satisfy myself* was his private law".[26] This "very lion of a man",[27] who dreamt "dreams of grandeur"[28] reflecting his own "sense of mastery [and] desire to dominate",[29] was literally a law until himself. His "emotional, egotistic, and artistic soul"[30] was offended by the inartistic animality of the common herd, for which he had nothing but contempt. Under different circumstances he "might have become a highly individualistic philosopher";[31] but as it was, this "cold", "hard", "forceful" man with his "will to existence",[32] struck those who met him as being "either devil, or prince or both",[33] as being "a kind of superman".[34] The term 'superman' probably reflects Dreiser's reading of Nietzsche, although the chapter-heading '"Man and Superman"' – given in quotation marks – is presumably borrowed from Bernard Shaw. But the word itself hardly matters. What is truly 'Nietzschean' is Dreiser's fascination with "the individual, in all his glittering variety and scope",[35] and more especially with the exceptional individual. Many of Frank Cowperwood's attitudes summarized above parallel, and indeed appear to echo, Nietzsche's attitudes. The Will-to-Power, not mentioned by name, is implicit in Cowperwood's every action. More generally, Cowperwood plays Aesthetic Man to his fellow-financiers' Theoretical Man; his religion is Art (women for him are a form of Art). Yet for all his aura of power, his egotism and amorality, he arguably remains a big-time small-town financier rather than a Zarathustran Superman, although the story of his life in *The Titan* does end in lines that have a clear Zarathustran ring: "In a mulch of darkness are bedded the roots of endless sorrows – and of endless joys. Canst thou fix thine eye on the morning? Be glad. And if in the ultimate it blind thee, be glad also. Thou hast lived." The conclusion is inescapable, however, that *The Titan*, for all its apparent Nietzschean echoes, is *not* the "magnificent Nietzschean document" which Mencken was pleased to call it, partly because the hero's life is successful only in a limited, material sense, and partly because Dreiser owes at least as much to Emerson, Whitman, and Schopenhauer, as to Nietzsche.

In *The Stoic* (1947) there are no 'Nietzschean' formulations, and indeed no signs of any indebtedness to Nietzsche. The presentation of the ageing Cowperwood is toned down considerably; as his vitality declines, Cowperwood is naturally no longer seen in superhuman terms, for he has now become 'human, all-too-human' in terms of physical frailty; he therefore reverts to his beginnings, to the type of *The Financier*. The tragic hero of *The Titan* is reduced to pathos when finally laid to rest in his neo-classical mausoleum, his worldly possessions scattered by other men's greed. In her sorrow his young mistress, Berenice, who had sought, Nietzsche-like, to make an art of life, turns to the Bhagavad-Gita for solace. The most Nietzschean figure in *The Stoic* is in fact arguably Berenice, who is a good example of the *Superwoman*, to borrow the ironical title of Arthur Symons' unpublished play of 1908. In retrospect it is clearer than ever that it is only when Frank Cowperwood is at the height of his powers that he is presented in 'Nietzschean' terms; indeed, any lingering doubt that *The Titan* reflects Dreiser's reading of Mencken's *The Philosophy of Friedrich Nietzsche*, is finally dispelled by *The Stoic*.

Theodore Dreiser sees life in terms of a struggle in which the strong crush the weak, and his trilogy shows him to be fascinated by the strong, amoral individual. In this he will have been confirmed rather than influenced by Nietzsche. When, in his essay 'Change' (in *Hey rub-a-dub-dub*, 1920) he tried for once to summarize his view of life, it was the *Umwertung der Werte* or "Dionysian will-to-renew" (A. R. Orage) which he stressed: "If I were to preach any doctrine to the world it would be love of change, or at least lack of fear of it. From the Bible I would quote: 'The older order changeth, giving place to the new,' and from Nietzsche: 'Learn to revalue your values.'" Dreiser and Nietzsche were, however, hail fellows well met chiefly because in the case of Dreiser too (as in that of Jack London) Nietzsche's superman-philosophy struck a personal chord; as W. A. Swanberg has said, Dreiser's ideology combined "A Nietzschean belief in the superman, complicated by the conviction that he was one of them", and "A fear that his supermanship was unrecognized".[36] It is a fair epitaph.

Chapter Thirteen
Zarathustran images: John Gould Fletcher

Among American poets the first important Nietzschean was John Gould Fletcher. Conrad Aiken's often-quoted comment on Fletcher's poetry – "remove the magic of phrase and sound and there is nothing left" – is in fact wide of the mark, for what is left, as Aiken should have been the first to realize, are extensive echoes of Nietzsche; moreover, much of Fletcher's imagery (cf. the "magic of phrase") appears to reflect his enthusiasm for *Thus Spake Zarathustra* – indeed, there is an interesting parallel with Isaac Rosenberg (see above) on this score.

Fletcher's captivation by Nietzsche dated from 1904–5, and was fired by his Harvard friend Lyman Willets Rogers. In his autobiography, *Life Is My Song* (1937), Fletcher wrote:

> Briefly, he [Rogers] was a Nietzschean; and the name of that philosopher, just then crossing the Atlantic in the excellent early

> translations of Thomas Common, first flashed across my mind in the year 1904–5, barely five years from Nietzsche's own physical death. Nietzsche had declared that the basis of the Christian religion was slave morality, naysaying to life; meekness, humility, poverty of spirit. He had affirmed, in the teeth of his own Christian heritage, in the teeth of his own weakness, that the basis for man's real religion – a religion worthy of humanity – should be a master morality, the affirmation of life, even the affirmation of life's endless recurrence; pride, power, audacity, abundance. That 'the weak and the ill-constituted shall perish' was the first word of Nietzsche's morality; and he condemned Christianity root and branch for being nothing but a decadent faith, inferior as such to Buddhism; which ... had become an incubus and a nightmare to the world since Luther had made it democratic. Nietzsche therefore would have done with Christianity once and for all and would put in its place the will to power and the religion of the superman. Such was Rogers' own disdainful creed; and all through 1904–5 I absorbed it in large doses, reading Nietzsche day after day at the Harvard Union, and dreaming about the superman at night![1]

Fletcher, then, like many of his contemporaries, came to Nietzsche as a result of his own growing religious doubt: "I had begun openly to doubt and even to despise the dogmas of the Christian religion."[2] In view of this and the fact that he first mentions Nietzsche in the context of Christian morality, it seems most likely that Fletcher's interest will have been caught initially (and, as we shall see, retained) by *The Antichrist*. By 1904 Thomas Common had published three volumes of Nietzsche in translation: *The Collected Works of Friedrich Nietzsche*, vol. II (*The Case of Wagner*, *Nietzsche contra Wagner*, *The Twilight of the Idols*, *The Antichrist*), 1896 (re-issued in 1899 as vol. III of the new edition); *Thus Spake Zarathustra*, 1900; and the selection *Nietzsche as Critic, Philosopher, Poet and Prophet*, 1901 (which includes selections from *The Antichrist*). In 1904/5 it therefore seems probable that Fletcher read the first or last of these volumes, although the phrase from *The Antichrist*[3] which was quoted above ("the weak and the ill-constituted shall perish") is not taken from Common's version. A little later that same winter he must also have read *Thus Spake Zarathustra*, for his nights were spent dreaming about the superman, and most of the Nietzschean echoes in his work derive from this most influential of Nietzschean texts.

The effect on Fletcher of his reading of Nietzsche day after day was twofold: Nietzsche completed Fletcher's break with the religion of his boyhood, and consolidated him in his desire to go on writing poetry:

> It was, I am convinced, partly because I could no longer find a support for belief in the organized religion of my day and time that I turned to poetry as a means of consolation [=Nietzsche's "metaphysical consolation"] ... Nietzsche was a better poet for believing that God – the God of his Evangelical Lutheran childhood – was dead, and that man had better prepare for the superman.
>
> In any case, my becoming a Nietzschean, and my break with the religion of my boyhood, made it certain that I would go on writing poetry. Men must believe in something; if they cannot believe in the accepted religion they will believe in art ... For my part, I believed, since severing my alliance with Christianity, all the more completely in art; and the part of Nietzsche's gospel that was most lost on me was his ... mockery of all artists as being mere play actors ... It seemed to me then that Nietzsche's mistrust of art sprang from a fear that art might, after all, be far more powerful than philosophy in revealing man to himself ... [4]

Fletcher here makes it clear – in mostly Nietzschean terminology – that Nietzsche gave him his basic adult philosophy and faith in the religion of Art. Nietzsche was very much his starting-point as a poet. And during the period when Fletcher lived mostly in Europe – 1908 to 1933 – Nietzsche was to be a considerable influence both on his ideas and on his style; this is true, especially, of the volumes *Irradiations* (1915), *Parables* (1925), *Branches of Adam* (1926), and *The Black Rock* (1928). Believing, as he does, in the religion of Art, there is in Fletcher more than a little of the aesthetic intensity of Pater and Nietzsche; and he expresses his aesthetic idealism in the same metaphor – with Pater's famous ideal "To burn always with this hard, gem-like flame" (in the Conclusion to *The Renaissance*), we may compare Zarathustra's commandment "Ready must thou be to burn thyself in thine own flame"[5] and Fletcher's reference to "we, the flame-seekers".[6]

Having said this, however, it must be added that at the beginning of his European period Fletcher reacted against his Harvard Nietzscheanism. In *Life Is my Song* he wrote: "It did not take me long [scil: in 1908/9] to discover that there had been serious flaws in my root-and-branch rejection of Christianity, *my half-baked Nietzscheanism*".[7] Evidently Fletcher now found his Nietzschean aestheticism too superficial and too extreme; he also discovered that he did not share "the childish and at bottom rather envious anti-feminism of Nietzsche".[8]

In Fletcher's earliest collections there is accordingly little sign of indebtedness to Nietzsche. In *Fool's Gold* (1913), the volume which he said dealt "more directly with personal experiences, and with my increasingly pessimistic and disillusioned attitude towards life in general",[9] there are a few Nietzschean echoes, e.g. of Eternal Recurrence:

Nothing alters, nothing is new:
Joy and pain and love and hate
In a vain circle 'round pursue.[10]

And the motifs of drunkenness, despair, and solitude sometimes carry Zarathustran undertones, as in these lines from 'Loneliness':

Let howl the cold sea;
Let the storm fill my soul;
Let the rudder bang free,
And the night be my goal.[11]

But in general the 'aesthetic pessimism' of the book seems to owe little to Nietzsche.

There is even less sign of Nietzsche in *Fire and Wine* (1913), although the poem "Dionysus and Apollo'[12] links with the impression made upon Fletcher by Nijinsky's dancing, which in turn points to *Irradiations* and his return to Nietzsche. In *Life Is My Song* Fletcher writes of the "pagan ecstasy" of Nijinsky's dancing in *Le Spectre de la Rose* (which so impressed Rilke) and – more especially – *L'Après-midi d'un Faune* in Paris in 1912:

> It seemed to me that in works such as these ... the conflict between Apollonian restraint and Dionysiac ecstasy that had gone on throughout the nineteenth century had been finally resolved into an art that was Apollonian only in that it expressed itself through the plastic relationship of the dancers' bodies, but was fundamentally and overwhelmingly Dionysiac in general effect.[13]

That Nijinsky's dancing made an indelible impression is clear, for

> In the manuscript of 'Irradiations' which I took back with me to London were tributes to Nijinsky, paeans to dancing, glorifications of the colour and intoxication of sheer life to put all the grim and monotonous pessimism of my early poems utterly to shame. It seemed to me that after so long a false start, I was just launched out on the yet uncharted sea of literary life, and that by accepting each moment as it came, without undue worry about the future, I was learning how to live. Nietzsche must have been right after all; only he who could learn how to dance with heart and legs would be able to triumph over the future. Man's greatest victory over adverse circumstances lay in the power to dance over tragedy. Dionysos had vanquished Apollo finally.[14]

In other words, Fletcher owed to Nietzsche both the false start of 1908–13 with the 'Apollonian' pessimism which he found increasingly inadequate, and the new start of 1915 with its 'Dionysian' affirmation. By 1915 Nietzsche had taught him how to live; but he had done so via the "pagan ecstasy" of Nijinsky's "overwhelmingly Dionysiac" dancing. Later in his autobiography Fletcher wrote of himself as the author of *Irradiations*, and commented: "It was not for nothing that I had admired Nietzsche." Unlike some of his later collections, *Irradiations, Sand and Spray* (1915) does not contain any obvious Nietzschean allusions, and at first sight even the "glorifications of the colour and intoxication of sheer life", even the "irradiant ecstasies" which gave the volume its title, seem to owe relatively little to Nietzsche. The affirmation of life –

> Sin that is splendour,
> Love that is shameless,
> Life that is glory,
> Life that is all.[15]

is Nietzschean enough in a general sense, though I doubt whether this would have been noticed if Fletcher had not drawn attention to it. But in fact it is the attitude of joyous acceptance of life, which underlies the volume and indeed made it possible, that constitutes his debt to Nietzsche here.

It is with the *Parables* of 1925 that we come to the beginning of Fletcher's most obviously and most deeply Nietzschean period. In the decade from 1915 to 1925 Nietzsche had not been a major influence. In *Goblins and Pagodas* (1916) there is virtually no sign of Nietzsche, while *The Tree of Life* (1918) is romantic, but not in the Nietzschean manner; the collection is concerned with love of woman, not with *amor fati*. By the mid-1920s, however, Fletcher had returned to Nietzsche; *Parables* shows him once more viewing his religious position in Nietzschean terms; and within three years, in *The Black Rock*, he was to have virtually identified himself with Zarathustra.

In *Life Is My Song* Fletcher stated that his *Parables* (1925) and *Branches of Adam* (1926) were both illustrations of a highly heretical point of view which

> stated that the path to 'the kingdom of heaven' lay in man himself, and not in the dogmas of the churches ... In the tidal wave of universal cynicism which swept over the world in the wake of that meaningless and senseless debauch of slaughter [in 1914–18], all that seemed left to man was the individual's private lust, his self-centred greed, his shameless and irresponsible self-seeking. By upholding man's search for God as the theme of all great poetry, in my *Parables* and my *Branches of Adam* I was committing myself to a final anachronism ... [16]

He was also committing himself to an entirely Nietzschean response to a Nietzschean analysis of contemporary man; Nietzsche's work as a whole illustrates nothing so much as "man's search for God". Fletcher returns to his basic point when he writes of Van Gogh that he "had lived a magnificently religious life, and had remained a complete skeptic",[17] and goes on: "And men like William Blake and Friedrich Nietzsche had followed a similar course. Like these, I preferred to remain a heretic, an outlaw from the churches."[18]

Parables consists of 'The Parables of Christ' and 'The Parables of Antichrist'. This opposition of Christ and Antichrist is both characteristic of the poet's religious dualism at this time, and also (in the context) directly Nietzschean. The *Parables* are in effect a kind of aphoristic prose preface to the poetry of the following collections. The influence of Nietzsche is strong: both the epigrammatic parable-form and the underlying opposition of Christ and Antichrist are Nietzschean, as are Fletcher's views on particular topics, e.g. Europe,[19] the Death of God,[20] etc. There are also a number of interesting references to Nietzsche. The first book, 'The Parables of Christ', has mottoes from the Bible, Nietzsche, and Blake; that from

Nietzsche ("What I desire above all, is wings, in order to be able to speak in parables") shows that even the title of the book derives from Nietzsche. The references in question also show that Fletcher sees a parallel between his own religious position in the mid-1920s and that of Nietzsche:

> Some fight for Antichrist in their minds but suffer Christ in their hearts: these are like Nietzsche, destroyers of themselves on the last summits of illusion ...
>
> Having seen all the heavens and the hells, I know that Hades and Dionysos are the same and that every path leads back to God ...
>
> We too have our martyrs; men who loved desperately, but who could only love with the spirit as with the flesh: ... Nietzsche ... [21]

For Fletcher at this time Nietzsche is partly object-lesson; but – increasingly – he also tends to compare his own poetic-religious struggles with those of Zarathustra (and of Blake's Orc). In 'The Parables of Antichrist', 'The New Beatitudes'[22] are essentially Zarathustran, as is the poem 'The Death of God'.[23]

Parables, then, shows Fletcher returning to his preoccupation with Nietzsche. The religious dualism which underlies and explains this preoccupation is expressed far more succinctly in the 'Preface' to his next collection, *Branches of Adam* (1926), although it is only in *The Black Rock* (1928) that Fletcher's newly-adopted Zarathustra-image is to be seen for what it is.

In the 'Preface' to *Branches of Adam* Fletcher expresses his Nietzschean point of view in these words: "The object of this poem is to show that good and evil exist in this world simultaneously; that good in fact depends upon evil and evil on good ... and that chaos and disunion, not law and order, are the principles of life which sustain all things".[24] This shows the extent of Fletcher's Nietzschean concern with relativity, which he even applies – using a metaphor from *Thus Spake Zarathustra* – to God:

> God, that is to say the ultimate unchangeable value which exists in each of us, must be either all-powerful or all good. If the root of life be power (as Nietzsche taught), then God must exert power over evil as well as good; he must in fact inflict evil ... On the other hand, if God be altogether good ... then God must refuse

> to work evil even against evil; he must permit evil to continue to the end of time. In the former case, God is a demon; in the latter, a cold abstraction ... I say there are two sides to God, the light-bearer and the darkness-bearer ... , the serpent and the eagle ... [25]

The root of life as Power, God as 'Apollo' *and* 'Dionysos', "the serpent and the eagle": this is *wholly* Nietzschean – does not Nietzsche, in the Foreword to *The Genealogy of Morals*, relate how in his first philosophical composition, written at the age of 13, he made God "the *father* of evil"? The serpent-and-eagle metaphor from *Thus Spake Zarathustra* points forward to *The Black Rock*, for it is in that collection that Nietzsche ceases to be a mere background influence and becomes a living presence in Fletcher's poetry. In *Branches of Adam* there is comparatively little in phrase and image that is specifically Nietzschean in the sense in which so much of *The Black Rock* is specifically Nietzschean. But the theme of the collection is man's search for God, and for Fletcher, Nietzsche was an archetypal God-seeker; the God whom man seeks is very close to Nietzsche's *later* Dionysos. Fletcher's Noah, in particular, has much in common with Fletcher the religious outlaw, and with Nietzsche and his Zarathustra; Noah is a summation of Fletcher's Zarathustra-self, while the imagery of Book IV of *Branches of Adam* is a summation of the Zarathustran images of the wanderer-seeker, the waters of life, and the mountain-summit reaching up into the heavens. It is no chance that when Noah smites the rock, the rock thunders back the message of Eternal Recurrence:

> Time is no more! All is destroyed, renewed,
> Passing from planet to planet and back to temporal death,
> All is recurrence ever.[26]

The Black Rock (1928) contains the poem 'From Portofino Point (In Memoriam Friedrich Nietzsche)', and also includes many other poems with Nietzschean echoes; in particular, the collection contains many poems whose imagery closely parallels the imagery of *Thus Spake Zarathustra*. Thus 'The Last Frontier'[27] has obvious Zarathustran connotations, while the phrase "Gods with white laughter ... thunderous laughter" in 'At Sunrise'[28] may well be an echo of Zarathustra's words "O my brethren, I heard a laughter which was not human laughter",[29] and an allusion to the "Olympian laughter" to which Nietzsche frequently refers. The following passage from 'Gates':

> It was noonday within my life,
> ...
> Grey calm on the glassy water,
> When I set forth to sea.
> I did not seek to wander,
> I merely drifted by,
> Towards the desolate ocean
> Which held for me my path[30]

has many parallels in Nietzsche's own poetry, and especially in the "Dionysos-dithyrambs" of 1888. Fletcher's "noonday" evidently has the Zarathustran connotation of the "great noontide" when man is in the middle of his course between animal and Superman: "*Dead are all the Gods: now do we desire the Superman to live.* – Let this be our final will at the great noontide!"[31]

One of the recurrent images common to Fletcher and Nietzsche is that of 'The Wanderer':

> For I was born to wander;
> Self-shaped and self-created,
> To move from city to city,
> Rejecting all.
> I know the vision I have hungered for
> Is held behind black mountains;
> But on the summits I shall seek it,
> I shall not fail.
>
> I shall go out alone
> Like a grey god,
> Striding on in the mist,
> Ravens flapping behind me;
> The rain will beat in my eyes
> Like blinding swords;
> The falling waters will take
> The rhythm of my laughter.[32]

The figure of the Wanderer, the image of the mountain-summits (representing his superhuman aspirations) and the abysmal waters from which they rise, the ravens, the Superman's self-creation, the tragic laughter – the whole paraphernalia of the poem is Nietzschean. The poem shows as clearly as any John Gould Fletcher's Zarathustra-self. Did not Zarathustra seek to "Link up all life in tragic dance"?[33]

The poem 'On My Own Face in the Glass' confirms that Fletcher saw himself as Zarathustra at this time:

> Poor pitiful fool! How great
> Your wish, how mean your fate,
> Slave, whipped by self-made rods,
> Destroyer and creator of all Gods,
> Dreamer of heaven, builder of the pit,
> One thing alone your doomed soul has uplit:–
> How when you scorned the law of Heaven unfurled,
> And by your secret inner wish was [sic] hurled
> Into the last, the perfect, uttermost abyss,
> Did you not whisper, 'Only here is bliss'?[34]

Were it not for the title, the reader would take this for a poem about Nietzsche's Zarathustra in one of his melancholy moments, for it is he who is the archetypal "Destroyer and creator of all Gods"; but as it is, the poem shows the remarkable extent to which Fletcher identified himself with Zarathustra some 20 years after first reading Nietzsche and becoming a self-confessed Nietzschean.

This brings us, appropriately, to the poem 'From Portofino Point (In Memoriam Friedrich Nietzsche)' which appears in 'Book IV: Cycle of Liguria' of *The Black Rock*. The context is significant: Fletcher's tribute to Nietzsche appears in the cycle which he himself considered "a sublimation of my own maturer ideas concerning life and death".[35] Yet not a few of these "ideas" are, in fact derived from *Thus Spake Zarathustra*. The line "Everything turns and returns"[36] alludes to Zarathustra's pronouncement of the mystery of Eternal Recurrence; the lines "Man has sat lonely and still/On his cold peak of despair"[37] and "beyond/There is naught but the silence of night"[38] take us straight back to Zarathustra's "One should live on mountains",[39] to his own "last summit",[40] and to his famous words "He who climbeth on the highest mountains, laugheth at all tragic plays and tragic realities".[41] The line "It is the still hour"[42] is an allusion to Zarathustra's 'Stillest Hour'. And so on. The most basic echo of Nietzsche, however, is in the phrase "True to the earth we have been",[43] which echoes Zarathustra's exhortation in his Prologue: "my brethren, remain true to the earth."

It is appropriate that John Gould Fletcher's most Nietzschean collection should end with 'Prayers to the Unknown God',[44] and more particularly with a poem, 'To the Unknown God' – written between 1916 and 1928, years when Fletcher was essentially a Nietzschean – which at once calls to mind Nietzsche's own poem of the same title. No other American or British poet is closer to Nietzsche the god-seeker than John Gould Fletcher; indeed, some of Nietzsche's own poems such as 'Seeking New Seas', 'From Lofty Mountains' and 'To the Unknown God' would not be out of place in *The Black Rock.*

Chapter Fourteen
"In his sphere, the master" (Eugene O'Neill)

The most 'Nietzschean' of modern English-language playwrights was not the ironical George Bernard Shaw, but the eclectic Eugene O'Neill. Of this there is no doubt. Asked in 1928 whether he had a literary idol, O'Neill replied: "The answer to that is in one word – Nietzsche".[1] Earlier, on 22 June 1927, O'Neill had written to his friend and fellow-Nietzschean Benjamin De Casseres:

> What you say of 'Lazarus Laughed' deeply pleases me – particularly that you found something of 'Zarathustra' in it. 'Zarathustra' ... has influenced me more than any other book I've ever read. I ran into it, through the bookshop of Benjamin Tucker, the old philosophical anarchist, when I was eighteen and I've always possessed a copy since then and every year or so I reread it and am never disappointed, which is more than I can say of almost any other book. (That is, never disappointed in it as a work of art. Spots of its teaching I no longer concede.)[2]

O'Neill, then, was introduced to the Tille translation of *Thus Spake Zarathustra* by Benjamin R. Tucker,* proprietor of The Unique Book Shop on Sixth Avenue, New York, probably in late spring 1907. Almost immediately the book became his personal catechism. Whatever his later reservations about "spots of its teaching", at 18 he swallowed it hook, line, and sinker. He made a habit of copying out passages from his copy of the book, kept it by his bedside, and took to carrying it around with him (cf. Edwin Muir). In his late 'teens he even began aping Nietzsche's style, and wrote some – weak – Nietzschean poetry. In her *Part of a Long Story* (N.Y., 1958), Agnes Boulton corroborates much of this:

> *Thus Spake Zarathustra* ... had more influence on Gene than any other single book he ever read. It was a sort of Bible to him, and he kept it by his bedside in later years as others might that sacred book. In those early years in the Village he often spoke of *Zarathustra* and other books of Friedrich Nietzsche, who at that time moved his emotion rather than his mind. He had read the magnificent prose of this great and exciting man over and over again, so that at times it seemed an expression of himself. I have some copies of Nietzsche that belonged to him, which he bought and read before I knew him, and which are copiously marked ... [3]

Though Agnes Boulton does not say which "other books of Friedrich Nietzsche" O'Neill enthused about to her, Barrett H. Clark adds that when he met O'Neill in 1926, the playwright carried "a worn copy of Nietzsche's *The Birth of Tragedy*" in his pocket,[4] and internal evidence from the plays confirms that O'Neill must have known *The Birth of Tragedy*. In 1912 O'Neill gave Maibelle Dodge an inscribed copy of *Thus Spake Zarathustra*. In *Long Day's Journey Into Night* (set in 1912), Edmund, the playwright's *alter ego*, keeps a copy of Nietzsche on his bookshelf and quotes from *Thus Spake Zarathustra* – presumably an accurate autobiographical detail. In 1914 O'Neill proceeded to read "the whole of *Also Sprach Zarathustra* in the original" with the aid of "a German grammar and a dictionary".[5] Some of the playwright's copious quotations from *Thus Spake Zarathustra* are now in the O'Neill Collection in Yale University Library.

* Editor of the periodical *Liberty*, which contains several articles on Nietzsche, including one dating from February 1908 which O'Neill presumably read.

It is therefore a matter of fact that "Eugene was enthralled by Nietzsche and remained so all his life", so that Nietzsche's philosophy became "an ineradicable part of his literary heritage".[6] O'Neill's views of tragedy, religion, ethics, etc. are essentially Nietzschean, and paraphrases and echoes of Nietzsche occur throughout his plays; most Nietzschean are the three interrelated plays, *The Fountain*, *The Great God Brown*, and *Lazarus Laughed*. It is a matter of fact, too, that O'Neill's diction and imagery in these and other plays is at times strikingly close to Nietzsche. The most fundamental parallel between the two writers, however, is that indicated by S. K. Winther: "O'Neill's tragedies are related to the philosophy of Nietzsche in … that they are an affirmation of life; they deal with life for the sake of living and not for the sake of eternity."[7]

Although he came to question a few aspects of Nietzsche's teaching, from 1907 onwards O'Neill's *Weltanschauung* was essentially Nietzschean. He accepted both Nietzsche's premisses and his conclusions. Thus his view that "man … has lost his old harmony with nature" echoes Nietzsche's view in *The Birth of Tragedy*, while the contrast, frequently made, between (wild) nature and (decadent) civilization, rugged landscape and megapolis, is no less Nietzschean.

O'Neill accepted Nietzsche's postulate that "God is dead"; it was no doubt because he had lost his own belief in God at the age of 13, and yet remained concerned above all with the relationship between man and God, that Nietzsche's work held such a powerful emotional and intellectual appeal for him. The passage in *Long Day's Journey Into Night* where Edmund says "Then Nietzsche must be right" and quotes from *Thus Spake Zarathustra* the words "God is dead: of His pity for man hath God died", is again clearly autobiographical in origin. O'Neill's position in this respect is made abundantly clear by his famous letter to the Nietzschean George Jean Nathan:

> The playwright today must dig at the roots of the sickness of today as he feels it – the death of the old God and the failure of science and materialism to give any satisfying new one for the surviving primitive religious instinct to find a meaning for life in, and to comfort its fears of death with.[8]

This is completely in line with Nietzsche's own quest for a religion for modern man, and O'Neill's answer to the problem is Zarathustra's answer: "The only way we can get religion back, is through an exultant acceptance of life".[9] General Mannon's condemnation of life-denying Puritanism in *Mourning Becomes Electra* directly echoes Zarathustra's discourse on 'The Preachers of Death'. For all his ostensible pessimism, O'Neill is essentially a Nietzschean yea-sayer; there is in him a will-to-live that is the living embodiment of Zarathustra's teachings. Of all the characters that he created, none is closer to his creator than Lazarus in *Lazarus Laughed*, most of whose attitudes come straight from *Thus Spake Zarathustra*. In *Lazarus Laughed* O'Neill starts, like Nietzsche, by sweeping away the traditional (Christian) moral values and replacing the Christian gospel of renunciation with Zarathustra's doctrine of affirmation. We shall see that this exultant affirmation of life even embraces the doctrine of Eternal Recurrence.

From the "death of God" there followed, for O'Neill as for Nietzsche, the relativity of all moral values. Among the passages which O'Neill copied from *Thus Spake Zarathustra* was this one: "Verily, I tell you: good and evil ... do not exist." It is a short step from this to Jack Townsend's Nietzschean philosophizing in *Abortion* (1914): "Some impulses are stronger than we are, have proved themselves so throughout the world's history. Is it not rather our ideals of conduct, of Right and Wrong, our ethics, which are unnatural and monstrously distorted?" The theme of the relativity of all moral values, the false values of modern so-called civilization, is recurrent in O'Neill's work; and, as in Nietzsche, it is linked with the lie-motif, modern man's falsity, his need for illusions and evasions.

Equally a consequence of the "death of God" is man's need to overcome himself and become Superman. We have seen that Wyndham Lewis criticized Nietzsche for possessing only the will-to-struggle, not the will-to-live. Nietzsche's view of tragedy, the "pessimism of strength", and of the tragic hero who gains victory through defeat, is shared by O'Neill:

> it [tragedy] is the meaning of life – and the hope. The noblest is eternally the most tragic.[10]

> A man wills his own defeat when he pursues the unattainable. But his *struggle* is his success! ... Such a figure is necessarily tragic. But to me he is not depressing; he is exhilarating![11]

O'Neill is here describing the struggle of the Superman, the man who, according to Zarathustra, has the courage to say "Was that life? Well, then – again!" It is in precisely these terms (*amor fati*) that Martha Jayson affirms life in *The First Man*: "Yes, it's been a wonderful, glorious life. I'd live it over again if I could, every single second of it – even the terrible suffering". But this is more than mere tragic or 'Dionysian' affirmation: it marks O'Neill's acceptance of the idea of Eternal Recurrence, which is well voiced by Cybel in *The Great God Brown*:

> Always spring comes again bearing life! Always again! Always, always forever again! – Spring again! – life again! summer and fall and death and peace again! ... but always, love and conception and birth and pain again – spring bearing the intolerable chalice of life again!

In *The Birth of Tragedy* tragic or higher man – the prototype of the Superman – is contrasted with theoretical man. O'Neill accepted this distinction, for Brown, in *The Great God Brown*, is "theoretical man":

> the visionless demi-god of our new materialistic myth – a Success – building his life of exterior things, inwardly empty and resourceless, an uncreative creature of superficial preordained social grooves, a by-product forced aside into slack waters by the deep main current of life – desire.[12]

O'Neill, then, not only shared Nietzsche's contempt for "theoretical man", but saw his age with Nietzsche's eyes as an age of "theoretical" culture. Underlying this veneer, for both writers, is Schopenhauer's irrational, insatiable Will.

Nietzsche's view that it is only in brief moments of Dionysian ecstasy that the "veil of Mâyâ" (the illusory phenomenal world) is torn aside to reveal true reality, "the Primordial Unity", is again shared by O'Neill. The best example of many is Edmund in *Long Day's Journey Into Night*, who experiences moments of "wild joy" when "the veil of things" seems to be torn aside and he has a sense of belonging to "Life itself": "For a second you see – and seeing the secret, are the secret. For a second there is meaning! Then the hand lets the veil fall and you are alone ... ".

Although O'Neill wrote in 1927 that he no longer conceded spots of Nietzsche's teaching in *Thus Spake Zarathustra*, he did not enlarge on this, and there is no conclusive internal evidence from his work to indicate exactly what reservations he may have come to have about Nietzsche's teachings, though it is a fair assumption that as he grew older and his own iconclasm was tempered, he came to have reservations about some aspects of Nietzsche's condemnation of Christianity. But having said this, the remarkable thing about this particular influence is that it was *not* modified to any considerable extent. Basically O'Neill became a thorough-going Nietzschean in 1907 and remained one to the end; we have his own word for it that he fell for Nietzsche in 1907, and Nietzsche's influence is seen at its strongest 20 years later, in *The Fountain* (1925), *The Great God Brown* (1926), and *Lazarus Laughed* (1928). The Nietzschean conflict between self and anti-self is experienced both by Juan in *The Fountain*, who is part 'theoretical', part 'aesthetic' man, and by Dion Anthony and Brown in *The Great God Brown*. But in the latter play the major conflict is between the life-denying spirit of Christianity and an exultant pagan acceptance of life, that is, the familiar conflict between 'Christ' and 'Dionysos'; in Brown's naturalistic creed the Christian concept of personal immortality is replaced by a form of 'eternal recurrence', and it is of this that Juan has his final mystical vision (cf. Zarathustra's vision). *The Great God Brown* in particular therefore anticipates the major themes of the most thoroughly Nietzschean of all O'Neill's plays, *Lazarus Laughed* – the very title of which echoes Zarathustra's words "Ye higher men, learn, I pray you – to laugh!" There is much of Zarathustra in Lazarus with his "wonderful exultant acceptance", and the play as a whole is constructed of Nietzschean ideas pondered for 20 years; here are the Nietzschean Superman (Lazarus), *amor fati*, eternal recurrence (O'Neill's doctrine may be one of cyclical regeneration rather than cyclical recurrence, but the debt to Nietzsche is obvious and considerable), Will-to-Power, self-overcoming, and so on, together with the Nietzschean attitude to 'life-denying' Christianity and its virtues, notably pity. Lazarus embodies the will-to-power which his wife, Miriam, denies; through self-mastery he re-creates himself as superman; his attitude is quintessentially the Nietzschean *amor fati*; his laughter, when his followers will their suicide, is "a triumphant blood-stirring call to that ultimate attainment in which all prepossession with self is lost in an ecstatic affirmation of Life." *Lazarus Laughed* is in fact the most thoroughly Nietzschean play ever written.

Partly because of some remarkable parallels between their lives,

O'Neill always felt an extraordinary sense of kinship with Nietzsche. This kinship is illustrated by Tom F. Driver's comment that "O'Neill was anti-religious only in so far as the object of the quest is concerned: he was extremely religious in terms of the quest itself"[13] for this is the case with Nietzsche himself. This sense of kinship helps to explain why O'Neill should have been so irresistibly attracted by Nietzsche's work once he had discovered it; he could not have been influenced by Nietzsche to the extent to which he was influenced without this underlying sense of kinship. As it is, Nietzsche exerted a stronger and more lasting influence over O'Neill than over any other British or American writer.

To examine all the many paraphrases, echoes and parallels that confirm the extent to which O'Neill was engrossed by Nietzsche, would require a separate book,* though it should be noted that Nietzsche is also in evidence in O'Neill's theoretical writings. For instance, in its oracular style, and in its concept of the mask, his 'Memoranda on Masks' (1932), with its 'dogma for the new masked drama', reflects his reading of *Thus Spake Zarathustra*; this is shown by the words: "One's outer life passes in a solitude haunted by the masks of others; one's inner life in a solitude hounded by the masks of oneself."

For the present, let us end by quoting from O'Neill's speech of acceptance of the Nobel Prize in 1936, when he paid Nietzsche one of the greatest and most public compliments he has ever been paid: "For me, he [Strindberg] remains, as Nietzsche remains, in his sphere, the master, still to this day more modern than any of us, still our leader." This is no less than just in that several of O'Neill's plays amount to expositions of Nietzsche's ideas. Whether this profound influence was beneficial, is another matter, for it could be argued that O'Neill failed to transmute Nietzsche's ideas into effective drama (because they *were* Nietzsche's ideas and not his own), and that Nietzsche's influence was pernicious in that it led the American playwright to concentrate on ideas at the expense of drama as such.

* The reader's attention is drawn to Esther Olson's *An Analysis of the Nietzschean Elements in the Plays of Eugene O'Neill* (University of Minnesota Dissertation, 1956), and Egil Törnqvist's article 'Nietzsche and O'Neill: A Study in Affinity' (*Orbis Litterarum*, XXIII (1968), 97–126).

Chapter Fifteen

"Formidable poetry" (Wallace Stevens)

To anyone who knows Nietzsche's work, Wallace Stevens' *Notes Toward A Supreme Fiction* will have a familiar ring: what is Nietzsche's whole work, what are his myths of the Superman, of Eternal Recurrence, and of Dionysos, if not "notes toward a supreme fiction", the most grandiose products of a mind that regards "our external world" as "a product of the fantasy"?

There is no existing evidence that Wallace Stevens was 'influenced' by Nietzsche, though he clearly knew something of Nietzsche's work – this is shown by echoes of Nietzsche in 'A Collect of Philosophy',[1] and by the poem 'Description without Place', in which he writes of Nietzsche:

> Things are as they seemed ...
>
> To Nietzsche in Basel ...

Nietzsche in Basel studied the deep pool
Of these discolorations, mastering

The moving and the moving of their forms
In the much-mottled motion of blank time.

His revery was the deepness of the pool,
The very pool, his thoughts the colored forms,

The eccentric souvenirs of human shapes,
Wrapped in their seemings, crowd on curious crowd,

In a kind of total affluence, all first,
All final, colors subjected in revery

To an innate grandiose, an innate light,
The sun of Nietzsche gildering the pool,

Yes: gildering the swarm-like manias
In perpetual revolution, round and round ...

The most explicit and interesting references to Nietzsche are found, however, in Wallace Stevens' letters, which show that he read Nietzsche as a young man and that his interest in Nietzsche was revived in 1942–5. On 12 June 1942 Stevens wrote to Henry Church: "About Nietzsche: I haven't read him since I was a young man. My interest in the hero, major man, the giant, has nothing to do with the Biermensch ... ".[2] Stevens returns to major man in a letter to José Rodriguez Feo dated 26 January 1945, where he writes: "The major men ... are neither exponents of humanism nor Nietzschean shadows";[3] this is a subject to which we shall return. In the meantime, Stevens' interest in Nietzsche seems to have been revived by Henry Church, for on 8 December 1942 he wrote to Church that he had been trying to obtain the English edition of Nietzsche (presumably meaning the Levy edition) from bookshops in London and New York; he added:

> I am very much interested in your preoccupation with Nietzsche. In his mind one does not see the world more clearly; both of us must often have felt how a strong mind distorts the world. Nietzsche's mind was a perfect example of that sort of thing. Perhaps his effect was merely the effect of the epatant. The incessant job is to get into focus, not out of focus. Nietzsche is as perfect a means of getting out of focus as a little bit too much to drink.[4]

The next letter to Henry Church in which Nietzsche is mentioned is dated 10 March 1944; after relating that he had ordered "a set of the English edition" from the London bookseller Hugh Rees, and had located a "complete set of Nietzsche" at the Hartford Theological Seminary, Stevens went on:

> I read only the first volume of Human All Too Human, and didn't think a great deal of that: not nearly what you thought. But I felt the vast difference between reading the thing in English with its total lack of voice and reading it in German with all of the sharp edges and intensity of speech that one feels in reading Nietzsche.[5]

From this it appears that some of Stevens' early reading of Nietzsche had been done in German; no details are known. The implication of this letter is that it was Nietzsche's *tone* that interested Stevens. In a letter to Leonard C. van Geyzel dated 29 January 1945 Stevens mentions that he received only five volumes of the "set of Nietzsche" that he ordered.[6]

The last reference to Nietzsche comes in a letter to Peter H. Lee dated 28 December 1954, in which Stevens wrote: "Even Nietzsche found happiness in the Swiss forests and Nietzsche was one of the inventors of the dark nights of the soul".[7] So Nietzsche has joined St. John of the Cross! Taken together these references from the *Letters* are significant in that they reveal that Wallace Stevens read Nietzsche at two different periods of his life; but they do not suggest a passionate interest.

In 'A Collect of Philosophy' (1951), Stevens several times refers to Nietzsche, whom we now know to have been in his mind at this time, and who is first quoted (with Bergson) as a modern example of "a poetic way of writing".[8] Stevens goes on: "When I say that writing in a poetic way is not the same thing as having ideas that are inherently poetic concepts, I mean that the formidable poetry of Nietzsche, for example, ultimately leaves us with the formidable poetry of Nietzsche and little more".[9] In other words, while in some ways admiring the "formidable poetry" of Nietzsche, Stevens makes it clear that in his view Plato, Bergson and Santayana are more attractive philosophers because their ideas are "inherently poetic concepts". Later in the same essay Stevens mentions that Jean Wahl wrote to him of "the idea of *Ewiges* [sic] *Wiederkehr* of Nietzsche", while in his Preface to Louis Séchan's *La Danse grecque antique*

(1930), he refers to Séchan's use of the distinction between the Apollonian and the Dionysian.[10] Now what does this tell us? That Stevens was familiar with Nietzsche's "formidable poetry" to some extent, though he seems not to have regarded Nietzsche's ideas as inherently poetic ones, and is only known to have read *Human, All Too Human* (vol. I); that he was familiar with the idea of eternal recurrence (to which he alludes in the poem 'Description without Place' already quoted); and that he was familiar with *The Birth of Tragedy*, at least at second hand. The very fact that Nietzsche is mentioned in company with Bergson and Santayana – Stevens' favourite philosophers – is perhaps as significant as his implied criticism of Nietzsche for lacking the *élan vital* of Bergson or the *douceur de vivre* which he found in Santayana. Santayana, of course, had written on Nietzsche in his *Little Essays* (N.Y., 1921),[11] and also mentioned him in his *Egotism in German Philosophy* (N.Y., 1916); the conflict between Puritanism and Nietzscheanism is central in Santayana's early work. A further passing reference to Nietzsche occurs in Stevens' essay 'Imagination as Value': "It [imagination] is the moderator of life ... Nietzsche walked in the Alps in the caresses of reality".[12]

As a 'philosophical poet', Wallace Stevens was particularly interested in 'poetic philosophers', whose ideas he would collect, sometimes from secondary sources, as *materia poetica*. Frank Doggett has pointed to Hans Vaihinger's *The Philosophy of 'As If'* (1924) as 'the best place to look [for influences]",[13] and this comment seems to be justified by the fact that Vaihinger's book contains close parallels for several terms and ideas in *Notes Toward A Supreme Fiction*, which, like many of Stevens' poems, is full of 'as-ifs'. What is significant in the present context is that these parallels are mostly contained in Vaihinger's essay on 'Nietzsche and his doctrine of conscious illusion' (or 'Nietzsche's Will to Illusion'). Hans Vaihinger was, of course, the author of *Nietzsche als Philosoph* (1902, 5th edn, 1930). That Nietzsche was linked in Stevens' mind with the problem of reality and illusion is proved by the poem 'Description without Place' already quoted, where he writes of Nietzsche's thoughts being "Wrapped in their seemings".

The *Entgötterung* of modern life, the "death of God" announced in rapturous despair by Nietzsche, is the basis of Wallace Stevens' work, for "The death of one god is the death of all",[14] and:

> To see the gods dispelled in mid-air and dissolve like clouds is one of the great human experiences. It is not as if they had gone over the horizon to disappear for a time; nor as if they had been overcome by other gods of greater power and profounder knowledge. It is simply that they came to nothing. Since we have always shared all things with them ... we shared likewise this experience of annihilation. It was their annihilation, not ours, and yet it left us feeling that in a measure we, too, had been annihilated. It left us feeling dispossessed and alone in a solitude ... What was most extraordinary is that they left no mementoes behind, no thrones, no mystic rings, no texts either of the soil or of the soul. It was as if they had never inhabited the earth. There was no crying out for their return.[15]

Though he does not link this 'great human experience' with Nietzsche, Stevens is here summarizing the experience of many of Nietzsche's readers. Now from this Nietzschean premiss, two equally Nietzschean propositions follow. God is dead, therefore (i) I am, and (ii) poetry is. Let us at this stage remember Stevens' view of poetry as expressed in *Opus Posthumous*:

> After one has abandoned a belief in God, poetry is that essence which takes its place as life's redemption ... In an age of disbelief, when the gods have come to an end, when we think of them as the aesthetic projections of a time that has passed, men turn to a fundamental glory of their own and from that create a style of bearing themselves in reality.[16]

There is no reason to suppose that this derives from Nietzsche's definition of art as "the last metaphysical activity within European nihilism" (to use Gottfried Benn's more explicit paraphrase again); but the parallel is very close and is no doubt to be explained partly by Stevens' indebtedness to Symbolism and its religion of art. How close the parallel with Nietzsche is, is shown by these lines from section V of 'The Man with the Blue Guitar':

> The earth, for us, is flat and bare.
> There are no shadows. Poetry
>
> Exceeding music must take the place
> Of empty heaven and its hymns,
>
> Ourselves in poetry must take their place[17]

Whether consciously or unconsciously, this is virtually a paraphrase of Nietzsche's definition of 'Dionysian art'. And when Stevens writes: "in an age in which disbelief is so profoundly prevalent ... poetry and painting ... are ... a compensation for what has been lost",[18] the parallel with Nietzsche's view of art as the last metaphysical activity of man is again clear; Nietzsche saw art as man's last chance of making sense of life and therefore his last source of 'metaphysical consolation'; Nietzsche, no less than Stevens, saw the connexions between poetry, religion, and philosophy. And Stevens' view of poetry as "life's redemption" exactly parallels Nietzsche's definition of art as "the redemption of suffering man".

While Nietzsche merely claimed that man "imagined" God, Stevens called the idea of God "the supreme poetic idea"; what Nietzsche called the "pathetic myth" of religion, Stevens called the "religious illusion". Stevens saw the nature of the modern godless, mythless world no less clearly than Nietzsche. Like Nietzsche he knew that "now both heaven and hell/Are one and here, O terra infidel".[19] Like Nietzsche he knew that heaven and hell are immanent states of mind and therefore 'fictions', necessary illusions; with Stevens' lines "men whose heaven is in themselves,/Or else whose hell",[20] compare Nietzsche's definition of heaven as "a condition of the heart". There being no god(s), it follows that "We seek/Nothing beyond reality. Within it,/Everything",[21] cf. Nietzsche's "non alia sed haec vita sempiterna"; and it follows, too, that good and evil are relative terms, as Nietzsche insisted: "We found,/If we found the central evil, the central good".[22]

Both Nietzsche and Stevens substitute self for the gods. There is much of Zarathustra in 'The Man with the Blue Guitar':

A substitute for all the gods:
This self, not that gold self aloft,

Alone, one's shadow magnified,
Lord of the body, looking down,

As now and called most high,
The shadow of Chocorua

In an immenser heaven, aloft,
Alone, lord of the land and lord

Of the men that live in the land, high lord.
One's self and the mountains of one's land,

Without shadows, without magnificence,
The flesh, the bone, the dirt, the stone.[23]

True, there are differences between Nietzsche's and Stevens' self-as-superman; but the solitude in which they dwell, the mountain air they breathe, is the same, and both are "a substitute for all the gods". This is why Stevens wrote that "Man must become the hero of his world",[24] which is exactly what Nietzsche meant when he said that man is something that must be overcome. For Wallace Stevens poetry is indeed man's "last metaphysical activity": it is an act of the mind, the "act of finding/What will suffice"; he who performs this act is "More than a man ... A man with the fury of a race of men,/A light at the centre of many lights,/A man at the centre of men".[25] He who makes "what will suffice" is "major man", the modern God; he is Man-the-Creator, he is the Nietzschean Superman and (Stevens' remark about the *Biermensch* does not alter this fact).

It is because he insists that the poetic creation of the world is the creation of reality that Stevens' poetry – like Nietzsche's – is centred on the self. And this self is seen in similar terms by both writers. Stevens' lines in section XII of 'The Man with the Blue Guitar':

I know that timid breathing. Where
Do I begin and end? And where,

As I strum the thing, do I pick up
That which momentously declares

Itself not to be I and yet
Must be. It could be nothing else.[26]

contain a view of the self that is also found, *inter alia*, in *The Birth of Tragedy*: "we must regard [ourselves] as the verily non-existent, that is to say, as a perpetual unfolding in time, space, and causality – what we label 'empirical reality' ".[27]

Man, superman, God – for Wallace Stevens these are all projections of self. In *Mattino Domenicale* (1954) he wrote: "If we are to think of a supreme fiction, instead of creating it, as the Greeks did, for example in the form of a mythology, we might choose to create it in the image of a man: an agreed on superman." Less central to Stevens' thought, though no less Nietzschean, is the opposition of "the highest man with nothing higher/Than himself" and "anti-master-gun" (in 'Examination of the Hero in Time of War'[28]), which closely parallels Nietzsche's distinction between 'higher' and 'lower' man, to say nothing of the later distinction between 'masters' and 'slaves' with their differing moralities. Stevens' "anti-master-man" or "subman" is corrupted by intellect (cf. Nietzsche's 'theoretical man'), which Nietzsche, like Bergson, saw as falsifying reality. These lines from 'Owl's Clover':

> We have grown weary of the man that thinks.
> He thinks and it is not true. The man below
> Imagines and it is true

exactly parallel Nietzsche's distinction between 'theoretical' (or Socratic) and 'tragic' (or aesthetic) man in *The Birth of Tragedy*, though Nietzsche would not have called his tragic-intuitive man "the man below". Common to both writers is a belief in the primacy of the (literary) creative imagination.

No parallel is more striking than that between Stevens' *Notes Toward A Supreme Fiction* and Nietzsche's view of reality. The very title of Stevens' poem recalls Nietzsche's view (quoted by Vaihinger) that "The whole perceptual and sensible world is the primordial poem of mankind"; besides, Stevens elsewhere speaks of "the universal mind, which, in the case of the poet, would be the imagination that tries to penetrate to basic images, basic emotions, and so to compose a fundamental poetry even older than the ancient world".[29] No one attached greater significance to human creativity than Nietzsche, who wrote: "our greatness lies in the supreme illusion." Section IV of Stevens' poem:

> There was a muddy centre before we breathed
> There was a myth before the myth began,
> Venerable and articulate and complete.
>
> From this the poem springs ... [30]

is based on this same image of the world as primordial poem. For both writers it is not only poetry, but reality itself, that is the "supreme fiction". Stevens' famous poem begins:

> Begin, ephebe, by perceiving the idea
> Of this invention, *this invented world*,
> The inconceivable idea of the sun.[31]

It may or may not be chance that the term "invented world" is Nietzsche's and is quoted in Vaihinger's essay. Vaihinger quotes many Nietzschean phrases that are suggestive in this context: "our concepts are inventions", "the true essence of things is an invention of the perceiving being", "our external world is a product of the fantasy", "the invented, rigid, conceptual world", "logical thinking represents the model-example of a perfect fiction", "the subject, the *ego* is only a fiction", and so on. Though the actual terminology is mostly different, the *ideas* here closely correspond to some of Wallace Stevens' basic ideas – and with Stevens it is arguably the *ideas* that count, particularly the idea that "The world is myself". Stevens writes "Life consists/Of propositions about life",[32] while Nietzsche for his part claimed that "We can only comprehend a world of our own making." Stevens sees Man as Fiction-Maker,[33] which is in line with Nietzsche's view that "The construction of metaphors is the fundamental instinct of man". With Nietzsche's "the true essence of things is an invention of the perceiving being", we may compare Stevens' line "things are as I think they are" ('The Man with the Blue Guitar';[34] the following section of the poem treats what Nietzsche calls "the illusion of identity"). Nietzsche writes that "our concepts are inventions", Stevens that "The first idea is an imagined thing".[35] Nietzsche writes "Matter ... is a subjective form", Stevens that "The world is myself." In *The Necessary Angel* (1951), Stevens wrote: "There is, in fact, a world of poetry indistinguishable from the world in which we live ... the poet ... gives to life the supreme fictions without which we are unable to conceive of it. ... few people realize that they are looking at the world of their own thoughts and the world of their own feelings",[36] and here too he is close to Nietzsche's view that the "world of Being" is an invention, a "mere fiction". Similarly the famous line in *Notes Toward A Supreme Fiction*, "The major abstraction is the idea of man", expresses an entirely Nietzschean concept, for Nietzsche himself wrote that " 'Mankind' does not even exist."

Clearly, then, Stevens' concepts of a "supreme fiction" and an "invented world" at least echo Nietzsche, and may reflect his reading of Vaihinger. With Nietzsche's view that "Man continually creates a fictional [or: an invented] world [*fingierte Welt*]", compare Stevens' line "What is there in life except one's ideas?",[37] or the final lines of 'Men Made Out of Words':

The whole race is a poet that writes down
The eccentric propositions of its fate.[38]

From this view of the "invented world" follows Nietzsche's statement that the distinction between the Thing-in-Itself and Appearances is an artificial one, and Stevens' lines voicing a similar idea:

If it should be true that reality exists
In the mind ...

Misericordia, it follows that
Real and unreal are two in one ... [39]

From the same view of the world there also follows Nietzsche's statement that "the 'unconditioned [absolute]' is a regulative fiction, to which reality must not be ascribed", which may be echoed and is certainly paralleled in Stevens' line "The fiction of an absolute – Angel".[40] It is also tempting to relate this line to Rilke's Angel, which embodies precisely this "fiction of an absolute".

In the third part ('It Must Give Pleasure') of *Notes Toward A Supreme Fiction*,[41] there is also a remarkable passage in which ideas highly reminiscent of Nietzsche's "supreme fictions" of the Superman and of Eternal Recurrence are combined in a truly Nietzschean way:

A thing final in itself and, therefore, good:
One of the vast repetitions final in
Themselves and therefore, good, the going round

And round and round, the merely going round,
Until merely going round is a final good.
...

... Perhaps
The man-hero is not the exceptional monster,
But *he that of repetition is most master*.[42]

It will surely be agreed that these parallels between Stevens and Nietzsche are striking. True, they concern only one complex of ideas, but that complex (the "Supreme Fiction") is central to the work of both writers. As I said at the beginning, there is no firm evidence to indicate that Wallace Stevens was actually influenced by Nietzsche's work in the way in which he was undoubtedly influenced by Santayana's. But these parallels, which again confirm Stevens' essential modernism, do suggest that he found in Nietzsche not only "formidable poetry", but inspiration for his own formidable poetry.

Postscript

The extent to which Nietzsche has left his mark on modern Anglo-American literature should by now be clear. From 1896 onwards, the year which saw the publication of Havelock Ellis's epoch-making study (still one of the best of its kind) and of the first English translations of his works, his ideas have affected many of the outstanding writers of the period. The critical myth[1] that Nietzsche influenced only a handful of writers, and those second-rate novelists, has been exploded. We have seen that Nietzsche was *the* formative influence on Eugene O'Neill, Herbert Read, and Edwin Muir; he was a major influence on John Davidson, W. B. Yeats, John Gould Fletcher, and Jack London, and an important influence on Wyndham Lewis, D. H. Lawrence, and J. C. Powys; he also left his mark on the work of a number of other important moderns, including Hart Crane and Wallace Stevens. And – let it be stressed again – virtually the whole of this unparalleled influence came about through universally decried translations (most translators would be happy to achieve a fraction of the effect achieved by Oscar Levy's band of devotees).

Nietzsche made his greatest impact in the years 1896–1914 when the 'transvaluation of values' chimed in with the birth-pangs of the twentieth century; give or take a year or so, there is much truth in F. Scott Fitzgerald's remark in a letter to Gertrude Stein that "the man of 1901, say, would let Nietche [sic] think for him intellectually".[2] The watershed in this history is 1914–18. After the First World War, in which he was posthumously involved, Nietzsche's reputation was never wholly freed from that of "the execrable 'Neech'" alias "the German monster Nietzsky"; his star began to wane in autumn 1914 as his English sales rose, and, although there were exceptions to the rule on both sides of the Atlantic, he was not, on the whole, to become a major influence on any writers of importance who had not already fallen under his spell by 1914.

This is not to say, however, that Nietzsche did not continue to preoccupy a number of writers who had discovered him before the war, or that some writers of the post-war generation did not enjoy an intellectual flirtation with his ideas. They did. The work of Louis MacNeice is a case in point.

MacNeice is a good example of a writer of the post-war generation who read Nietzsche, approved (to the extent of 'worshipping' him), and moved on. MacNeice later wrote of himself in his first year at Oxford in 1927:

> I was building myself an eclectic mythology ... This world was girded with odd pieces from the more heterodox Greek philosophers, especially Heraclitus and Pythagoras ... I ... was delighted ... by Nietzsche's *Birth of Tragedy*, though I knew it to be perverse and historically upside-down. It made the Greeks seem much more human because it made them as gloomy as the moderns and as orgiastic as D. H. Lawrence. 'Up Dionysus!' became my slogan ... [3]

The Birth of Tragedy was clearly partly a "side-dish" in which the classical scholar took a perverse delight because it sweetened the academic diet which he regarded as "on the whole repellent". But for a time Nietzsche exerted a real fascination. Nor did MacNeice forget *The Birth of Tragedy*; in his *The Poetry of W. B. Yeats* (1941), he wrote:

> Nietzsche in *The Birth of Tragedy* argued that Greek tragedy is a blend of what he calls the Apollonian and Dionysian elements, Apollo tending to stress distinctions, Dionysus to obliterate them. This is not the place to criticize Nietzsche's topsy-turvy application of this doctrine; what is pertinent is his recognition of Apollo – of the rational genius.[4]

Here already is an attitude to which MacNeice returned in his 'Memoranda to Horace':

> Though elderly poets profess to be inveterate
> Dionysians, despising Apollonians,
> I find it, Flaccus, more modest
> To attempt, like you, an appetitive decorum.[5]

In 1927–8, however, it was Nietzsche's 'Dionysianism' which appealed to the young poet; in his *Modern Poetry* (1968), MacNeice wrote of himself: "I [in 1928] subscribe to Nietzsche's eulogy of 'Dionysianism' in 'The Birth of Tragedy' ".[6] Nor was MacNeice's enthusiasm reserved for *The Birth of Tragedy*; that he both read more Nietzsche, and took his reading seriously, is shown by a slightly later comment:

> Apart from my instincts I was now [1928] almost without principles ... So-called altruism was merely a projection of egotism. Spinoza and Nietzsche had been right to repudiate pity. On this basis it was hard to choose – unless one's appetites came into it – between one course of action and another.[7]

This comes straight from *Human, All-Too-Human*. That MacNeice was in fact something of a Nietzschean in summer 1928 is shown both by this quotation and by the letter which he wrote to Anthony Blunt on 21 July 1928 from Molde (Norway), which contained the words "*Also Sprach Zarathustra* is exciting poetry ... *I worship Nietzsche* and I can't abide blonde beasts and husky Uebermensch [sic]".[8] The end of it all was that on 20 September 1928 his stepmother "threw Nietzsche downstairs this morning and the archdeacon said he was only fit to light candles with".[9] Clearly his son's 'Dionysianism' was too much for the Archdeacon!

If Louis MacNeice was so delighted by Nietzsche as philosopher and poet in 1927/8, what kind of impact did Nietzsche have on the poems he was writing then? In *Blind Fireworks* (1929) there is only one fairly clear echo of *The Birth of Tragedy*: the lines "Here no golden mean is, here no damned middle:/All is purity of extremes"[10] appear to echo Nietzsche's contrast of the Apolline and the Dionysian and to involve "Nietzsche's eulogy of 'Dionysianism'" to which MacNeice subscribed in 1928. The lines in the same poem:

> And the Chinese puzzles of reincarnations,
> Where one undoes and undoes the wrappings of brown paper
> But only finds flesh in innumerable gradations ... [11]

could involve an allusion to the idea of eternal recurrence; but though MacNeice enthused over *Thus Spake Zarathustra* as poetry, there is no evidence that he was struck by this particular poetic idea. What probably does reflect his reading of Nietzsche in a general way is the motif of the dead/dying gods ("A stark stranded wreck I see,/ The bones of dead divinity"; "And gods as fires go out, and all goes out")[12] which is elaborated in a poem with a 'Nietzschean' title, 'Twilight of the Gods':

> This is our twilight, the eternal phoenix dying,
> ... the dark shapes are fading,
> Down the stony vista the shadows are receding.
> The snowflakes of Nirvana drop about my being,
> ...
> Covering the blear sad eyes of the sages,
> Covering this and that and the other thing,
> Anything, everything, all things covering.[13]

In *Blind Fireworks*, then, there are no more than a few faint echoes of Nietzsche, though the young poet's attitude is clearly 'tragic' and 'aesthetic'; indeed, in view of MacNeice's 'worship' of Nietzsche in 1928, it is perhaps surprising that Nietzsche did not leave more of a mark on these rather immature poems; but this may simply mean that although MacNeice was affected both intellectually and emotionally by his reading of Nietzsche, he was not very deeply affected.

What is not surprising, and what tends to bear out this interpretation, is the fact that there is very little sign of Nietzsche in MacNeice's later poetry. There are but two allusions to Nietzsche: in *Autumn Journal* (1938) the line "Who knows if God, as Nietzsche said, is dead?",[14] and the motto prefacing Section VI (1939–40) of *The Collected Poems* ("ein Zwiespalt und Zwitter von Pflanze und von Gespenst"), which explains the title of the poem 'Plant and Phantom'[15] and the collection of that name (1941). The motto is interesting because it reflects MacNeice's enthusiastic reading of *Thus Spake Zarathustra* a decade earlier; the phrase he quotes comes from 'Zarathustra's Prologue':

> Even the wisest among you is only a disharmony and hybrid of plant and phantom. But do I bid you become phantoms or plants?
> Lo, I teach you the Superman!
> The Superman is the meaning of the earth. ...
> I conjure you, my brethren, *remain true to the earth* ...

MacNeice's motto thus involves a hidden allusion to the Superman-idea; but it remains an incidental allusion to an idea about which he was not exactly enthusiastic (compare his comment on the "husky Uebermensch"). Otherwise there are a few parallels such as:

> We need no metaphysics
> To sanction what we do.[16]

But these parallels are of no further significance. For Louis MacNeice Nietzsche was evidently only a phase through which he passed. Given that MacNeice had once 'worshipped' Nietzsche, and given the highly allusive nature of his poetry, the virtual absence of allusions to Nietzsche or to Nietzschean ideas, shows that the German philosopher had no permanent place in MacNeice's Pantheon; the young poet whose gleeful slogan was "Up Dionysus!" came to confess himself an "Apollonian".

Louis MacNeice, it will be agreed, merely enjoyed a brief flirtation with Nietzsche's ideas; he did not really fall under Nietzsche's spell in the way in which so many writers of the pre-1914 world had done. But then he belonged to a totally different age. Different ages have different prophets, and the prophet of the post-1918 world was to be Karl Marx. And all too soon Nietzsche himself was to be appropriated as the false prophet of Nazism. It was, therefore, inevitable that later poets should see Nietzsche far more coolly and objectively:

> O masterly debunker of our liberal fallacies, how
> Well you flayed each low Utilitarian

And all the arid prudence of their so-called Rational Man
That made envy the one basis of all moral acts.

All your life you stormed, like your English forerunner Blake,
Warning, Nietzsche, against that decadent tradition
Which in Luther appeared a fragrant and promising bloom:
Soon Europe swarmed with your clerical followers.

In dim Victorian days you prophesied a reaction,
And how right you've been. But tell us, O tell us, is
This tenement-gangster with a sub-machine gun in one hand

Really the Superman your jealous eyes imagined,
That dark Daemonic One whose voice would cleave the rock
open
And offer our moribund era the water of life?

(W. H. Auden[17])

Notes

Chapter One

1. Wyndham Lewis, 'Nietzsche as a Vulgarizer', in his *The Art of Being Ruled* (1926), repr. in *Wyndham Lewis. An Anthology of His Prose*, ed. E. W. F. Tomlin (1969), 116.
2. J. Willett, *Expressionism* (1971), 21.
3. Wallace Stevens, *Opus Posthumous* (1957), 158.
4. Quoted from the Penguin edition (1959), 276.
5. G. Saintsbury, *History of Criticism*, vol. III (1904), 578.
6. *Encounter*, CIX (October 1962), 32.
7. *Op. cit.*, 63; see also 23, 85, 121.
8. *The Academy*, 1 August 1896, 75.
9. Nos 2, 3, 4, April/July/August 1896.
10. 30 April 1903.
11. *Op. cit.*, 148–9.
12. XLIV (October 1910), 425–38.
13. 299–328.
14. *Fabian News*, VIII (5 July 1898), 17.
15. *Ibid.*
16. 8 July 1899, 746–8.
17. *Ibid.*, 746.
18. *Ibid.*, 747.
19. IV, no. 20 (August 1898), 115.
20. Quoted from *The Monthly Review*, XII (August 1903), 100, 104.
21. 414.
22. In the *North American Review*, CLXXIX (1904), 842–59.
23. *The Quarterly Review*, CLXXXIV (October 1896), 303–4.
24. *The Nation*, 29 March 1906, 259.
25. 12 June 1913, 590.
26. Herbert Read, *The Contrary Experience* (1963), 68.
27. *Anglia*, LIII (1929), 217; my translation.
28. *Op. cit.*, 185.
29. *Ibid.*, 197.
30. *Op cit.* 65, 73, 190 ff.

Chapter Two

1. 'A Craving for Hell', *Encounter*, CIX (October 1962), 32.
2. Arthur Ransome, *Portraits and Speculations* (1913), 135–41.
3. Walter Pater, *Greek Studies* (repr. 1928), 24–5.
4. *The Birth of Tragedy*, sections 1 and 4.
5. *Ibid.*, sect. 4.
6. *Ibid.*, sect. 8.
7. *Ibid.*
8. *Ibid.*, sect. 21.

9. 'A Study of Dionysus', in his *Greek Studies*, 25.
10. *The Birth of Tragedy*, sect. 4.
11. G. C. Monsman, *Pater's Portraits* (1967), 18.
12. *The Birth of Tragedy*, sect. 5.
13. *Ibid.*, sect. 23.
14. Monsman, *op. cit.*, 19.
15. *Ibid.*
16. *Op. cit.*, sect. 9.
17. *Ibid.*, sect. 10.
18. *Ibid.*
19. Monsman, *op. cit.*, 19.
20. *The Quarterly Review*, CLXXXIV (October 1896), 308–9.
21. See R. T. Lenaghan, 'Pattern in Walter Pater's Fiction', *Studies in Philology*, LVIII (1961), 88–9.
22. See his *Early Greek Philosophy*.
23. English translation: *The History and Antiquities of the Doric Race*, tr. Henry Tufnell and George Cornewall Lewis, 2 vols, 1830, 2nd edn 1839.
24. sect. 4.
25. Müller, *op. cit.*, vol. I, 317.
26. See *The Note-Books and Papers of Gerard Manley Hopkins* (1937), xxiii.
27. W. H. Gardner, *Gerald Manley Hopkins*, vol. I (1948), 7.
28. *Op. cit.*, 11.
29. R. Lhombreaud, *Arthur Symons. A Critical Biography* (1963), 80–1.
30. *Op. cit.*, 220.
31. Tr. Jean Marnold and Jacques Morland (Paris, 1901).
32. 30 August 1902, 220.
33. *Op. cit.*, 188.
34. sect. 21.
35. *Plays, Acting and Music*, 67.
36. In *Studies in Seven Arts* (1906).
37. *Ibid.*, 321ff.
38. *Ibid.*, 193.
39. sect. 16.
40. Arthur Symons, *William Blake* (1907), 1.
41. *Ibid.*, 7–8.
42. *Ibid.*, 2, 4, 6, 7.
43. *Ibid.*, 82, 246.
44. *Ibid.*, 1.
45. *The Romantic Movement in English Poetry*, 46.
46. Quoted by Lhombreaud, *op. cit.*, 182.
47. From *Amoris Victima*.
48. *Op. cit.*, sect. 3.
49. *Ibid.*
50. Quoted by Richard Ellmann, *The Identity of Yeats* (1954), 166.
51. In 'Ballet, Pantomime, and Poetic Drama', *Dome*, I (October 1898), 66.

Chapter Three

1. 1912, repr. 1947, 122ff.
2. *Op. cit.*, 257.
3. *Ibid.*
4. CVI (1914), 674–80; see also his review, 'The Best Book on Nietzsche', *New Statesman*, 28 June 1919, 318–20.
5. See *Letters from George Moore to Éd. Dujardin* (1929).
6. Moore, *Conversations in Ebury Street* (1924; rev. edn 1930), 179.
7. Vol. I, *Ave* (1911, repr. 1947), 49.
8. See *Ave*, 155.
9. *Salve*, 165.
10. *Ibid.*, 172.
11. *Confessions* (repr. 1928), 117.
12. *Ibid.*, 119.
13. *Ibid.*, 174.
14. *Ibid.*, 116.
15. *Ibid.*, 116, 117.
16. *Thus Spake Zarathustra*, sections XLIX, LIII.
17. *Confessions*, 118.
18. In *Human, All Too Human*, vol I, sect. 32.
19. *Op. cit.*, 8, 99, 100, 116.
20. *Vale* (1914, repr. 1947), 103.
21. *Op. cit.*, 199.
22. *Ibid.*, 7.
23. *Ibid.*, 201.
24. Hone, *op. cit.*, 142.
25. No. 2546 (12 August 1876), 219.
26. Stimulatingly discussed by William F. Blissett in *George Moore's Mind and Art*, ed. Graham Owens (1968), 53–76.
27. Hone, *op. cit.*, 257–8.
28. *Evelyn Innes* (1898), 417–18.
29. *Op. cit.*, sect. 279.
30. *Op. cit.*, 418.
31. *Op. cit.*, 122–3.
32. *Op. cit.*, 11th edn (1928), 251, 269–70.
33. *Op. cit.*, sect. 341.
34. *Op. cit.*, sect. LVII.

Chapter Four

1. H. Fineman, *John Davidson. A Study of the Relation of his Ideas to his Poetry* (1916), 32.
2. 'Frédéric Nietzsche [sic], le dernier métaphysicien', *La Revue Politique et Littéraire*, XLVIII (1891), 586–92.
3. *Ibid.*, 586.
4. Summer 1890.
5. *Sentences and Paragraphs*, 72–4, 82, 84.
6. *The Speaker*, 28 November 1891.

7. *Glasgow Herald*, 18 March 1893.
8. John Davidson, 'A Poetic Disciple of Nietzsche', *Daily Chronicle*, 23 May 1902.
9. John A. Lester, Jr, 'Nietzsche and John Davidson', *Journal of the History of Ideas*, XVIII (1957), 421.
10. Holbrook Jackson, *The Eighteen Nineties* (1913), 230–1.
11. *Op. cit.*, 66, 68.
12. "Eternal cirque of heinous agony": *The Testament of an Empire-Builder* (1902), 73.
13. From *Ballads and Songs* (1895), 22.
14. *The Testament of John Davidson* (1908), 18.
15. J. B. Townsend, *John Davidson, Poet of Armageddon* (1961), 204.
16. 7 June 1902, 572.
17. 14 June 1902, 598.
18. Townsend, *op. cit.*, 481.
19. Quoted from Grant Richards, *Author Hunting* (1934), 224.
20. In *John Davidson, A Selection of His Poems* (1961), 49.
21. In *The Complete Works of Friedrich Nietzsche*, vol. 18 (Index), (1913), xxi.

Chapter Five

1. B. Bergonzi, *The Early H. G. Wells* (1961), 11.
2. See 'Human Evolution, V – According to Nietzsche', *Natural Science*, x (June 1897), 393–4.
3. *Op. cit.*, 244.
4. Tr. Helen Zimmern (1909), xiii.
5. G. K. Chesterton, *Heretics* (1907), 84.
6. Bergonzi, *op. cit.*, 11.
7. *Ibid.*, 107.
8. *The Sleeper Wakes and Men Like Gods* (n.d.), 138.
9. See *Life and Letters of Thomas Henry Huxley*, ed. L. Huxley, vol. II (1900), 360.
10. *The Nation*, 29 March 1906, 259.
11. *Op. cit.*, 64.
12. G. K. Chesterton, *George Bernard Shaw* (1909), 203–7.
13. Vol. I; *Form and Actuality*, tr. C. F. Atkinson (1926).
14. *Ibid.*, 368, 372, 374.
15. *The Sunday Times*, 20 March 1910.
16. James G. Huneker, in his Introduction to Shaw's *Dramatic Opinions and Essays*, vol. I (N.Y., 1928), xv.

Chapter Six

1. W. B. Yeats, *Letters* (1954), 379.
2. *Ibid.*
3. *Op. cit.*, 201.
4. *The Poetry of W. B. Yeats* (1941), 56.
5. *Letters*, 403.

6. *Ibid.*, 402.
7. *Prolegomena to the Study of Greek Religion* (repr. 1961), 446.
8. M. I. Seiden, *William Butler Yeats. The Poet as Mythmaker 1865–1939* (1962), 49.
9. *Op. cit.*, 25.
10. R. Ellmann, *The Identity of Yeats* (1954), 93.
11. *Thus Spake Zarathustra*, sect. LVIII.
12. F. A. C. Wilson, *Yeat's Iconography* (1960), 180.
13. *Ibid.*
14. p. 122; the passage is from *The Genealogy of Morals.*
15. Wilson, *op. cit.*, 182.
16. *Collected Poems*, 141.
17. See *The Wanderings of Oisin* (1889), 68.
18. W. K. C. Guthrie, *Orpheus and Greek Religion* (2nd edn, 1952), 226.
19. Quoted from Charles M. Brakewell, *Source Book in Ancient Philosophy* (N.Y., 1907), 33.
20. See Simplicius on Aristotle, *De caelo.*
21. Heraclitus, quoted by Nietzsche in his *Philosophy in the Tragic Age of the Greeks.*
22. sect. 260.
23. I, sections 16, 17.
24. Common, *op. cit.*, 109.
25. *Ibid.*, 110.
26. *Ibid.*, 111.
27. *Ibid.*
28. *Ibid.*, 113.
29. *Ibid.*, 129.
30. From *The Antichrist; ibid.*, 132.
31. *Ibid.*, 134.
32. G. S. Fraser, *W. B. Yeats* (1958), 8.
33. Common, *op. cit.*, 133; Yeats underlined this passage.
34. *Ibid.*, 193.
35. *Ibid.*, 230–1.
36. *Ibid.*, 131.
37. *The Birth of Tragedy*, sect. X.
38. W. B. Yeats, *Essays and Introductions* (1961), 254.
39. *Ibid.*, 245.
40. *Ibid.*, 255.
41. *Ibid.*, 298.
42. 'Yeats and Nietzsche', *Encounter* (December 1969).
43. A. Norman Jeffares, *W. B. Yeats, Man and Poet* (1949), 152.
44. Yeats' annotation in Common, *op. cit.*, 129.
45. *Yeats's Iconography*, 177.
46. *A Vision* (1937), 128.
47. *Op. cit.*, 10.
48. In his *W. B. Yeats* (1958), 8.
49. *Op. cit.*, sect. LXXI.
50. In *The Yeats We Knew*, ed. F. McManus (1965), 86–7.

51. Jeffares, *op. cit.*, 294.
52. J. M. Hone, *W. B. Yeats 1865–1939* (1942), 400.
53. *Letters*, 773.
54. *Op. cit.*, 21.
55. Common, *op. cit.*, 124.

Chapter Seven

1. Herbert Read, *The Contrary Experience* (1963), 62.
2. Tr. Th. Common, 1909; 2nd edn, 1911.
3. *The Tenth Muse* (1957), 175; 'On First Reading Nietzsche' was originally broadcast on the BBC Third Programme in February 1947.
4. *The Contrary Experience*, 165–7.
5. *Ibid.*, 161.
6. *The Tenth Muse*, 174.
7. *The Contrary Experience*, 187.
8. See *The Nation*, 12 June 1913, 589.
9. *The Contrary Experience*, 203.
10. *Ibid.*, 70.
11. *The Tenth Muse*, 176.
12. *The Contrary Experience*, 70.
13. *Ibid.*, 69.
14. *Ibid.*, 71.
15. *Ibid.*, 125.
16. *Op. cit.*, 178.
17. sect. 188.
18. *The Tenth Muse*, 179.
19. *Ibid.*
20. 'The Law', from *The Narrow Place* (1943).
21. Willa Muir, *A Memoir* (1969), 45.
22. Edwin Muir, *An Autobiography* (1954), 126–7.
23. *Ibid.*, 140.
24. *Ibid.*, 127.
25. *Ibid.*, 116.
26. *Ibid.*, 117.
27. *Ibid.*, 144.
28. *Ibid.*, 146.
29. *Ibid.*, 170.
30. *Ibid.*, 151.
31. Herbert Read, *The Contrary Experience*, 133.
32. Muir, *An Autobiography*, 151.
33. *Op. cit.*, 68.
34. *Ibid.*, 16.
35. *Ibid.*, 233–4.
36. In *The New Age*, 20 September 1917; repr. in A. R. Orage, *Selected Essays and Critical Writings*, ed. Herbert Read and Denis Saurat (1935), 165, 166, 168.
37. See Willa Muir, *A Memoir* (1969), 13.

38. *Ibid.*, 48.
39. According to an article in *The New Age*, January 1924.
40. *An Autobiography*, 169.
41. Quoted by P. H. Butter, *Edwin Muir: Man and Poet* (1966), 40.
42. *A Memoir*, 137.
43. Muir, *An Autobiography*, 128; my italics.
44. Michael Hamburger, 'Edwin Muir', *Encounter*, xv (6 December 1960), 49.
45. *Ibid.*
46. John Holms, quoted by Muir in *An Autobiography*, 168.
47. 'Twice-Done, Once-Done', from *The Voyage* (1946).

Chapter Eight

1. *D. H. Lawrence, Artist and Rebel* (1963), 8.
2. E. T. (Jessie Chambers), *D. H. Lawrence, A Personal Record* (2nd edn, 1965), 120.
3. Tr. Helen Zimmern (1907).
4. Tr. Th. Common (1896).
5. Tr. Johanna Volz (1903).
6. Tr. W. A. Haussmann (1899).
7. Tr. John Gray (1899).
8. Tr. A. Tille (1899).
9. 'The Theatre', in *Twilight in Italy* (1916), 132.
10. In *Phoenix* (1936), 304.
11. *Ibid.*, 490–1.
12. *Op. cit.*, 156.
13. *Phoenix*, 491.
14. *Letters*, 237.
15. *Phoenix*, 469.
16. *Aaron's Rod* (1922), 310–11.
17. C. B. O'Hare, *The Role of European Literature in the Prose Works of D. H. Lawrence* (Ann Arbor, 1966), 336.
18. 1923, 178.
19. In *The Tales* (1934), 796.
20. In *Phoenix* (1936), 272.
21. From the poem 'Medlars and Sorb-Apples'.
22. *The Utopian Vision of D. H. Lawrence* (1963), 159.
23. *Op. cit.*, 65.
24. *Ibid.*, 251.
25. *Phoenix*, 461.
26. J. C. Powys, *Autobiography* (1934), 359.
27. *Ibid.*, 386.
28. *Ibid.*, 395.
29. *Ibid.*
30. *Ibid.*, 398–9.
31. H. P. Collins, *John Cowper Powys, Old Earth-Man* (1966), 44.
32. *Op. cit.*, 201, 206.
33. *Ibid.*, 199.

34. *Ibid.*, 197–8.
35. *Op. cit.*, 541.
36. *Ibid.*, 559.
37. *Ibid.*, 542.
38. *Ibid.*, 555.
39. *Ibid.*, 553, 556, 557.
40. *Obstinate Cymric* (1947), 90.
41. *Autobiography*, 565.
42. *The Pleasures of Literature*, 555.
43. *Autobiography*, 432.
44. *Visions and Revisions* (1915, repr. 1955), 149.
45. *Ibid.*, 209.

Chapter Nine

1. *Letters from Edward Thomas to Gordon Bottomley*, ed. R. George Thomas (1968), 152.
2. *Ibid.*, 154.
3. II, sect. 24.
4. Edward Thomas, *Richard Jefferies* (1909), 207.
5. p. 140.
6. Quoted by Joy Grant, *Harold Monro and the Poetry Bookshop* (1967), 269.
7. *Poetry and Drama*, 1, June 1913, 128.
8. *Ibid.*, September 1913, 262.
9. *Liverpool Daily Courier*, 22 January 1909.
10. *Ibid.*, 23 July 1909.
11. L. Abercrombie, *Romanticism* (1926), 149.
12. *Ibid.*, 122.
13. *Ibid.*, 154.
14. *Ibid.*, 145, 154.
15. *Ibid.*, 122.
16. *The Poems of Lascelles Abercrombie* (1930), 357.
17. From *Interludes*; see *The Poems*, 21–37, 57–73.
18. From *Twelve Idyls*; see *The Poems*, 340–60.
19. *Ibid.*, 349.
20. *Ibid.*, 351.
21. *Ibid.*, 352.
22. *Romanticism*, 149.
23. *The Poems*, 352ff.
24. *Ibid.*, 355.
25. *Ibid.*
26. *Op. cit.*, 72.
27. The Earl of Lytton, *Wilfred Scawen Blunt* (1961), 15.
28. Robert Speaight, *The Life of Eric Gill* (1966), 32.
29. Stephen Graham, *Part of the Wonderful Scene. An Autobiography* (1964), 69.
30. *Ibid.*, 70.
31. *Op. cit.*, 137.

32. *Ibid.*, 156.
33. *Op. cit.*, 420.
34. *Ibid.*
35. E.g. in his *Recent Tendencies in Ethics* (1904), 18–26, 47ff.
36. C. H. Sorley, *Letters from Germany and from the Army* (1916), 115.
37. *Ibid.*, 119.
38. *The Letters of Rupert Brooke*, ed. Geoffrey Keynes (1968), 63–4.
39. Quoted by Christopher Hassall, *Rupert Brooke* (1964), 244.
40. *The Letters of Rupert Brooke*, 363.
41. *Ibid.*, 300.
42. Quoted by Hassall, *op. cit.*, 253.
43. *The Collected Works of Isaac Rosenberg*, ed. G. Bottomley and D. Harding (1937), 265–6.
44. *Ibid.*, 251.
45. *Ibid.*, ix.
46. *Ibid.*, 6.
47. *Thus Spake Zarathustra*, sect. VII.
48. *The Collected Works of Isaac Rosenberg*, 8.
49. *Ibid.*, 9–10.
50. *Ibid.*, 11.
51. *Ibid.*, 17.
52. *Ibid.*, 20.
53. *Ibid.*, 61.
54. *Ibid.*, 41.
55. *Ibid.*, 51.
56. Sect. LXVI.
57. *The Collected Works*, 63.
58. *Ibid.*, 62.
59. *Ibid.*, 100.
60. *Ibid.*, 185.
61. *Ibid.*, 118.

Chapter Ten

1. See *Blast*, no. 2, 10.
2. *Ibid.*
3. Also in *Blast*, no. 1, q.v.
4. The essay also appeared in German: 'Nietzsche als Popularphilosoph', *Der Querschnitt*, VII (1927), 90–6.
5. From *The Art of Being Ruled*; repr. in *Wyndham Lewis. An Anthology of His Prose*, ed. E. W. F. Tomlin (1969), 117.
6. *Ibid.*, 116.
7. *Ibid.*, 121.
8. In *Herbert Read, A Memorial Symposium*, ed. Robin Skelton (1970), 22.
9. A. R. Orage, *Friedrich Nietzsche: The Dionysian Spirit of the Age* (1906), 11–14.
10. Wallace Martin, *The New Age under Orage* (1967), 18.

11. Herbert Read, *The Contrary Experience*, 167.
12. Quoted by M. A. Mügge, *Nietzsche, His Life and Work* (4th edn, 1914), 351.
13. In *Speculations* (1924, repr. 1936), 113–40.
14. Alun R. Jones, *The Life and Opinions of T. E. Hulme* (1960), 41.
15. Quoted from Jones, *op. cit.*, 190.
16. *Speculations*, 217.
17. Published in Michael Roberts, *T. E. Hulme* (1938), 300.
18. p. 82.
19. LXIX (March 1917), 321–31.
20. *Op. cit.*, 330.
21. In *Notes & Queries* (October 1964), 386–7.
22. pp. 426–7.
23. Richard Ellmann, *James Joyce* (N.Y., 1959), 147.
24. Quoted from Florence Emily Hardy, *The Life of Thomas Hardy* (1962), 364.
25. Quoted from Oscar Levy's letter on 'Thomas Hardy and Friedrich Nietzsche', *The Outlook*, LXI (18 February 1928), 217.
26. From Part I of *Thus Spake Zarathustra.*
27. *Loc. cit.*, 218.
28. See P. Bridgwater, 'German Poetry and the First World War', *European Studies Review*, I no. 2 (1971), 147–86.
29. *Op. cit.*, 15
30. *Op. cit.*, 76.
31. *Blast*, no. 2 (July 1915), 10.

Chapter Eleven

1. C. N. Stavrou, *Whitman and Nietzsche* (1964), 2.
2. 5 December 1896, 300–8; the article was reprinted from *The Quarterly Review*, where it appeared in October 1896.
3. See *The Dial*, XXII (16 June 1897), 359.
4. *Athenaeum*, 7 March 1903, 298.
5. In *Current Literature*, XLIV (March 1908), 295.
6. *Ibid.*, XLIX (July 1910), 15.
7. *Ibid.*
8. *Op. cit.*, 147.
9. Ludwig Lewisohn, *Expression in America* (N.Y., 1932), 350.
10. *Steeplejack* (N.Y., 1920), v.
11. *Ibid.*, 224.
12. In *The Smart Set* (July 1915).
13. See *The Intimate Letters of James Gibbons Huneker* (1936), 36.
14. *Op. cit.*, 109.
15. *Ibid.*
16. *Ibid.*, 115.
17. *Ibid.*, 118.
18. *Ibid.*, 120.
19. *Ibid.*
20. *Op. cit.*, 268.

21. *The Influence of Friedrich Nietzsche on American Literature* (1963), 82, 83.
22. Brom Weber, *Hart Crane* (1948), 19.
23. See *The Smart Set*, November 1909; February 1910; March 1912; March 1915, etc.
24. In a letter to Edward Stone, and quoted in his *Henry Louis Mencken's Debt to Friedrich Nietzsche* (1937), iv.
25. In Isaac Goldberg, *The Man Mencken* (N.Y., 1925), 11.
26. See W. H. Nolte, *H. L. Mencken, Literary Critic* (Middletown, 1966), 34.
27. *Op. cit.*, 18.
28. See *Little Review Anthology* (1957), 18–21.
29. Quoted by Brom Weber, *op. cit.*, 21.
30. In *The Letters of Hart Crane 1916–1932*, ed. Brom Weber (1965), 66–7.
31. *Ibid.*, 99.
32. Weber, *Hart Crane*, 18–19.
33. *The Letters of Hart Crane*, 358.
34. *The Complete Poems and Selected Letters and Prose of Hart Crane*, ed. Brom Weber (N.Y., 1966), 138.
35. *Ibid.*, 27–33.
36. *Hart Crane's Sanskrit Charge: A Study of The Bridge* (Ithaca, 1960), 14.
37. See 'General Aims and Theories', in *The Complete Poems . . .*, 217–23.
38. *Ibid.*, 219ff.
39. *Ibid.*, 66.
40. *Op. cit.*, 13.
41. *Ibid.*, 23; from *Thus Spake Zarathustra*, sect. LVI.
42. *King Coffin*, 48–9; cf. *Beyond Good and Evil*, sect. 265.
43. *King Coffin*, 197.
44. *Op. cit.*, 227.
45. See S. S. Alberts, *A Bibliography of the Works of Robinson Jeffers* (N.Y., 1933), 37–8.
46. *Op. cit.*, 400.
47. *Ibid.*, 404.
48. *Ibid.*, 402.
49. *Ibid.*, 407.
50. *Ibid.*, 412.
51. *Ibid.*, 403.
52. *The Loyalties of Robinson Jeffers* (1956), 45.
53. *Op. cit.*, 270.
54. *The Strenuous Life*, 1.

Chapter Twelve

1. Quoted by Joan London, *Jack London and His Times* (1968), 183.
2. *Ibid.*, 186.
3. *Ibid.*, 209.

4. *Ibid.*
5. Richard O'Connor, *Jack London: A Biography* (1965), 121.
6. In Georgia Bamford, *The Mystery of Jack London* (Oakland, Cal., n.d.), 210.
7. LeRoy C. Kauffmann, *op. cit.*, 81.
8. *The Golden Day: A Study in American Experience and Culture* (1927), 248–9.
9. *Ibid.*, 240.
10. *Letters from Jack London*, ed. K. Hendricks and I. Shepard (1966), 483.
11. O'Connor, *op. cit.*, 194.
12. Quoted by O'Connor, *ibid.*
13. Joan London, *op, cit.*, 253.
14. *Letters from Jack London*, 361.
15. *Ibid.*, 463.
16. Quoted by Joan London, *op. cit.*, 329–30.
17. *Ibid.*, 356–7.
18. *The Golden Day*, 250.
19. *Letters of Theodore Dreiser*, ed. R. H. Elias, vol. I (Philadelphia, 1959), 97.
20. *Ibid.*, 98.
21. *Letters of H. L. Mencken* (1961), 45.
22. *Op. cit.*, 15.
23. *Ibid.*, 27.
24. *Ibid.*, 8.
25. *Ibid.*, 32.
26. *Ibid.*, 9.
27. *Ibid.*, 437.
28. *Ibid.*, 59.
29. *Ibid.*, 107.
30. *Ibid.*, 59.
31. *Ibid.*, 11.
32. *Ibid.*, 393.
33. *Ibid.*, 165.
34. *Ibid.*, 468.
35. *Ibid.*, 551.
36. *Dreiser* (N.Y., 1965), 416.

Chapter Thirteen

1. *Op. cit.*, 20.
2. *Ibid.*
3. Sect. 2.
4. *Life Is My Song*, 21.
5. *Thus Spake Zarathustra*, sect. XVII.
6. *The Black Rock*, 19.
7. *Op. cit.*, 35; my italics.
8. *Ibid.*, 45.
9. *Ibid.*, 53.

10. *Fool's Gold* (1913), 19.
11. *Ibid.*, 23.
12. *Op. cit.*, 46.
13. *Op. cit.*, 65.
14. *Ibid.*, 68–9.
15. *Op. cit.*, 37.
16. *Op. cit.*, 296.
17. *Ibid.*, 307.
18. *Ibid.*
19. *Op. cit.*, 32
20. *Ibid.*, 118–19.
21. *Parables*, 65, 69, 123.
22. *Ibid.*, 75–6.
23. *Ibid.*, 118–19.
24. *Op. cit.*, 9.
25. *Ibid.*
26. *Op. cit.*, 79.
27. *Op. cit.*, 18.
28. *Ibid.*, 20, 21.
29. *Thus Spake Zarathustra*, sect. XLVI.
30. *The Black Rock*, 27–8.
31. *Thus Spake Zarathustra*, sect. XXII.
32. *The Black Rock*, 35: second and third stanzas of 'The Wanderer'.
33. *Ibid.*, 78.
34. *Ibid.*, 86–7.
35. *Life Is My Song*, 315.
36. *The Black Rock*, 160.
37. *Ibid.*
38. *Ibid.*, 161.
39. *Thus Spake Zarathustra*, sect. LIII.
40. *Ibid.*, sect. XLV.
41. *Ibid.*, sect. VII.
42. *The Black Rock*, 163.
43. *Ibid.*, 160.
44. *Ibid.*, 165–88.

Chapter Fourteen

1. See 'A Eugene O'Neill Miscellany', *New York Sun*, 1 December 1928.
2. Quoted from Egil Törnqvist, 'Nietzsche and O'Neill: A Study in Affinity', *Orbis Litterarum*, XXIII (1968), 97–8. The original letter is in the O'Neill Collection of the Baker Memorial Library, Dartmouth College (U.S.A.).
3. *Op. cit.*, 61.
4. See Barrett H. Clark, *Eugene O'Neill: The Man and His Plays* (N.Y., 1947), 4–5.
5. *Ibid.*, 25.
6. A. and B. Gelb, *O'Neill* (N.Y., 1962), 121, 110.
7. *Eugene O'Neill. A Critical Study*, 2nd edn (N.Y., 1961), 22.

8. In *American Mercury*, January 1929, 119.
9. Gelb, *op. cit.*, 520.
10. In *New York Tribune*, 13 February 1921.
11. In *American Magazine*, November 1922, 120.
12. In *New York Evening Post*, 13 February 1926.
13. In *O'Neill*, ed. J. Gassner (Englewood Cliffs, 1964), 119.

Chapter Fifteen

1. In *Opus Posthumous* (N.Y., 1957).
2. *Letters of Wallace Stevens*, ed. Holly Stevens (1957), 409.
3. *Ibid.*, 485.
4. *Ibid.*, 431–2.
5. *Ibid.*, 462.
6. *Ibid.*, 486.
7. *Ibid.*, 863.
8. *Opus Posthumous*, 184.
9. *Ibid.*, 187.
10. *Ibid.*, 282.
11. pp. 212–14.
12. *The Necessary Angel* (1960), 150; cf. also *Collected Poems* (1955), 216, where Nietzsche may have provided the model for "The pensive man ... He sees that eagle float/For which the intricate Alps are a single nest."
13. See *The Act of the Mind*, ed. R. H. Pearce and J. Hillis Miller (Baltimore, 1965), 20.
14. *Collected Poems*, 381.
15. *Opus Posthumous*, 206–7.
16. *Ibid.*, 158.
17. *Collected Poems*, 167.
18. *The Necessary Angel*, 171.
19. *Collected Poems*, 315.
20. *Ibid.*, 186.
21. *Ibid.*, 471.
22. *Ibid.*, 251.
23. *Ibid.*, 176.
24. *Ibid.*, 261.
25. *Ibid.*, 239–40.
26. *Ibid.*, 171.
27. *Op. cit.*, sect. 4.
28. *Collected Poems*, 273–81.
29. *The Necessary Angel*, 145.
30. *Collected Poems*, 383.
31. *Ibid.*, 380; my italics.
32. *Selected Poems*, 98.
33. For his views on metaphor as fictive agent, see *The Necessary Angel*, 77.
34. sect. XXVIII.
35. 'Notes Toward A Supreme Fiction', sect. VIII.

36. *Op. cit.*, 31, 66.
37. 'The Man with the Blue Guitar', XX.
38. *Collected Poems*, 356.
39. 'An Ordinary Evening in New Haven', XXVIII: *ibid.*, 485.
40. In 'Notes Toward A Supreme Fiction': *ibid.*, 404.
41. sect. IX.
42. *Collected Poems*, 405–6; my italics.

Postscript

1. Still being perpetuated, see John McCormick, *American Literature 1919–1932* (1971), 206.
2. In J. M. Brinnin, *The Third Rose. Gertrude Stein and Her World* (Gloucester, Mass., 1968), 241.
3. Louis MacNeice, *The Strings Are False* (1965), 110.
4. *Op. cit.*, 87.
5. *The Burning Perch* (1963), 50–1.
6. *Op. cit.*, 67.
7. *The Strings Are False*, 115.
8. Quoted by William T. McKinnon, *Apollo's Blended Dream. A Study of the Poetry of Louis MacNeice* (1971), 20; my italics.
9. *The Strings Are False*, 269.
10. From the poem 'Coal and Fire', *Blind Fireworks*, 47.
11. *Ibid.*, 46.
12. *Ibid.*, 13, 38.
13. *Ibid.*, 77–80.
14. *The Collected Poems* (1966), 137.
15. *Ibid.*, 159.
16. *Ibid.*, 162.
17. W. H. Auden, 'Nietzsche', in his *New Year Letter* (1941), 96.

Bibliography

Places of publication are given only for books published outside the United Kingdom.

Abercrombie, Lascelles
'The Thought-Shaker', 'Nietzsche Again', and 'Nietzsche's Work', *Liverpool Daily Courier*, 20 November 1908, 22 January 1909, and 23 July 1909.
Romanticism (Martin Secker, 1926).
Poems (Oxford University Press, 1930).

Aiken, Conrad
Earth Triumphant and Other Tales in Verse (Macmillan Co. New York, 1914).
King Coffin (J. M. Dent & Sons, 1935).

Anon.
'A Prophet of Nietzsche' (review of John Davidson, *The Testament of an Empire-Builder*), *The Academy and Literature*, LXII (7 June 1902).

Anon.
'Barker, Nietzsche and Shaw', *The Sunday Times*, 20 and 27 March 1910.

Anon.
'The Ideals of Anarchy – Friedrich Nietzsche', *The Quarterly Review*, CLXXXIV (October 1896); repr. in *Littell's Living Age*, 5 December 1896.

Archer, William
Fighting a Philosophy [A Study of the Influence of Nietzsche on German Policy], (University of London Press [1915]).

Auden, W. H.
'Nietzsche', in his *New Year Letter* (Faber & Faber, 1941).

Badcock, J.
Slaves to Duty (W. Reeves, 1893).

Bamford, Georgia
The Mystery of Jack London (private publication, Oakland, Cal., 1931).

Barbellion, W. N. P. [Pseudonym of Cummings, Bruce Frederick]
The Journal of a Disappointed Man (Chatto & Windus, 1919).

Barry, W. F.
Heralds of Revolt (Hodder & Stoughton, 1904).

Baumgarten, Eduard
Das Vorbild Emersons im Werk und Leben Nietzsches (Heidelberg, 1957).

Beecham, Thomas
[letter] *Manchester Guardian*, 9 October 1914.

Bell, Clive
Civilization (Chatto & Windus, 1928).

Bergonzi, B.
The Early H. G. Wells (Manchester University Press, 1961).

Bland, Hubert
'Frederick Nietzsche: a Child in a China-Shop', *Fabian News*, VIII no. 5 (July 1898).

Bottome, P.
The Master Hope (Hurst & Blackett, 1904).

Bridgwater, Patrick
'The Strong Enchanter: W. B. Yeats and Nietzsche', in *Affinities. Essays in German and English Literature*, ed. R. W. Last (Oswald Wolff, 1971).

Butter, P. H.
Edwin Muir: Man and Poet (Oliver & Boyd, 1966).

Butterfield, R. W.
The Broken Arc: A Study of Hart Crane (Oliver & Boyd, 1969).

Chesterton, G. K.
Heretics (John Lane, London and New York, 1905).
Orthodoxy (John Lane, London and New York, 1909).
George Bernard Shaw (John Lane, London and New York, 1910 [1909]).

Clarke, Austin
Essay on Yeats in *The Yeats We Knew*, ed. F. MacManus (The Mercier Press, Cork, 1965).

Collins, H. P.
John Cowper Powys, Old Earth-Man (Barrie & Rockliff, 1966).

Common, Thomas (ed.)
Nietzsche as Critic, Philosopher, Poet and Prophet. Choice Selections from his Works (Grant Richards, 1901).

Crane, Hart
'The Case Against Nietzsche', *The Pagan*, April/May 1918.
The Letters of Hart Crane 1916–1932, ed. Brom Weber (University of California Press, Berkeley and Los Angeles, 1965).
The Complete Poems and Selected Letters and Prose of Hart Crane, ed. B. Weber (Anchor Books, New York, 1966).

[Davidson, John]
'The New Sophist', *The Speaker*, 28 November 1891.

Davidson, John
'Frederick Nietsche [sic]', *Glasgow Herald*, 18 March 1893.
Sentences and Paragraphs (Lawrence & Bullen, 1893).
'Tête-à-tête', *The Speaker*, 17 June 1899.
'A Poetic Disciple of Nietzsche', *Daily Chronicle*, 22 May 1902.
'Letter on Nietzsche', *The Academy and Literature*, LXII (June 1902).
The Testament of John Davidson (Grant Richards, 1908).

De Casseres, Benjamin
Forty Immortals (J. Lawren, New York, n.d.)
The Superman in America (University of Washington Bookstore, Seattle, 1929).
I Dance with Nietzsche (Private publication, New York, [1936]).

Dell, Floyd
Moon-Calf, A Novel (A. A. Knopf, New York, 1920).

Dembo, L. S.
Hart Crane's Sanskrit Charge: A Study of The Bridge (Cornell University Press, Ithaca, N.Y., 1960).

Douglas, Norman
How about Europe? (Chatto & Windus, 1930; American edn: *Goodbye to Western Culture*, Harper Bros., New York, 1930).

Dreiser, Theodore
The Titan (John Lane Co., New York, 1914; Constable & Co., 1928).
Hey rub-a-dub-dub (Boni & Liveright, New York, 1920; Constable & Co., 1931).
Letters of Theodore Dreiser, ed. R. H. Elias, 3 vols (University of Philadelphia Press, Philadelphia, 1959).

'E. T.' [Chambers, Jessie]
D. H. Lawrence. A Personal Record (2nd edn, Cass, 1965).

Eliot, T. S.
Review of A. Wolf, *The Philosophy of Nietzsche* (London, 1915), *International Journal of Ethics*, April 1916.

Ellis, Havelock
'Friedrich Nietzsche', *The Savoy*, nos 2, 3 and 4, April/July/August 1896.
'Nietzsche', in his *Affirmations* (Walter Scott Ltd, 1898; repr. in his *Selected Essays*, Dent, 1936).
'The Genius of Nietzsche', in his *Views and Reviews, First Series: 1884–1919* (Desmond Harmsworth, 1932).

Ellis, Mrs Havelock [Edith]
'Nietzsche and Morals', *Forum*, XLIV (October 1910).
Three Modern Seers (Stanley Paul & Co., 1910).

Ellmann, R.
The Identity of Yeats (Macmillan, 1954).

Fineman, H.
John Davidson. A Study of the Relation of his Ideas to his Poetry (Dissertation, University of Philadelphia, 1916).

Fletcher, John Gould
Irradiations, Sand and Spray (Houghton Mifflin Co., Boston and New York, and Constable & Co., 1915).
Parables (Kegan Paul & Co., 1925).
Branches of Adam (Faber & Gwyer, 1926).
The Black Rock (Faber & Gwyer, 1928).
Preludes and Symphonies (Macmillan Co., New York 1930).
Life Is My Song (Farrar & Rinehart, New York and Toronto, 1937).

Foner, Philip S.
Jack London: American Rebel (Seven Seas, Berlin, 1958).

Foster, George Burman
'The Prophet of a New Culture', *The Little Review* [ed. Margaret C. Anderson], no. 1 (March 1914).

Garnett, Edward
'Views and Reviews – Nietzsche', *Outlook*, 8 July 1899.
Friday Nights (Jonathan Cape, 1929).

Gassner, J. (ed.)
O'Neill (Prentice Hall, Englewood Cliffs, 1964).

Gill, Eric
The Necessity of Belief (Faber & Faber, 1936).

Goodheart, Eugene
The Utopian Vision of D. H. Lawrence (University of Chicago Press, Chicago and London, 1963).

Grant, Joy
Harold Monro and the Poetry Bookshop (Routledge & Kegan Paul, 1967).

Graves, Robert
'Nietzsche', in his *The Crowning Privilege* (Cassell & Co., 1955).

Gregory, H. and Zaturenska, M.
A History of American Poetry 1900–1940 (Harcourt, Brace & Co., New York, [1947]).

Groshong, James
G. B. Shaw and Germany: the Major Aspects (Dissertation, University of Stanford, 1957).

Hamburger, Michael
'A Craving for Hell', *Encounter*, October 1962.

Hardy, Thomas
[letter] *Daily Mail*, 27 September 1914.

[letter] *Manchester Guardian*, 7 October 1914.
[letter] *Manchester Guardian*, 13 October 1914.

Hardy, Florence Emily
The Life of Thomas Hardy (Macmillan & Co., London; St Martin's Press, New York, 1962).

Hassall, Christopher
Rupert Brooke, A Biography (Faber & Faber, 1964).

Hecht, Ben
Erik Dorn (G. P. Putnam's Sons, New York and London, 1921).
Humpty Dumpty (Boni & Liveright, New York, 1924).

Heller, Erich
'Yeats and Nietzsche', *Encounter*, December 1969.

Hone, Joseph M.
'Nietzsche and Culture', *Contemporary Review*, CVI (1914).
The Life of George Moore (Victor Gollancz, 1936).
W. B. Yeats 1865–1939 (Macmillan & Co., 1942).

Hubbard, Stanley
Nietzsche und Emerson (Verlag f. Recht u. Gesellschaft, Basle, 1958).

Hulme, T. E.
'German Chronicle', *Poetry and Drama*, June 1914.
Speculations, ed. H. Read *et al.* (Kegan Paul & Co., 1924, repr. 1936).

Huneker, James G.
Overtones: A Book of Temperaments (T. Werner Laurie Ltd, New York and London, 1904).
Egoists: A Book of Supermen (T. Werner Laurie Ltd, 1909).

Jackson, Holbrook
All Manner of Folk: Interpretations and Studies (Grant Richards, 1912).
The Eighteen Nineties (Grant Richards, 1913).

Jeffares, A. Norman
W. B. Yeats, Man and Poet (Routledge & Kegan Paul, 1949).

Jeffers, Robinson
The Selected Poetry of Robinson Jeffers (Random House, New York, [1938]).

Kauffmann, LeRoy C.
The Influence of Friedrich Nietzsche on American Literature (Dissertation, University of Pennsylvania, 1963).

Kennedy, J. M.
The Quintessence of Nietzsche (T. Werner Laurie Ltd, 1909; rev. edn 1914 entitled *Nietzsche*).
Nietzsche. His Maxims of Life (T. N. Foulis, [1913]).

Keynes, Geoffrey (ed.)
The Letters of Rupert Brooke (Faber & Faber, 1968).

Klenze, C. von
'A Philosopher Decadent', *The Dial*, 16 June 1897.

Knight, G. Wilson
Christ and Nietzsche (Staples Press, 1948).

Lawrence, D. H.
The Trespasser (Duckworth & Co., 1912).
Twilight in Italy (Duckworth & Co., 1916).
Aaron's Rod (Martin Secker, 1922).
Reflections on the Death of a Porcupine (Centaur Press, Philadelphia, 1925; Martin Secker, 1934).
The Plumed Serpent (Martin Secker, 1926).
Phoenix (The Viking Press, New York, 1936).
The Collected Letters of D. H. Lawrence, ed. Harry T. Moore, 2 vols (Heinemann, 1962).

Lee, Vernon
'Nietzsche and the "Will to Power"', *North American Review*, December 1904.
Gospels of Anarchy and other Contemporary Studies (T. Fisher Unwin, London and Leipzig, 1908).

Lees, F. N.
'T. S. Eliot and Nietzsche', *Notes & Queries*, October 1964.

Lenaghan, R. T.
'Pattern in Walter Pater's Fiction', *Studies in Philology*, LVIII (1961).

Lester, John A. (Jr)
'Nietzsche and John Davidson', *Journal of the History of Ideas*, XVIII (1957).
Journey Through Despair, 1880–1914 (Princeton University Press, Princeton, N.J., 1968).

Levy, Oscar (ed.)
The Complete Works of Friedrich Nietzsche, 18 vols (T. N. Foulis, 1909–13).

Levy, Oscar
'Thomas Hardy and Friedrich Nietzsche', *The Outlook*, LXI (18 February 1928).

Lewis, Wyndham
'Editorial', *Blast*, no. 2, July 1915.
The Art of Being Ruled (Chatto & Windus, 1926).
Paleface (Chatto & Windus, 1929).
Men Without Art (Cassell & Co., 1934).
'Nietzsche as a Vulgarizer', repr. in *Wyndham Lewis, An Anthology of his Prose*, ed. E. W. F. Tomlin (Methuen & Co., 1969).
'Nietzsche als Popularphilosoph', *Der Querschnitt*, VII (1927).

London, Jack
The Sea-Wolf (Macmillan Co., New York, and Macmillan & Co., 1904).
The Iron Heel (Macmillan Co., New York, 1907; Everett & Co., 1908).
Martin Eden (Macmillan Co., New York, 1908; William Heinemann, 1910).
Burning Daylight (Macmillan Co., New York, 1910; William Heinemann, 1911).
Letters from Jack London, ed. K. Hendricks and I. Shepard (MacGibbon & Kee, 1966).

London, Joan
Jack London and His Times (Doubleday, Doran & Co., New York, 1939).

Ludovici, A. M.
Who is to be Master of the World? An Introduction to the Philosophy of Friedrich Nietzsche (T. N. Foulis, 1909).
Nietzsche, His Life and Works (Constable & Co., 1910).
Nietzsche and Art (Constable & Co., 1911).

Lytton, The Earl of
Wilfred Scawen Blunt (Macdonald, 1961).

MacNeice, Louis
Blind Fireworks (Victor Gollancz, 1929).
The Strings Are False (Faber & Faber, 1965).

Magee, William [Pseudonym of Eglinton, John]
Anglo-Irish Essays (Talbot Press, Dublin, and T. Fisher Unwin, London, 1917; John Lane Co., New York, 1918).

Mallock, W. H.
Aristocracy and Evolution (A. & C. Black, 1898).
The Veil of the Temple (John Murray, 1904).

Marcuse, L.
'Nietzsche in Amerika', *Neue Schweizer Rundschau*, XVIII (1950).
'Nietzsche in America', *South Atlantic Quarterly*, L (July 1951).

McManus, F. (ed.)
The Yeats We Knew (The Mercier Press, Cork, 1965).

Mencken, H. L.
The Philosophy of Friedrich Nietzsche (J. W. Luce & Co., Boston, and T. Fisher Unwin, London, 1908; 3rd edn, 1913, repr. Kennikat Press, Port Washington, New York, 1967).
'What about Nietzsche?' *The Smart Set*, November 1909.
(ed.), *The Gist of Nietzsche* (J. W. Luce & Co., Boston, 1910).
'Friedrich Nietzsche. The Prophet of the Superman', *The Smart Set*, March 1912.
'Transvaluation of Morals', *The Smart Set*, March 1915.
'Friedrich Nietzsche', in *H. L. Mencken's Smart Set Criticism*, ed. W. H. Nolte (Cornell University Press, Ithaca, 1968).

'Introduction' to his transl. of F. W. Nietzsche, *The Antichrist* (A. A. Knopf, New York, 1923).
Letters, ed. Guy J. Forgue (A. A. Knopf, New York, 1961).

Moore, Edward [Muir, Edwin]
We Moderns: Enigmas and Guesses (George Allen & Unwin, 1918).

Moore, George
Confessions of a Young Man (3rd edn, T. Werner Laurie, 1904).
Evelyn Innes (T. Fisher Unwin, 1898).
Memoirs of My Dead Life (William Heinemann, 1906).
Hail and Farewell, vol. 2: *Salve* (William Heinemann, 1912; repr. 1947).

Moore, Harry T.
The Life and Works of D. H. Lawrence (George Allen & Unwin, 1951).

More, Paul Elmer
Nietzsche (Houghton Mifflin Co., Boston and New York, 1912).

Morgan, Margery M.
'Shaw, Yeats, Nietzsche and the Religion of Art', *Kosmos*, I (1967).

Morland, M. A.
'Nietzsche and the Nineties', *Contemporary Review*, CICIII (April 1958).

Muir, Edwin
Latitudes (Andrew Melrose Ltd, [1924]).
Transition (L. & V. Wolff, 1926).
An Autobiography (Hogarth Press, 1954).

Muir, Willa
A Memoir (Hogarth Press, 1969).

Mumford, Lewis
The Golden Day: A Study in American Experience and Culture (Humphrey Milford, 1927).

Murry, John Middleton
Between Two Worlds (Jonathan Cape, 1935).

Nevinson, H. W.
Changes and Chances (Nisbet & Co., 1923).

Nietzsche, F.
The Collected Works of Friedrich Nietzsche, ed. A. Tille, 3 vols (Henry & Co., 1896–7).
The Works of Friedrich Nietzsche, ed. A. Tille, 4 vols (T. Fisher Unwin, 1899–1903).
The Complete Works of Friedrich Nietzsche, ed. Oscar Levy, 18 vols (T. N. Foulis, 1909–13).

Nolte, W. H.
H. L. Mencken, Literary Critic (Wesleyan University Press, Middletown, Connecticut, 1966).

Nordau, Max
Degeneration (William Heinemann, London, and D. Appleton & Co., New York, 1895).

Notes for Good Europeans, ed. Thomas Common, 1903–9.

O'Connor, Richard
Jack London: A Biography (Victor Gollancz, 1965).

O'Hare, C.B.
The Role of European Literature in the Prose Works of D. H. Lawrence (University Microfilms, Ann Arbor, 1966).

Olson, Esther
An Analysis of the Nietzschean Elements in the Plays of Eugene O'Neill (Dissertation, University of Minnesota, 1956).

Orage, A. R.
Friedrich Nietzsche. The Dionysian Spirit of the Age (T. N. Foulis, 1906; A. C. McClurg & Co., Chicago, 1911).
Nietzsche in Outline and Aphorism (T. N. Foulis, 1907; A. C. McClurg & Co., Chicago, 1910).
Consciousness, Animal, Human, and Superhuman (Theosophical Society, 1907).
Readers and Writers (George Allen & Unwin, London, and A. A. Knopf, New York, 1922).
Selected Essays and Critical Writings, ed. H. Read and D. Saurat (Stanley Nott, 1935).

Pater, Walter
'A Study of Dionysus', *Fortnightly Review*, December 1876.

Pearce, R. H. (ed.)
The Act of the Mind. Essays on the Poetry of Wallace Stevens (John Hopkins Press, Baltimore, 1965).

Petzold, Gertrud von
John Davidson und sein geistiges Werden unter dem Einfluss Nietzsches (Dissertation, University of Leipzig, 1928).
'Nietzsche in englisch-amerikanischer Beurteilung bis zum Ausgang des Weltkrieges', *Anglia*, LIII (1929).

Powys, John Cowper
The War and Culture (G. Arnold Shaw, New York, 1914; English edn entitled *The Menace of German Culture*, W. Rider & Son, 1915).
Visions and Revisions. A Book of Literary Devotions (G. Arnold Shaw, New York, and W. Rider & Son, London, 1915; repr. Macdonald, 1955).
A Philosophy of Solitude (Jonathan Cape, 1933; American edn entitled *The Philosophy of Solitude*, Simon & Schuster, New York, 1933).
Autobiography (John Lane, 1934).
The Pleasures of Literature (Cassell & Co. Ltd, 1938; American edn entitled *Enjoyment of Literature*, Simon & Schuster, New York, 1938).
Obstinate Cymric (Druid Press, 1947).

Lucifer (Macdonald, 1956).

Pütz, Peter
Friedrich Nietzsche (Metzler, Stuttgart, 1967).

Ransome, Arthur
Portraits and Speculations (Macmillan & Co., 1913).

Read, Herbert
Songs of Chaos (Elkin Mathews, 1915).
The Tenth Muse (Routledge & Kegan Paul, 1957).
The Contrary Experience (Faber & Faber, 1963).

Reichert, H. W. and Schlechta, K. (eds)
International Nietzsche-Bibliography (2nd edn, University of North Carolina Press, Chapel Hill, 1968).

Rix, Walter T.
'Nietzsches Einfluss auf Shaw', *Literatur in Wissenschaft und Unterricht*, IV, 2 (1971).

Rolleston, T. W.
'Modern Forces in German Literature', *The Quarterly Review*, CCXXI (July 1914).

Roosevelt, Theodore
The Strenuous Life (Century Co., New York, 1900; Grant Richards, 1901).

Rosenberg, Isaac
The Collected Works of Isaac Rosenberg, ed. G. Bottomley and D. Harding (Chatto & Windus, 1937).

Royce, Josiah
'Nietzsche', *Atlantic Monthly*, LXIX (March 1917).

Santayana, George
Little Essays (Constable & Co., London, and C. Scribner's Sons, New York, 1920).

Shaw, G. B.
'Nietzsche in English', *The Saturday Review*, 11 April 1896.
[Letter re Nietzsche Society], *The Eagle and the Serpent*, 15 April 1898.
'Giving the Devil his Due', *The Saturday Review* (Supplement), 13 May 1899.
'Epistle Dedicatory' to *Man and Superman* (A. Constable & Co., 1903).
'Preface' to *Major Barbara* (A. Constable & Co., 1909).

Skelton, R. (ed.)
Herbert Read: A Memorial Symposium (Methuen, 1970).

Snider, Nancy V.
An Annotated Bibliography of English Works on Friedrich Nietzsche (University Microfilms Inc., Ann Arbor, 1962).

Sorley, C. H.
Letters from Germany and from the Army (Private publication, 1916).

Speaight, Robert
The Life of Eric Gill (Methuen, 1966).

Spengler, Oswald
The Decline of the West, vol. I: *Form and Actuality*, tr. C. F. Atkinson (George Allen & Unwin, [1926]).

Squires, Radcliffe
The Loyalties of Robinson Jeffers (University of Michigan Press, Ann Arbor, 1956).

Stavrou, C. N.
Whitman and Nietzsche (University of North Carolina Press, Chapel Hill, 1964).

Stevens, Wallace
Letters of Wallace Stevens, ed. Holly Stevens (Faber & Faber, 1967).

Stone, Edward
Henry Louis Mencken's Debt to Friedrich Nietzsche (University of Texas M.A. thesis, 1937).

Swanberg, W. A.
Dreiser (Scribner's, New York, 1965).

Symons, Arthur
'Nietzsche on Tragedy', *The Academy and Literature*, 30 August 1902.
Plays, Acting, and Music (Duckworth, 1903).
Studies in Seven Arts (Constable, 1906).
William Blake (A. Constable & Co. Ltd, 1907).
'Blake et Nietzsche', *Fontaine*, XI (May 1947).

Tedlock, E. W. (Jr)
D. H. Lawrence, Artist and Rebel (University of New Mexico Press, Albuquerque, 1963).

The Eagle and the Serpent, ed. Erwin McCall, 1898–1902.

Thomas, Edward
'Nietzsche', *The Bookman*, June 1909.
Richard Jefferies (Hutchinson & Co., 1909).
Letters from Edward Thomas to Gordon Bottomley, ed. R. George Thomas (Oxford University Press, 1968).

Tille, A. (ed), see under Nietzsche, F.

Törnqvist, Egil
'Nietzsche and O'Neill: A Study in Affinity', *Orbis Litterarum*, XXIII (1968).

Townsend, J. B.
John Davidson, Poet of Armageddon (Yale University Press, New Haven, 1961).

Trevelyan, R. C.
The New Parsifal. An Operatic Fable (Chiswick Press for the author, 1914).

Vaihinger, Hans
The Philosophy of 'As If', tr. C. K. Ogden (Kegan Paul & Co., 1924).

Weber, Brom
Hart Crane (Bodley Head, New York, 1948).

Wells, H. G.
'Human Evolution, III – Mr. Wells Replies', *Natural Science*, April 1897.
The Island of Dr. Moreau (William Heinemann, 1896).
The Food of the Gods and how it came to earth (Macmillan & Co., 1904).
The Sleeper Wakes (Nelson, 1910).
Men Like Gods (Cassell & Co., 1923).

Wilson, F. A. C.
W. B. Yeats and Tradition (Victor Gollancz, 1958).
Yeat's Iconography (Victor Gollancz, 1960).

Wright, Willard H.
What Nietzsche Taught (B. W. Huebsch, New York, 1915).

Wyzewa, T. de
'Frédéric Nietsche [sic], le dernier métaphysicien', *La Revue politique et littéraire*, XLVIII (1891).

Yeats, W. B.
Collected Poems (Macmillan, 1933; 2nd edn, 1950).
The Collected Plays (Macmillan, 1934).
A Vision (Macmillan, 1937).
The Letters of W. B. Yeats, ed. Allan Wade (Hart-Davis, 1954).

Zwerdling, A.
Yeats and the Heroic Ideal (Peter Owen, 1966).

Index

Abercrombie, Lascelles, 114, 116, 117–22
Aiken, Conrad, 155, 159–60, 173
Anderson, Margaret, 153
Auden, W. H., 206–7

Barbellion, W. N. P., 124
Barker, Granville, 61
Beecham, Thomas, 147
Bell, Clive, 148
Blunt, Wilfred Scawen, 115, 122–3
Bridges, Robert, 143, 145
Brooke, Rupert, 15, 114, 125–7

Chesterton, G. K., 18–19, 51, 57, 59–60
Clarke, Austin, 87
Crane, Hart, 117, 155, 156–9, 202

Davidson, John, 11, 14, 18, 30, 36, 41, 47, 48–55, 61, 62, 68, 73, 88, 90, 96, 110, 202
De Casseres, B., 153, 155, 168, 184
Dell, Floyd, 155
Dobell, Bertram, 145
Douglas, Norman, 148
Dreiser, Theodore, 155, 165, 170–2

Egerton, George, 11
Eglinton, John, 37, 38, 39, 46
Eliot, T. S., 114, 132, 139–42
Ellis, Edith, 13
Ellis, Havelock, 12–13, 14, 17, 30, 34, 37, 67–8, 127, 150, 152, 165

Fitzgerald, F. Scott, 203
Fletcher, John Gould, 20, 36, 131, 153, 155, 156, 173–83, 202

Garnett, Edward, 15
Gill, Eric, 15, 123
Gogarty, Oliver St John, 142
Graham, Stephen, 123–4
Graves, Robert, 10, 71

Hardy, Thomas, 106, 109, 132, 143–5, 147
Hecht, Ben, 155
Hopkins, Gerard Manley, 26–8
Hulme, T. E., 11, 132, 137–9
Huneker, J. G., 14, 48, 150, 151–3, 155, 211

Jackson, Holbrook, 51, 136
Jeffers, Robinson, 155, 156, 160–1
Joyce, James, 11, 132, 142, 156

Lawrence, D. H., 104–9, 159, 202, 203
Lee, Vernon, 16, 17
Lewis, Wyndham, 9, 11, 132–5, 145, 147–8, 153, 187, 202
London, Jack, 18, 81, 155, 163–70, 172, 202

MacNeice, Louis, 69, 203–6
Mallock, W. H., 15–16
Mencken, H. L., 117, 145–6, 150, 151, 153, 154–5, 156, 161, 162, 170, 172
Monro, Harold, 114, 117
Moore, George, 31, 36, 37–47
More, Paul Elmer, 151
Muir, Edwin, 11, 18, 89, 96–103, 135, 137, 166, 185, 202
Murry, John Middleton, 115, 124

Nevinson, W. H., 147
Nordau, Max, 11, 12, 19, 150

O'Neill, Eugene, 18, 85, 153, 154, 155, 156, 184–90, 202
Orage, A. R., 11, 65, 91, 96, 97, 99, 116, 123, 132, 135, 136–7, 172

Pater, Walter, 21–9, 30, 36, 39, 41, 47, 175
Pound, Ezra, 19–20, 98, 117, 132, 153
Powys, John Cowper, 109–13, 202

Ransome, Arthur, 22, 89
Read, Herbert, 11, 18, 32, 67, 91–6, 97, 98, 135–6, 137, 202
Roosevelt, Theodore, 161–2
Rosenberg, Isaac, 20, 115, 125, 127–31, 173
Royce, Josiah, 139

Santayana, George, 193, 194
Shaw, G. B., 10, 14, 15, 30, 39, 55, 58–66, 68, 73, 91, 126, 171, 184
Shephard, Morgan, 85–6
Sorley, Charles, 115, 125
Stevens, Wallace, 9, 86, 155, 156, 190–201, 202, 221
Symonds, John Addington, 16–17
Symons, Arthur, 17, 21, 29–36, 37, 69, 118, 172

Thomas, Edward, 114, 115–17
Trevelyan, R. C., 122

Wells, H. G., 14, 56–8, 126, 138

Yeats, W. B., 10, 11, 18, 31, 32, 34, 35, 36, 37, 38, 40, 46, 51–2, 67–90, 91, 109, 128, 137, 142, 165–6, 202, 203